Christina Aguilera
A Star Is Made

The Unauthorized Biography

PIER DOMINGUEZ

COLOSSUS BOOKS

Phoenix
New York   Los Angeles

Christina Aguilera: A Star is Made The Unauthorized Biography

by Pier Dominguez

Published by:
Colossus Books
A Division of Amber Communication Group, Inc.
1334 East Chandler Boulevard, Suite 5-D67
Phoenix, AZ 85048
amberbk@aol.com
www.amberbooks.com

Tony Rose, Publisher/Editorial Director   Samuel P. Peabody, Associate Publisher
Yvonne Rose, Senior Editor   The Printed Page, Interior & Cover Design
Edited by Yvonne Fleetwood

ALL RIGHTS RESERVED

No part of this book may be reproduced or transmitted in any form or by any means—electronic or mechanical, including photocopying, recording or by any information storage and retrieval system without written permission from the authors, except for the inclusion of brief quotations in a review.

The publication is designed to provide accurate and authoritative information in regard to the subject matter covered. It is sold with the understanding that the Publisher is not engaged in rendering legal, accounting or other professional services. If legal advice or other expert assistance is required, the services of a competent professional person should be sought.

COLOSSUS BOOKS are available at special discounts for bulk purchases, sales promotions, fund raising or educational purposes.

© Copyright 2003 by Pier Dominguez and Colossus Books
ISBN #: 0-9702224-5-9

Library of Congress Cataloging-In-Publication Data

Dominguez, Pier.
  Christina Aguilera : a star is made : the unauthorized biography /
Pier Dominguez.
     p. cm.
Summary: A biography of the pop singer, focusing on her journey of
self-discovery and struggle to find her artistic identity.
Includes bibliographical references.
  ISBN 0-9702224-5-9
  1. Aguilera, Christina, 1980- 2. Singers--United States--Biography.
[1. Aguilera, Christina, 1980- 2. Singers. 3. Women--Biography.] I.
Title.
  ML3930.A36 D66 2003
  782.421649'092--dc21

2002041408

10 9 8 7 6 5 4 3 2 1

First Printing January 2003

"A REVEALING AND CONTROVERSIAL PORTRAIT"

No pop star has ever risen to the pinnacle of the music world and exploded onto the international scene in such an exciting frenzy as Christina Aguilera. A controversial and elusive figure, Christina has polarized and mesmerized audiences since the beginning.

While fans praise her sultry, soulful voice, a growing contingent of detractors finds her whole persona tacky. Even other artists, including Eminem have openly proclaimed their dislike of her; and her idol, Mariah Carey, refused to talk to her.

Love her or hate her, Christina's success is without precedent. Millions and millions of her albums sold worldwide. It seems that everything she touches turns platinum.

In *Christina Aguilera: A Star is Made*, author Pier Dominguez traces the construction of a 21st century star and provides a shrewd, psychological portrait—the first analytical look at her life and rise to the pinnacle of the pop world. This biography reveals Christina Aguilera in a most intimate light, chronicling her early years, exploring her motivations and tracing the development of her career. It strips away the media hoopla and exposes the *Real Christina*.

▼ Fled her abusive father at age 5
▼ Cut out her first manager and later refused to give her credit
▼ Dropped her first boyfriend as her fame was reaching its most glorious crescendo
▼ Became the puppet of her record label, which attempted to downplay her ethnicity and helped her keep her romantic life secret
▼ Fired the manager who took her to the top of the charts

After an almost two-year hiatus, and after having her stardom carefully constructed by the RCA label, Christina has come back with an album "Stripped" that is almost entirely her own creation. The question Dominguez provocatively poses is, "Will she shine as brightly on her own?"

> "Before the 11 piercings, the countless barely there outfits, and the infamous "Dirrty" video, Christina Aguilera was just another sweet little girl…her transformation is detailed in A Star is Made by 19-year-old author Pier Dominguez"
> —The New York Post

Nineteen year-old journalist Pier Dominguez has written for New York Newsday, is the author of *Amy Fisher: Anatomy of a Scandal.*

Outstanding Acclaim for Pier Dominguez

...There is something that sets him apart. He's a college student with a dream and a clear vision of success....Dominguez is a rising star.
—**New York Times**

"Pier Dominguez shines new light on the star."
—**Publisher's Weekly**

"[Dominguez is] ...A precocious pop intellectual...."
El Heraldo, Colombia

"Christina Aguilera is lucky to have such a phenomenal biographer in Pier Dominguez... One day he will be as big a star as his subjects. He brings extraordinary gifts to his work—immense curiosity, fine writing skills, intrepid reporting, thorough research, and indefatigable energy."
—Kitty Kelley, #1 *New York Times* best-selling biographer

"Pier Dominguez is one of the best young writers I know."
—Jack Olsen, Edgar award-winning *New York Times* best-selling true crime author

"Comprehensive... [Dominguez] display[s] an easy-to-read style and takes an inquisitive approach that will appeal to Aguilera fans craving details about the former Beaver County girl's meteoric rise to the top...Though pointing out a few unflattering 'diva' moments in her career, Dominguez paints a mostly sympathetic portrait of Aguilera as a young woman unwilling to compromise her artistic vision...Worth the quick read if you're a fan of the singer or someone trying to make sense of her curious on- and off-stage actions"
—**Beaver County Times**

"Dominguez has pieced together a look at the girl who once called Wexford home from available sources and through interviews...An interesting look behind the scenes. He touches on rumors of romance, the development of "Genie in a Bottle" and later hits, and how she wound up giving voice to both "Mulan" and "Moulin Rouge." ...Although it might seem early to chronicle Christina, it turns out she's done enough in her few years in the spotlight to actually fill the volume. There's a good selection of photos, from her earliest years through achieving fame."
—**The Daily News** (PA)

"[Pier Dominguez is]...A quickly rising star..."
—*Move* magazine

Dedication

*To my parents, for teaching me the importance of family.
To my brothers, Tony and Eric, for being
the most important forces in my life.*

Author's Note

Before I began writing this biography, I suspected that writing a book about somebody who is relatively young might be complicated because it is hard to place events in perspective when a significant portion of the events of a person's life—and career— have yet to take place. It is also more complicated to deconstruct a personality when a person is only 21 years old because they have not yet started exhibiting behavioral patterns...so I thought.

I soon realized that when the person is somebody remarkable enough to have risen to worldwide superstardom at the age of 18, obtained a Grammy at 19 and sold 23 million records by the age of 21, the job is made a lot easier. Especially when their "meteoric" and "instantaneous" rise to stardom was preceded by a decade-long career of struggle and hard work.

After writing a book about Amy Fisher, which chronicled her emotional evolution as well as the scandal that engulfed her life and cast her as the "Long Island Lolita" in the eyes of the American public, doing an unauthorized biography of Christina *seemed* like a less ambitious undertaking...so I thought.

As I researched Christina's life—immersing myself in newspaper archives, lawsuits, court records, tapes, transcripts and attempting to interview as many people as I could—a very real, defined and consistent portrait emerged of her. Despite the apparent wealth of information on the singer, it was harder to find the "real" Christina than it was to find the real Amy.

Although much has been written about Christina, this is the first analytical, serious and uncensored look at her life and her rise to the pinnacle of the pop world. This is not a typical fluff biography in which "fun facts" and figures are stuffed between myriad pictures. Although I am younger than all of the authors who have done books on Christina, or any other pop star, (or any biography for that matter!) previously, I, unlike them, would not have the audacity to call my book an "unauthorized" look at Christina's life if it read like a press release from her manager. After Amy Fisher's lawyer threatened a lawsuit if I proceeded with the publication of my book about her, I learned that when writing about notorious figures, authorization is not the way to go.

I believe that the biographical enterprise is an inherently interesting and constructive genre from which much can be learned. In part, in writing this book, I hope that younger people who buy it decide to give other biographies a chance.

There are new revelations in this book culled from careful research and dedicated analysis, and some of them do not cast Christina in a particularly positive light. It was certainly not my objective to taint Christina's image or "expose" the negative aspects of her life. The "unauthorized" in the title refers to my exposure of Christina's psychological underpinnings, her motivations, her real personality and her relationships.

I firmly believe that after reading this book, the readers will have come a lot closer to answering for themselves the *multi*-million-dollar question, "What is she *really* like?"

In trying to answer that question, and writing this book, I relied on the help and cooperation of many people.

For taking the time to answer questions, however briefly or brusquely, I would like to extend my gratitude to *Seventeen* magazine's Heidi Sherman; the *Pittsburgh Post-Gazette's* pop critic Ed Masley, whose articles on Christina shed much light on her personality; and *Billboard's* Leila Cobo, whose analyses of the singer's career have consistently been the most accurate and complete. I would also like to thank former Mickey Mouse Club member Lindsey Alley, for her time and sincerity. Good luck with your plays! Robbie Nicholson, thank you for the pictures and your fan story, and Gareth Edwards, your expertise on English singer Seal provided much needed background information.

Christina's fan and Webmaster of www.christinaaguilera.to, Kerry Walsh objectively and honestly answered all my questions about the fans' problems with Christina's official website. For her honesty and graphics design expertise, I salute her!

To my mentors: Jack Olsen, of course, without your encouragement the first book would never have happened, and by extension, neither would this one. (R.I.P.) Kitty Kelley, the most famous, successful biographer in the world: I cannot thank you enough, period. Alvaro Diaz—author and extraordinary teacher, who, after reading my first essay instilled in me the belief that my writing was superior.

I would like to thank my parents for always providing me with the support I need. My brothers, Tony and Eric, the two most important people in my life, are always encouraging and I was moved by their excitement when I sold this book. My beautiful—and articulate—aunt Monica, who is never at a loss for words and from whom, somehow, I believe I inherited my way with words. My cousin Rachel—whose excitement over the first book was probably one of my own psychological underpinnings in writing this one—and Loren, whose year-long absence from my life made me realize how much I love her.

Miek Coccia, of the James Levine agency, thanks for your advice and encouragement—even as you passed on the book! Ditto for Marcela Landres of Simon and Schuster.

Mr. Tony Rose, publisher and editor *extra ordinaire*, who had the vision to believe in my writing and future, Thank you so much for giving the book a chance!

In researching Christina's story, I realized how important it is to be surrounded by a healthy group of people in one's formative years at school. I feel truly blessed to have been surrounded by the most intelligent, loving, respectful and classy group of friends I could ever have asked for. Thus, I would like to thank the people who in spending 14 years of my life with me had an inevitably forceful impact on my life. Throughout our years at Karl C. Parrish School, inadvertently, they taught me that the possibilities in my life are boundless. I love you, I am eternally grateful, and you will be a part of my life FOREVER.

Contents

Chapter 1. A Star is Born	1
Chapter 2. The Little Girl with The Big Voice	13
Chapter 3. A Beaver County Mouseketeer	23
Chapter 4. The Demo Tape	33
Chapter 5. The Mysterious Management Deal	37
Chapter 6. The Teen Pop Machine	45
Chapter 7. The Selling of Christina	57
Chapter 8. Pop! Goes the Genie	69
Chapter 9. The Seduction of Fame	79
Chapter 10. Rumors, Romance & Controversy	93
Photo Gallery	117
Chapter 11. On Tour & In Love	141
Chapter 12. Exit Steven Kurtz	161
Chapter 13. Her Kind of Christmas	183
Chapter 14. Seizing Control	195
Chapter 15. Not Your Pop Tart	201
Chapter 16. A New Beginning	219
Discography	227
End Notes	233

Christina Aguilera: A Star is Made

The transformation is complete: from sweet pop princess as a teenager to controversial superstar as a young woman. With the release of her sophomore album, Christina finally exposed her true self.

Introduction

I'm not going to sit there and lie.
Whether you like me or hate me, that's me.
—Christina Aguilera in an interview with MTV

The first question that most people asked when I said I was writing an unauthorized biography of Christina Aguilera was: "Why her?" Many individuals followed up on this question by noting that Britney Spears would probably be a better subject. I welcome introspection and decided to ponder why it was Christina who caught my attention. I suppose that I should note that my previous book was an unauthorized biography of Amy Fisher, which I wrote when I was 17 years old. But I did not really *choose* to write about Amy. The circumstances simply lent themselves for such a project and I embraced it passionately.

Christina, on the other hand, was the first person that I actually *chose* to write about. As I did the preliminary research for this book, my underlying reason for selecting Christina over her equally famous contemporary became ever clearer: Unlike Britney, Christina is raw. In her case, the guarded woman behind the façade is more interesting and complex than the media caricature could ever hope to become. When you remove the carefully orchestrated hype surrounding Britney Spears which has inflated her popularity to unimaginable levels, the laid-bare woman-girl is even blander than her over-produced music. Spears' entire public persona is a construction of the public imagination aided and abetted by an unquestioning media that feeds a phenomenon it doesn't quite understand. A perceptive article in an English publication placed her in perspective:

> "'I love junk food,' says Britney unrepentantly. Which is just as well, because, come to think of it, that's pretty much what Britney is. Like junk food, she sells instant gratification and, in doing so, she triumphantly Americanizes the supine earth. She should come wrapped in greaseproof paper, with a straw, or perhaps a flute, to make ingestion easier."

Despite the unrelenting comparisons from an unenlightened press corps, Christina Aguilera is Britney's diametrical opposite. From her childhood to her stage presence, from her piercings to her voice, Christina's story is not shrouded in hype or ensconced in lies, at least not thanks to the efforts of the petite singer herself. As I prodded, poked and unraveled the carefully constructed media image that her record company had crafted, I found that underneath the beautiful mane of blond hair and behind the piercing blue eyes, lay a consummate professional struggling to find her artistic identity as she discovered herself more fully.

Initially, Christina's record label intended for her to appear bland and took pains to hide most of her uniqueness from the public. Like the old Hollywood studio system that ran the lives of their stars; arranging dates, announcing divorces and planning marriages, Christina was, along with Britney Spears, one of the first teen pop stars to be churned out by this image factory in the late 90's. They wanted to appeal to the largest audience; they molded the singer into a white canvas over which an entire public could project their own expectations of what she should be. She was a role model for little girls, a teen pin-up for teenage boys, and a superior vocalist in the eyes of adult record buyers. RCA Records conscientiously controlled her image and her music, and tuned it in to the pop music trend that emerged in 1999.

After the release of her self-titled debut album, *Rolling Stone* magazine praised her "powerhouse pipes," *Time* magazine called her "One of the most strikingly gifted singers to come along since Mariah Carey," and *The New York Times* praised her "striking vocal power" while auguring greater success in the future.

It was not surprising that on the day she attended her first Grammy Awards ceremony, on February 23, 2000, Christina Aguilera found herself at the center of a media buzz. Before the ceremony, the House of Versace had spent 28 hours fitting the slinky metallic sheath she would wear. Once she arrived at the Staples Center, Christina looked as amazing as she claimed she felt. Her face was illuminated, her sleek hair looked particularly radiant, the heavy dress flattered her lithe figure and appropriately accentuated her bosom. She looked striking. As she walked down the red carpet, she glittered, looking dignified and in control.

In fact, Christina's poise and apparent command of her own artistic endeavors was entirely superficial. For one, Christina preferred her hair curly but she had it straightened in deference to the record company. "Unfortunately, pop is often about eye-candy," she later explained knowingly. "My record company told me to have straight hair even though I prefer it curly."

Although Christina was already fighting to take charge of her own image and music, her dilemmas were clearly on display that night. As she took her seat next to her manager inside the Staples Center, Christina found herself nominated for Best Female Pop Vocal Performance for "Genie In A Bottle." In fact, "Genie In A Bottle" was a song she had not even wanted to record. "To tell you the truth…I don't know, maybe I shouldn't say this, but I really didn't want to really record 'Genie In A Bottle' to be my first single," Christina later admitted. That night, Christina did not win the Grammy for Female Pop Vocal Performance, but she took home the statuette for Best New Artist, a category she had watched her idol, Mariah Carey, win exactly nine years before.

After the ceremony, Christina stepped inside her black stretch limo, placing her delicate pink heels in the car, and drove off into the night. Christina turned to the reporter in the car with her. "Did I sound Okay onstage?" she asked. "I was in shock. I was preparing at that moment to put on my loser face."[1] Still reeling from the excitement, she picked up her cell phone and called her mother, Shelly Kearns. She also called MTV personality Carson Daly, whom she was rumored to be dating. In fact, by the time of the 2000 Grammy Awards, Christina had already fallen in love with one of her dancers, Jorge Santos. In an attempt to maintain Christina's image as a single teen pin-up, the record company and Christina successfully kept this hidden from the public, until the relationship was exposed later that year by Heidi Sherman, an inquisitive writer for *Seventeen* magazine.

Wearing gold pants and a belly-baring top, Christina was all smiles at a post-Grammy party thrown by her record company's parent corporation, BMG. The young vocalist held court at the party, aware that she was the label's glittering gem.

Two years later, on February 27, 2002, Christina Aguilera arrived at the 44th Annual Grammy Awards celebration. A lot had happened to Christina since that night three years earlier. This year, her appearance on the red carpet was meant to shock. In the words of the New York *Daily News*, Christina "continued the trend started two years ago by Jennifer Lopez. The Staten Island songbird came close to baring her bust in a black vintage Madame Gres gown with a scooped-out bodice. She was obviously shooting for a Hollywood glamour look with red lipstick, penciled eyebrows and platinum blond curls."

She was at the Grammy ceremony with two nominations in the same category of Best Pop Collaboration with Vocals. This time, however, the nominations had come in for two songs, including her duet with Ricky Martin "Nobody Wants to Be Lonely," that Christina herself had decided to participate in. In the case of the other song, it had been despite her record company's pleas to the contrary. RCA felt that "Lady Marmalade," the lead single off the *Moulin Rouge* movie soundtrack, would be too left field for Christina. The song was an R&B confection that included vocal performances by rapper Lil' Kim, R&B artists Mya and Pink, and featured production by Missy Elliot. It appeared to be a 180-degree turn for Christina. In the end, her own instincts proved correct after the track became the first airplay-only song in the history of the *Billboard Hot 100* to spend more than one week at No. 1. In fact, it perched itself at the top position for 5 weeks—the same amount of time that "Genie" had spent at the top—and became the best-selling single of 2001.

When she performed at the Grammys that night, before taking home her third such award, she was wearing fringed white hot pants and a small black top that barely covered her body. In the eyes of the general public, Christina's "new look" was shocking and unexpected. Her body was more revealed than ever and her hair was finally done up in the rebellious curls she favored. "Sexuality is a beautiful thing.... It's something that's just a part of me," she said later in an interview with MTV. "It's one of the better parts of being a woman. We're sexier than guys."

Despite the apparent breach between Christina's two images, in truth, these clothes and music represented who she truly was. By this time, Christina had finally managed to take control of her identity and expose her true self.

During the years of personal fulfillment and artistic growth between the two Grammy Award ceremonies, Christina had been involved in numerous controversies. Eminem, a hip hop rapper known for his hard-core lyrics, had dissed her on his hit single "The Real Slim Shady" provoking a firestorm of speculation about her alleged promiscuity. She had been called a "bitch" by English boy band Westlife. 80's teen pop star Deborah Gibson said she "lives and breathes the sexual image," and fellow teen pop star Jessica Simpson noted that "she definitely knows she has sold eight million records and I don't really like that in people." She had also almost gotten involved in a physical altercation with grunge-rocker turned Academy award-nominated actress, Courtney Love. Writing in her website's diary, Shirley Manson of alternative rock band Garbage, chastised: "Why don't you make an effort to be a better person, Christina? Maybe that might bring you a little closer to God, because there are rumors coming from numerous and credible sources that you are a stuck-up bitch."

The tabloids were equally aggressive and kept relentless tabs on her dating habits, trumpeting relationships with Carson Daly, Enrique

Iglesias, Limp Bizkit's Fred Durst, and even DMX. Christina herself fanned the heat of some of these rumors, inadvertently allowing these myths to become an integral part of her public image.

Despite the brouhaha, her career thrived. She remixed two of her album tracks, "What A Girl Wants" and "Come On Over," and both reached No. 1 on the *Billboard* chart when released as singles, taking her album sales to the 8-million plateau. Although her record label had initially attempted to downplay her Hispanic heritage in an attempt to sell her to the largest audience, they trumpeted it when she released a Latin album that topped *Billboard's Latin 50* chart for 19 weeks. In the process she became the first female singer ever to hold the top spot of the *Billboard Hot 100* and the *Hot Latin Tracks* chart simultaneously when her fourth single, "Come On Over" knocked Madonna's "Music" out of the No. 1 spot. She put out a Christmas album that became the top-selling Holiday record on *Billboard's Holiday Album* chart. Her worldwide record sales reached 23 million and she received a Latin Grammy for her Spanish-language album. In three years, Christina had amassed the kind of record sales and industry accolades that many artists spend a lifetime trying to obtain.

There had been personal breakthroughs as well. After almost collapsing during her first tour, Christina decided to take control of her own affairs and fired her manager, Steven Kurtz, the savvy businessman under whose tutelage Christina had shot to superstardom. She had survived her tour's punishing schedule, but not before alienating countless fans who were disappointed with the singer's negative attitude at backstage "meet-n-greets." On the other hand, she made peace with her father, Fausto, whom her mother had divorced when Christina was only seven years old. She had momentarily allowed love in her life and her relationship with Jorge Santos became public and flourished. By the time she attended her third Grammy ceremony, the relationship was over. But Christina had been taking creative and personal risks that had produced successful results in both her emotional and professional lives. After much struggle, she found herself at the helm of her career. "Now I have total control," Christina told *Time* Magazine in late 2001. "Before, I had to stay with that perfect pop image. But I'm glad I went through it. I'm stronger now."

Christina's compulsive perfectionism and overwhelming need to be in charge of her affairs, which led her on the path to self-discovery that culminated with the sharp turn in her musical direction, were characteristics firmly rooted in her childhood. Her early years were played out against a backdrop of domestic violence and shattering instability, which caused the singer to steer clear of any situations in which she could be vulnerable. In school, her jealous classmates taunted her mercilessly as the determined little girl's career started its meteoric climb to the top with a Star Search performance at age 8, a televised National Anthem singing at age 9; a Mickey Mouse Club membership at age 12; and a recording contract at age 17. Despite the success, the stinging rejection from her peers left lingering doubts inside her that did not go away and gnawed at her security.

Christina's seemingly meteoric rise to stardom was preceded by a decade-long career in the entertainment industry. It was a fascinating journey that Christina had undertaken in her search for the mass adulation and admiration that had eluded her among her contemporaries. This biography reveals Christina Aguilera in a most intimate light, chronicling the early years, exploring her motivations and tracing the development of her career. It strips away the media hoop-la and exposes the young woman at the center of it all.

ONE
A Star is Born

Christina Maria Aguilera was born on December 18, 1980 in Staten Island, one of New York City's most unassuming boroughs. Even her name, the anglicized *Christina*, from the Spanish *Cristina* and the typically Hispanic middle name *Maria*, represented a compromise between the two cultures that she would grow up in. She was the daughter of Fausto Wagner Xavier Aguilera, a U.S. Army sergeant of Hispanic descent stationed in the United States, and his Irish-American wife, Shelly Loraine Fidler. At the time of Christina's birth, Shelly was only 20 years old and her new husband was almost 32 years old. Although Christina would later sing of being a product of her mother's love affair with a Latin lover who left her barefoot and pregnant, in reality, Shelly was married when she was expecting Christina.

It is hard to surmise what effect it would have on Christina to be born in 1980, which meant she would grow up during the apex of "Reaganomics." High inflation rates and unemployment plagued the country during many of those years, and nothing epitomized president Ronald Reagan's philosophy more than a comment he made to a group of college students: "What I want to see, above all, is that this remains a country where someone can always get rich."[1] Although neither one of Christina's parents, and certainly not her college-bound mother, embraced that philosophy, it would appear that Christina managed to take it to heart.

Neither one of Christina's parents were part of the ruling class that became even richer during the Reagan years. Fausto Aguilera had been born in Guayaquil, Ecuador. He had moved to Staten Island, escaping a rather dreary future of poverty in his native country with his parents and siblings, a brother and sister, when he was 19 years old. He enlisted in the army because he did not have any other means of support and did not attend college.

Shelly was part Irish and half German; her great grandfather could not even speak English. Her own mother, Delcie Fidler, was predominantly Irish-Welsh and part Dutch. In her youth, Shelly had been a talented violin and piano player. Encouraged by her mother, when she was 16 years old she toured throughout Europe with the Youth Symphony Orchestra. Although other mothers, especially at that time, might have been reticent about letting a daughter wander off to another continent, Delcie had no such qualms. Perhaps because her husband had died when Shelly was only twelve years old, she herself possessed a wonderful sense of independence that she passed on to her daughter, and that Shelly would pass on to her own children as well.

At that point her future husband had settled in the United States, the only reason Shelly was able to communicate with Fausto in his native language and steal his heart, was because Shelly was going to college to be a Spanish translator and mastered the language to perfection. Furthermore, she was deeply fascinated with the entire Latin culture and drove her college friends crazy talking about all that she had learned about the foods, traditions and customs that are a part of it.

Despite their apparently diverging personalities: a disciplined military man and a free-spirited, open-minded musician, the couple had fallen in love. They married disregarding their almost ten-year age gap, and more importantly, dismissing their cultural differences at a time when the United States was not as welcoming of Latin Americans as it later became. The significant growth of the Latino population of New York began in 1980, increasing by 33% ten years after Christina's birth. The total number of people living in Staten Island in 1980 was 351,866. Of those, only 19,353 were of Hispanic origin. Although it constituted less than 6% of the total population, the growth, at least in numbers, had begun.[2]

The young couple's hope for the future was illuminated with the birth of their first baby, which made them a family. She had beautiful blonde hair and blue eyes. Although her mother and father were both dark-haired, she inherited both characteristics from her father's side, as Walter, an uncle she would never get to meet, was blonde-haired with blue eyes as well. Soon after Christina's birth, in 1981, the Aguileras were living in New Jersey. In a picture taken around that time, Christina, who exhibited no trace of her Hispanic ethnicity as a toddler, sits in her mother's lap and the sheer happiness of Shelly, who had long auburn hair, is clearly visible.[3]

Ever since she was a toddler, Christina loved singing. "Practically since I was out of diapers I wanted to become a singer," she would later recall. If she was to succeed in the music business at the ripe age of 18, her love for her work had to begin at the earliest stage possible. "I mean, this is my ultimate love. Ever since I've been out of diapers, I've loved to sing."[4] She was not exaggerating. Once, when she was three years old, riding the bus with her mother, Christina started singing to herself. The passengers all commented on how her voice was "unusually good for such a tiny girl."[5]

Even the shower—one of the few places most people not blessed with prodigious voices used to express themselves artistically—did not escape Christina's voice. It rattled off the walls, and Christina later recalled "those childhood stories of spreading towels on the floor and using bottles of shampoo as an 'ikaphone.'"

Fortunately for Christina, her father's cultural heritage combined with her mother's love of the culture, provided her the base she would later use to sing in Spanish. "I grew up hearing [Spanish] being spoken in my household. My father being from Ecuador, I'm half Latin," Christina would later explain. At that young age, Christina was already singing in Spanish and she would speak in that language with her parents. She was very proud of her Latin heritage. Later, she would recall "hearing a lot of Spanish being spoken and a lot of Julio [Iglesias] on the record player." Little did she know that, years later, she would find herself romantically linked with the Latin crooner's son in the tabloids, or that she would perform with him at the Super Bowl's half-time show.

Because Fausto was part of the army, he was stationed at different places all over the world. Beginning in 1982 the Aguilera family had to move on numerous occasions: from New York to Texas to New Jersey to Japan. "I spent some years growing up there [in Japan] when I was in my younger childhood," Christina explained later. They lived in a city called Sagamihara where Shelly worked teaching English to Japanese students. On one occasion, one of Shelly's students came over with some of his paintings. He spread them on the floor and just to steal the attention away, little Christina started playing hopscotch all over them."

Her attention-grabbing ways arose early in life, and would only be exacerbated when more people were added to her family and she had to come up with ploys to grab her mother's scattered attention. Although Christina would later grow up with a number of siblings, her initial five years, a determining and formative time in a youngster's life, were played out as an only child. As such, she would later display the self-possessed characteristics associated with only children, who, like Christina, are usually more mature, more advanced and more ambitious than their peers. Such an attitude would cause friction between Christina and her contemporaries all of her life.

Christina recalled, "Right after Staten Island…I've lived everywhere from Texas, to Japan for three years, to New Jersey. I'm this traveling girl. My father was in the Army, so I guess I'm an Army brat."[6] She did not spend enough time in one place that she could call "home," and the almost non-stop traveling could not have been healthy for an already shaky marriage between Shelly and Fausto.

Watching Julie Andrews in *The Sound of Music* when she was five years old, proved to be inspiring for the young girl. "*The Sound of Music* was my real music inspiration…at like 5 years old," she would later recall fondly.[7] Watching Andrews run through the hills as the music plays in the movie and Andrews sings her heart out had a deep impact on Christina. Julie Andrews "was free and alive," she later said, "rebellious against the nuns. I know it sounds really cheesy, but that was my escape."[8]

The freedom that Andrews conveys as she sings was something that the little girl could easily identify with, and she would soon be using music to break free of an ugly situation that started brewing at home. "When I discovered Julie Andrews and *The Sound of Music*, I immediately fell in love. I had the soundtrack on a little tape. I'd put it in my boombox in my room. And I would just, like, close my door and open my window and just sing out. I don't know. It was such a release for me, growing up, for any bad energy or anything that was going on, tension or pain that I was going through. Singing was a way of releasing that. It really made me happy. I would just sing that all over the place."[9]

Her mother later recalled that Christina loved watching the movie over and over again. Shelly also explained that while other girls dreamed of being nurses or princesses, Christina's heart was set on a singing career. Christina would sing out of her window to strangers and, if human ears simply weren't available, Shelly recalled that "she'd surround herself with stuffed animals, and they'd be her audience."

By the time Christina was five years old, her parent's marriage had turned rocky. Fausto himself admitted, "My relationship with [Shelly] was tense and I wasn't perfect…Shelly and I disagreed on a lot of things and we both had hot tempers." Whether the difficulties between the couple arose from the inherent differences in their backgrounds is something Christina herself has not addressed. Certainly, Fausto Aguilera, a son of South American parents, may have expected a certain kind of wife that Shelly, who had taken his name, was not willing to become. Although Christina has been understandably cryptic about it, the truth was that Fausto was hitting Shelly in front of a frightened, unprotected and cowering Christina. On a couple of occasions, Christina, the only daughter, even tried to intercede on behalf of her mother and found herself being victimized as well.

There was a disturbing tension in the Aguilera household and Christina could sense it. The little girl viewed music as her salvation. Whenever her parent's arguments became loud enough so that their voices trespassed their bedroom door, Christina shut it out by singing. But the perceptive and sensitive little girl was not oblivious to what was going on around her. Every night when her mother put her to bed, they followed a similar routine.

"Mommy, please, can't we go to live with Grandma tomorrow?" Christina would ask Shelly quietly. "Please! I don't want to live with Daddy!" Shelly herself was deathly scared of Fausto's rages and slept with a can of mace under her bed. She had been saving all the money that she could to finance their trip out of New Jersey, where they were living after their overseas intermission.

Christina later added that she had to "witness many…arguments at times and [music] was my way of getting out of that situation."[10] Music provided a sort of safe haven for Christina. Whatever was troubling her, she was able to channel it out of her system by breaking into song. Unfortunately, this healing power was deceptive because it was nothing more than a child-like escape from a pervasive problem that was a part of the little girl's every day reality.

After she became famous, she explained somewhat reluctantly: "I definitely try whenever I can to donate to charities involving abused children and battered women. That's a cause that I really feel strongly about and where I can help out…That's something I've felt really strongly about, because I've been around certain situations myself."[11]

In an interview with *Latina* magazine she was slightly more explicit. "I saw certain things growing up that really affected me," Christina said, choosing her words carefully. "It's too easy to give in to peer pressure, to listen too much to the male's opinion. I receive letters from fans writing about certain abusive situations that they are in, and that is why I want to reach out."

On another occasion she elaborated: "I'd like to really— actually go to schools and talk to kids who may be in those situations and open up some of my own experiences and try to, you know, reach out to other kids and help them get out of those situations."[12] Some time after Christina's rise to fame, Shelly herself addressed the situation, admitting: "Well, she witnessed my ex husband being quite abusive—emotionally and physically—to me and grew up determined that, if God blessed her with her dream of fame, she'd use it somehow to help people in that situation."

Remembering years later, Fausto Aguilera was less dramatic than his famous daughter. "I love Christina and her sister Rachel," he said. "I never abused them in any way and they know that." Regarding his abuse of Shelly, he replied: "I'm sorry to have ever raised a hand to my wife, but it was never brutal like Ike and Tina Turner. Still, even though it's been exaggerated, I respect Shelly and Christina's right to remember things differently."

Be that as it may, the effect that viewing the violence inflicted on her mother—and perhaps even herself, depending on whom you believe—must have been devastating for little Christina. According to the Domestic Violence Data Source, "The psychological harm caused by domestic violence can in some cases have a more long lasting impact than the injuries sustained, even when those injuries are severe." Even if Christina herself was not a victim of her father's abuse, the psychological injuries were equally harsh. Christina herself actually said: "It's not only physical abuse, but there's damage inside—mental abuse."[13] Furthermore, the impact on Christina was even greater because she had to carry all of the weight on her diminutive shoulders, as her sister was not yet born and was barely one year old when they finally left Fausto. Christina's personality as a teenager, which included a take-charge nature and a seemingly rebellious independence, was not superficial. These were character traits deeply rooted in her troubled childhood, when she felt a need to protect her mother and take care of herself.

Domestic violence also impacts the friends and family of the people who are abused. In Shelly's case, it appears that this was not an issue because she did not remain with her husband long enough for any real patterns to emerge. She fled the situation, giving her daughter the right message of self-respect and teaching her that she did not have to put up with unacceptable behavior from men. It is a message that Christina learned well and which she would later infuse into her music, as both of her No. 1 hits included references to girl power and dealt with demanding respect from men.

Right before Christina's seventh birthday, and shortly after the birth of her sister in 1986, Shelly finally left Fausto. The cultural differences and, most importantly, the domestic violence became too much for the young mother to bear. After she had saved enough money to finance her trip, Shelly fled with Christina and her barely one-year-old sister Rachel. They drove to the middle-class Pittsburgh suburb of Wexford. After the divorce, Christina lost absolutely all contact with her father who was stationed at a base in Colorado. Inevitably, the estrangement from her father led to an initial severing of her ties to her paternal grandparents, who still lived in Staten Island. However, Christina later noted: "I used to sing in Spanish when I was younger. My grandparents really supported me and helped me be proud of my Latin roots. It was just a part of who I was growing up."[14]

Christina later confided to Rudy Perez, the man who produced her Spanish-language album, that she had been so traumatized by her estrangement from her father, that she blocked out all of the Spanish she had learned. "After the separation, she had a lot of regret and she blocked out the whole Spanish thing," Perez said. "It didn't help she was also growing up in Pittsburgh and that all her friends were American. There aren't too many Latinos there."[15]

Initially, the young, traumatized family moved in with Shelly's mother, Delcie Fidler. Despite her young age, Christina was quite aware of the fact that it was not an ideal living arrangement. "I always envied people who had childhood friends and memories of growing up together because I never really had that," she later said regretfully. "Then the divorce and hard times at school, all those things combined to mold me, to make me grow up quicker. And it gave me the drive to pursue my dreams that I wouldn't necessarily have had otherwise."[16] That is quite a positive way of looking at it. On the other hand, children who witness violence at home often display emotional and behavioral disturbances as diverse as withdrawal, low self-esteem, nightmares, self-blame and aggression against peers, family members and personal belongings. But it appears to have had the opposite effect in Christina, who grew up craving the spotlight and wanted nothing more than acceptance from her peers. Unfortunately, such acceptance did not come easily.

The sudden uprooting was not Christina's only problem. In elementary school, as a result of Christina's singing ability, the other children were so "horrible that she was without friends," Shelly later recalled bitterly. Penny Householder, Christina's first grade teacher tried to shelter her from the other children's mockery. "She was just so much better than everybody else—head and shoulders above everybody," the teacher later said. "They were just, you know, normal children. And she had this wonderful talent."

Christina's childhood friend, Marcie Craig Reilly, clearly recalled the shocking harassment she was subjected to. "I remember one time in gym class they were trying to kick balls at her, to deliberately try to hurt her. It was just a jealousy thing."

Katie Heffner, another childhood friend, surmised why there was such an attitude toward Christina. "She had a lot of self confidence," Heffner explained, "which sometimes can be mistaken for arrogance." Such self-confidence would continue to create problems for Christina with fellow performing artists once she became famous.

More than once, Christina had arrived home in tears and desolate because she had received threats or somebody had been mean to her. Shelly started questioning the wisdom of letting her little girl embark on a show business career. "Well sweety, are you sure you want to do this?" Shelly asked Christina concerned. "I'm behind you a hundred percent if you want to, but make sure." Christina looked at her mother and said: "Well how come they can do cheerleading and I can't do singing? I thought it was about what you want to do." Shelly recalled thinking, "Well, okay, she makes more sense than anyone else."[17]

Christina's love of song did not exactly help her in her quest to make friends, though. Other children from the block would come over to her house wondering whether she wanted to play with them. Shelly would tell them that singing was Christina's own special game. Looking back on it later, Christina noted, "My mom would tell them that was my play, singing all by myself. I guess I was weird."

The constant harassment finally marked the end of their stay in Rochester. By the time Christina was eight years old, Shelly decided that they would all be better if they moved to Pittsburgh.

The credit for Christina's healthy self-esteem and the seeming normalcy of her childhood despite aggravating circumstances must go to Shelly and her family. Christina became particularly close to her grandmother as well as to her maternal aunts and uncles. She was enveloped in the protective cocoon of her family, who provided Christina with the emotional nourishment that she would take with her, and continue to crave, after she shot to superstardom. Shelly, along with her the help of siblings, made a commendable effort to maintain a sense of normalcy for her daughter.

Although cynical critics later suggested that Christina's interest in her Hispanic background only surfaced after she had decided to record an album in Spanish, clearly her ethnicity was an important part of her identity from an early age, thanks to her mother.

It was Shelly who made the little girl feel proud of who she was and where she had come from. "Growing up in a predominantly Irish area, it was easy to always honor the Irish customs and family traditions," Shelly later explained. She added, "After my marriage had ended in divorce, I always made sure, for my girls' sake, that we incorporated versions of the Aguilera family's South American traditions into their lives as well. Even though they never saw their dad and the grandparents never visited or anything, I still wanted them to be proud of all aspects of who they are."[18]

Fausto's parents told Shelly that every year at midnight on Christmas Eve, their family would sit down to eat an elaborate Christmas dinner. Since neither Christina nor her sister Rachel liked to sit down to eat a full course dinner, "I let the kids stay up till midnight and I serve[d] a huge variety of homemade cookies and hot chocolate, and we read the Nativity story together," Shelly later wrote in an online journal for her daughter's website. Christina loved the holiday season, and occasionally sang Christmas tunes even when the holiday was long gone. "I used to go around with a Christmas hymn book when I was really little and sing them for fun, all the time, whether it was Christmas or not," she later said.[19]

Christina also recalled, rather awkwardly in Spanish, Shelly's efforts to give their household a Latin flavor. "My mom would make a lot of traditional Latin dishes. My mom loves the Latin culture as well.

[For Christmas] we would put up a manger...she really tried to raise us as well as she could with what we had."[20]

Quite remarkably, the fragile-looking little girl turned out to be tougher than she seemed. She took the frustration she felt as a result of the divorce and the isolation of a sudden separation from her father, and channeled it toward working for her talents. It is a stunning display of Christina's resilience, that unlike a significant number of children who witness domestic abuse at home, she was apparently able to hold it together.

Perhaps the one indication that Christina was not entirely unscarred by the divorce, but had certainly been disturbed by the domestic violence she had witnessed, was the little girl's persistent fear of the dark, possibly motivated in part by the nightmares that are characteristic of children in abusive environments. Even when she was already well into her teens, she requested that the lava lamp in her basement room be left on as she fell asleep so she wouldn't have to be afraid. She also noted, "My priest gave me this cross from back home, which I keep under my pillow sometimes. I'm afraid of the dark, so...it's just as a little bit of protection."[21] (Christina was actually very close to her priest, Father Rick Thompson. "God has blessed us all in calling you to the priesthood," she later wrote of the man who counseled her when she lived in Pittsburgh. "Thank you so much for keeping me in your thoughts and prayers, giving me guidance and making a difference to many.")

What Christina hated was the insecurity, the uncertainty that pervaded her when she found herself in a darkened room. It was reminiscent of the feelings of insecurity and vulnerability that plagued her when her father hit her mother, which had probably resulted in her having horrible nightmares. Christina developed a remarkably childlike yet endearing defense mechanism: visions of a guardian angel whom she described as "this guy in an all-white outfit, just kind of glowing. He had a white beard and was looking down at me calmly."[22]

Certainly, Christina is still very young and it is not surprising that no real emotional problems have surfaced as a consequence of the abuse that she witnessed at home. Only time will tell if Christina is able to come into her own as a woman without the problems that have plagued other divas with precociously early beginnings who found themselves being molded into superstars before they had discovered themselves fully as human beings.

It was in Wexford that Shelly Aguilera met James Kearns, who worked as a paramedic. Shelly found herself falling in love with the kind, gentle man and they got married on May 12, 1991. Christina was only 10 years old, and sister Rachel was 4. As he eased into the young family, Shelly called her husband "Jim" but Christina, who soon grew very attached to this new father figure, started calling him "Dad." Jim had two children of his own from a previous marriage, five-year-old Stephanie and seven-year-old Casey.

"I call my hometown Pittsburgh, Pennsylvania, because that's basically where I ended up from age eight on," Christina later recalled of her years there. Her earliest Christmas memory dates back to her times in Wexford. "I remember when I was eight, running down the stairs, looking under the tree and finding the Barbie kitchen I wanted so badly. That's my coolest Christmas memory." At this point, Christina had no idea that one day she herself would be immortalized as a collectable plastic doll.

It is no accident that Christina's happiest memory dates to the time after she had gotten out of her father's life. It must have been a refreshing change for the little girl to find herself in a stable home with a caring stepfather who made her mother very happy. On the other hand, Christina now found herself battling for her mother's attention with two new additions to the family. Considering her closeness to her mother, it could not have been an easy situation.

TWO
The Little Girl with The Big Voice

Christina began performing at age six in talent shows. One such early tape shows Christina in a black dress, her blonde hair seemingly brighter as a result of the contrast with the darker clothes. The little girl is animatedly waving some kind of cardboard signpost as the audience reacts cheerfully. Jude Pohl, the director of the Pittsburgh theater company Pohl Productions, later remembered Christina from local talent showcases he used to run. Even then, the little girl knew how to stand out. "This eight-year-old girl was the undefeated champion," he recalled. "The thing about her was that she wasn't just a cute little girl with a big little girl's voice," he said, "She was a little girl with an adult voice."[1] He was floored by a videotape of a nine-year-old Christina. "We were just amazed," he recalled. "We called her right away, but we already had our people scheduled for the year, so we just had her come and perform as a guest performer at the finals."

The following year, Christina won all the awards after a powerful rendition of "Break It To Me Gently." The sheer force of her talent so impressed a fellow performer that the little girl refused to go on after hearing Christina sing. "We could have had her compete in the adult female vocalist contest if she had been behind a curtain," Pohl later said.[2] One former competitor, Noelle Bannister, still remembered

Christina more than a decade after their encounter. "I knew she wasn't—just your average nine-year-old," she said in a television interview. "She had the talent, and the drive, and the focus of someone who was going to do something."

It was in one of these performances that Walt Maddox, a professional singer in Pittsburgh who was one of the members of the group The Marcels (whose claim to fame was the song "Blue Moon"), discovered Christina. He was impressed by her voice and command of the stage, and decided to take Christina along with him to performances, recording studios and wherever his job happened to take him. It was an eye-opening experience for Christina, who was not yet nine years old, and not only because of what she learned as an artist. It was also the beginning of a pattern, whereby Christina felt more comfortable in the presence of adults who were very positive, even gushing, about her talent, as opposed to her jealous contemporaries. "Once you saw Christina and heard Christina," Maddox recalled, "there was just no way you could ever forget the voice of this little kid." Later, Christina sang with Maddox at a "Kids Against Drugs" benefit.

Shelly's mother, grandma Delcie Fidler, also noticed that Christina's pitch and performance were more polished than those of other children who were phasing out of their "I-want-to-be-a-singer" periods. In her grandmother's mind, Christina's performances suggested real talent. She told Shelly that the little girl had the chops to become a professional singer. Christina believed it as well. Whenever adults asked her what she wanted to be when she grew up, the tiny girl would reply with complete conviction: "A singer." On one occasion when Christina was at a party thrown by one of her neighbors, she was asked to sing and she cheerfully broke into song. Slowly, the people in the room began gravitating toward her. By the time she was finished with her song, her neighbor asked her for her autograph. Christina never forgot how good she felt to have such a request made of her.[3] While it was Christina's womanly voice that made others take notice of her talent, beneath it lurked an insecure little girl who desperately craved love and recognition. Christina's focused drive from such an early age suggests that she was desperately seeking validation through her talents; indicating that she felt that she was worthy not simply for being, but for being a good singer.

Regardless of the psychological underpinnings motivating Christina's success, it was as a result of her self-assured performances at talent shows and block parties, that friends and fellow mothers of Christina's classmates…as well her grandmother…insisted that Shelly send a tape of the girl's performances to Star Search, the nationally syndicated talent search program. Not really expecting anything to come of it, Shelly sent the tape. The show's producers were delighted with the blonde little girl. Christina was only eight years old when she traveled to the studios of the program, hosted by legendary emcee, Ed McMahon. Christina was thrilled to meet him, and it was her first time in Los Angeles.[4] The same man who introduced Britney Spears to a national audience asked the studio audience for a big round of applause for Junior Vocalist challenger Christina Aguilera.

The little girl was stunningly in command as soon as she came out on the stage. Wearing one of her mother's old disco day blouses—made of a black, shiny material—as a dress, held on tightly with a large, glittering belt, Christina precociously belted out Whitney Houston's "Greatest Love Of All." She had a startlingly deep voice that seemed to soar up and down as she started demonstrating the mannerisms (which the press would later dub "Mariahisms") that would become a trademark of her performance style.

After receiving a big round of applause from a pleased studio audience, Christina had one of her first career disappointments. She lost to a boy, all decked out in a tuxedo, who was actually older than her. When she lost, Christina thought "No fair!" Regardless, Shelly wanted to teach Christina how not to be a sore loser, and she insisted: "You gotta go over there and shake his hand." Christina later recalled "…with tears streaming down my eyes, I was like eight years old, saying 'Congratulations, I'm really happy for you'." A poignant scene, but Shelly did not want her eight-year-old to become enveloped by the jealousy, competitiveness, and frustration that can surface during the trials and tribulations of attempting to establish a professional singing career.

Although Christina lost her first important competition, it was hardly a setback for the determined little girl. Showing the same character, good spirit and dogged determination that she would exhibit as a young adult, she decided to use her runner-up winnings to buy a portable sound system that allowed her to sing in a park near her home. That same year, Christina won her first important talent show, singing another Whitney Houston standard, "I Wanna Dance With Somebody." Christina was even interviewed on the Pittsburgh talk show "Himelstein One On One," and she performed on the KDKA morning show with Larry Richert.

Unfortunately, the success Christina achieved was not a source of pride for everyone. As Christina's name became more prominent in the local press, the jealousy of her classmates and of their parents grew proportionately. According to Christina, they slashed the tires on her mother's car and some of her classmates started ignoring her. She was experiencing firsthand some of the drawbacks that being a singer and, more importantly to other people, a celebrity, would entail.

Although Christina learned to put a smile on her face and dealt with the problems as best she could, the rejection of her peers left her with lingering feelings of self-doubt that could not be easily dismissed, even with her mother's words of comfort. These feelings of inadequacy fueled Christina's desire to make it as a singer, and more importantly, to become a star. The strong relationship Christina would later develop with her fans had its roots in her childhood, when she decided that she would achieve the stardom that she desperately wanted to prove to herself and her contemporaries, that she was worthy of their attention.

One morning after breakfast, Shelly and her mother were looking through *The Pittsburgh Post-Gazette*, the local paper, and there was a tiny ad in the back section, soliciting the presence of girls and boys to audition for *The New Mickey Mouse Club*, a children's variety show with skits, music and choreography, that would air on the Disney Channel.

Shelly told Christina about the open casting call, and the nine-year-old girl was excited at the chance of performing on television. Christina decided she wanted to audition. Shelly took the young girl to the casting location. Lynne Symons, then executive director of original programming for the Disney Channel, recalled that in the audition they were on the lookout for "triple threats who could do it all." During the auditioning, which lasted almost all day, an energetic Christina made cut after cut after cut. Although there were more than 400 Pittsburgh children who auditioned for the show, she was one of only four (six, according to Shelly) selected to shoot an audition tape. In the end, however, Christina was deemed too young to be on the show. Her audition tape was appropriately archived and noted, so that they could call her in case they decided to have another casting call. Christina could not have known that a brown-haired little girl with big brown eyes from Louisiana had also auditioned and been told she was too young. That little girl, whose name was Britney, would soon be following Christina's footsteps into the show.

Two years after *The New Mickey Mouse Club* debacle and numerous talent show performances later, Christina sang before a crowd gathered for a Pittsburgh charity banquet. Just as it had continuously happened in Christina's life that one opportunity opened the doors for more, that performance led to her being asked to sing the National Anthem for the Pittsburgh Steelers and Penguins. Later, she remembered the experience fondly. "I did a lot of singing of the National Anthem at sporting events between the ages of nine and eleven," she recalled with a laugh. "I was the youngest anthem singer ever, for a while." Because of her singing, "I became a huge hockey fan," Christina recalled. In fact, at the time, her bedroom walls were lined with hockey sticks and Penguins posters.

Apparently, she was quite the charm for the Penguins. "It was a funny thing. They'd actually win whenever I sang the anthem." After she was invited back to sing on October 10, 1992, New York Newsday noted: "Trying to import some much-needed good luck, the Pirates invited one of the Stanley Cup champion Penguins' national anthem singers last night: 11-year-old Christina Aguilera from nearby Wexford, Pa. One of Aguilera's neighbors is Sid Bream, the former Pirates first baseman who plays for the Braves." Christina sang "The Star-Spangled Banner" at every home game during the '92 season when the Penguins won the Stanley Cup.

Despite her "perfect record," not everyone was thrilled about Christina singing the anthem. The Minneapolis *Star Tribune* pointed out, "there was growing optimism after two games in Atlanta that we could get through the National League playoffs with only adults singing 'The Star-Spangled Banner.'...The revolting trend that started in Minnesota a year ago—to have a dolled-up munchkin sing the anthem—will be repeated tonight when Game 3 of the series is played in Three Rivers Stadium. Christina Aguilera, 11, of Wexford, PA, has drawn the anthem assignment. Good news: The forecast is for rain and 45-degree temperatures. Maybe the sight of a drenched twerp will put a merciful end to baseball's cuteness craze." At 11 years of age, the budding singer experienced the first backlash from the press.

Throughout all these ups and downs, Shelly was always very much in the background; offering her daughter love and support, but refusing to force her into shows or performances. She has always refuted the view that she was a pushy mother, "'cause there's a lot of stage mothers out there," she explained, "but you want to see an angry kid…you let two weeks pass by [with no performances booked for Christina].[5] Shelly would certainly suggest or ask when she saw something in the paper, but it was always Christina's enthusiasm that cinched the deals.

Christina later explained that, if anything, *she* was a "stage child" always pushing and prodding her mother to take her to auditions, "but she knew that I wanted to do this and she really helped me out."[6] Shelly did not require much needling because, from the beginning, she was entirely supportive of her daughter. She had been a musician herself and could identify with her daughter's passion. She even read any material she could get her hands on that explained what she could do to help her daughter further her career. "When Christina was young I kind of learned real quickly that this was sort of out of my control, that she was going to be this, that God was kind of guiding everything. Stuff would land in our laps and I thought, 'Oh, okay I'm supposed to do this.' So I kind of figured this was what she wanted to be and she never, ever wanted to be anything else. I didn't know what to do at all, I was clueless," Shelly explained. "So, I went to bookstores and libraries; and read everything I could get my hands on written by professionals in the industry. That helped tremendously."[7]

One day, Christina was hanging out in her room listening to the radio and singing along to the songs as she usually did. Suddenly, Mariah Carey's four-week No. 1 hit, "Vision of Love" came on. Christina ran down the stairs and tugged at Shelly's outfit. "Mommy, Mommy," Christina yelled excitedly. "I just found the greatest person in the world! I just heard the greatest new voice!" Thus it was then that her immense admiration for Mariah Carey's vocal acrobatics began.[8]

Christina entered 6th grade at North Allegheny's Marshall Middle School, one of three middle schools in North Allegheny. Located at 5145 Wexford Run Road, in Marshall Township, the school was a second home to approximately 800 students in grades six, seven, and eight. By the time she had reached the 7th grade, Christina had finally made some friends. She even became part of what she termed the "cheerleader clique." In one of the only times she decided to attempt to partake in typical teenage activities, she decided to try out for the squad herself.

"Two friends that were cheerleaders encouraged her to try out one year," Shelly later explained. "She did, and she made it, but was a cheerleader for literally one week. Their practice schedule was extremely strict. Christina knew she'd miss much more than half the practices due to her traveling so much for her singing, so she turned her spot over to someone else."[9]

Once again, Christina had sacrificed a spot on her school's popularity totem pole for her singing. She explained, "A lot of times, I didn't want to talk about just boys, I didn't want to talk about cheerleading practice. You know what I mean? I wanted to be fully into music."[10] Although many would later dismiss Christina's youthful success by suggesting that she had not paid her dues, anecdotes like these demonstrate that it was only through her determination, drive and early focus that she was able to achieve her dream at such an early age. Christina did make important sacrifices that must have seemed monumental to a teenage girl desperately craving acceptance. On the other hand, her eschewal of other activities desirable and healthy for

19

somebody her age was prompted by her inability to connect with her contemporaries. Because she was unable to gain acceptance by being herself, she would achieve popularity through her talent. Christina's recollection of this period of her life leaves no doubt as to what her priorities were: "I always pretty much did something in entertainment; acting, dancing, but mainly singing. On the side I went to school and did babysitting around my hometown. That's basically it."[11]

It was her talent, however, that proved a double-edged sword. Although it would propel her name to the top of the pop charts, it did not improve her standing among her classmates. On one occasion, when Christina was at the movies with some friends, a group of students asked her tauntingly: "Sing for us! Sing for us!" When she broke down and finally sang for them, they started talking among themselves: "Oh, she's showing off again." But Christina just couldn't win. On other occasions, when Christina refused to sing for them, they shouted mockingly, "Oh, she's too good to sing for us."

According to Shelly, an astute observer and a stay-at-home mom, "In school, Christina had some friends who were among the popular girls." She described her friend Marcie as a friend for a lifetime, and her other friend Craig would drive Christina around whenever Shelly was busy. "For all the times you've driven me around," Christina later said. "I owe you a car." Many "popular" girls were horribly nasty to her; and some who weren't in the popular group were nasty to her as well. "Some went to extremes," Shelly would later recall, adding that they "…still do to this day…as we get word of a few that work in local malls and try hard to spread false dirt about her, using the fact that they went to middle school with her as some sort of supposed credibility on their part."[12]

Academically, Christina had the typical disdain for mathematics. She rather predictably enjoyed her English classes, and, interestingly, she was also particularly fond of her Science class. The latter two subjects came easiest to her. Although her intellectual curiosity was much less intense than her artistic talents, and she focused all of her drive and ambition into her efforts to have an artistic career, she would later dabble in psychology classes and ponder studying psychology in college.

Although Christina was hurt by her classmates' rejection of her, it also taught her how to keep a smile on her face in the midst of difficult circumstances. Christina herself, whose affinity for psychology was accompanied by a fondness of introspection, admitted once: "I put on a pretty good front, but I'm pretty sensitive. I would say that I'm thick-skinned. I'm a pretty sensitive person, but I can take heat."[13]

When Christina was twelve years old, her mother received a curious phone call. It was from one of the producers of Disney's *The New Mickey Mouse Club*. They had seen Christina's audition tape and wanted to know whether Christina was still available for casting on the show. "Before, she was too young, but we'd like her to come back and audition for us again," Christina recalled the producer asking. Casting agent Matt Cassella told Christina's mother that when she first auditioned, she was a bit too young for a part. Now that she had turned 12, she was old enough. Shelly was ecstatic, and so was Christina. She "...freaked out" and was "jumping up and down."[14]

Christina and her mother went back to the casting location. That winter, 15,000 potential Mouseketeers all over the United States auditioned for what were only seven new slots on *The New Mickey Mouse Club*. In fact, Christina would be joining Keri Russell (of the WB's *Felicity*) and J.C. Chasez (of 'N Sync), who were both older and already part of the show by the time she was selected. It is a testament to Christina's enormous talent that out of thousands of teenagers, she had made the cut after passing two rounds of tryouts. After the selection, there was a camp at Disney World where all the finalists met and went through auditions and screen tests.

THREE
A Beaver County Mouseketeer

Christina earned a 5-year contract with Disney. The Pittsburgh *Post-Gazette* proudly announced that one of their own would become a Mouseketeer; A BEAVER COUNTY MOUSEKETEER, read the headline on October 2, 1993. "Christina Aguilera is going to Disney World," the article began. "That's where *The New Mickey Mouse Club* tapes its shows, and Christina, 12, of Rochester, Beaver County, is a new Mouseketeer on the show, which begins its new season Monday on the Disney Channel."

Christina only attended part of the 7th grade in Wexford, as the rest was in Florida while she lived there during taping seasons of *The New Mickey Mouse Club*. The show was taped on the Disney/MGM Studio Lot. Christina and her family relocated to Orlando from May to late October and filmed all of the episodes for the year. Shelly had to give their dog, a Newfoundland named Sampson, to a friend because it was too big for their Florida apartment. Once they arrived in Orlando, they got a smaller Shetland Sheepdog, which they named Fozzie. They have kept the dog to this day.[1]

When they arrived in Orlando, each Mouseketeer family was able to select an apartment. Despite having a choice of several complexes, most of the Mouseketeers lived in the same apartment building. It was more practical and convenient because many cast members hung out and traveled to and from the studio lot together.

A typical day as a Mouseketeer included three hours of schooling in the "Mouseketeer Bungaloo" and then several hours of rehearsing and taping on the set. In the Bungaloo, each Mouseketeer had a separate cubby desk, and there was one tutor who monitored all of them at one time. Since their ages ranged from 11 to 18 years old, students worked independently during the three-hour session.

Christina recalled: "The show was like summer camp, all of us coming together. We'd start the school year late, and leave school early in the spring."[2] When students at Christina's Marshall Middle School put their books away for the summer on June 10, she would also put hers away in the Bungaloo until school reopened August 29. "Christina's tutor is constantly in touch with her teacher at Marshall, so that she can come back in the fall and jump right back into her regular schooling," Shelly explained to the *Post-Gazette* at the time. They covered the same course materials and received the same homework assignments as classmates in their home schools would. That way, they wouldn't fall behind by the time they returned to their real classrooms in October.

Being on *The New Mickey Mouse Club* was an eye-opening experience for Christina. Like a sponge, she soaked up everything. She was honing her show business chops. Christina later said that in retrospect, "It was a great way to grow up. I got the most incredible education, both in terms of who I wanted to be as an artist and in terms of how the business works. It gave me the focus I needed…" The show included dance numbers, singing and acting and Christina was slowly becoming an entertainment triple-threat. The time that Christina spent on the set varied depending on whether she was performing in the skits scheduled for that day. Most shows weren't filmed from start to finish. "We tape it in little parts," Christina explained after taping her first season. "We might do a skit one day and a dance number the next day. We sometimes do a lot of openings and closings in one day."

The New Mickey Mouse Club ran daily at 5:30 after *Kids Incorporated* (which featured Jennifer Love Hewitt). It was a half hour of music, comedy skits and celebrity guests. Each day had a special theme. Monday was "Music Day," which featured artists like Exposé, TLC and Jon Secada. Actor Luke Perry made an appearance during a Guest Day on Tuesday. Wednesday was "Anything Can Happen Day" and Thursday was "Party Day." The week ended with "Hall of Fame Day," where regular kids performed and then were inducted into the Mickey Mouse Hall of Fame. They even inducted kids who had battled alcohol addiction, drug abuse, or bulimia.

A typical episode would include Christina dancing and singing with Britney and the others, and in one particularly memorable show, J.C. threw a pie in her face. "My parents are clowns," Christina said, rolling her eyes in exaggeration, "we throw pies all the time." The shows were hard work, but Christina never considered it work at all. Coincidentally, J.C. Chasez would later remember little Christina as a singing machine who loved to imitate Whitney Houston's high notes.

Christina enjoyed listening to Whitney, whose songs had played such an important role in her career, even if it had been from afar. As a Mouseketeer, she got to meet Houston when she performed on the show one time. She was also fascinated with Mariah Carey, who had the biggest influence on her vocal styling. Mariah Carey was almost ten years older (she was born in 1970) than Christina, and the young girl was 10 years old when Mariah's first, gospel-style album came out.

It is interesting that Christina would cite Mariah as an important influence in her early musical development. As Mariah's career progressed and the singer became more in control of her life, she veered toward R&B-influenced music and tighter clothing which broadened her appeal to younger crowds. At the time of her debut, however, her discoverer, Sony Music chief Tommy Mottola, carefully choreographed her album and image and that image was anything but youthful. In demure black dresses and flowing skirts, the singer actually looked older than her years. Perhaps Christina's interest was spurred by the fact that Mariah was also of mixed heritage; her father was a black man from Venezuela, and like Shelly, Mariah's mom was of Irish descent. The marriage of Mariah's parents, like that of Shelly and Fausto, also ended in divorce by the time she was three years old.

As Christina's career progressed, the similarities between her and the biggest selling artist of the 90's would become striking.

Another favorite singer of Christina's was Janet Jackson. She later recalled of the latter superstar, "I remember watching MTV when I was a little girl. To me, Janet had it all; amazing videos, hot songs and the sexiest voice."[3] As far as consummate entertainers went, Madonna was also someone that Christina looked up to. Little did she know that the music channel that had propelled Madonna's rise to pop superstardom, and that she avidly watched, would also have an important role in her own career. What is of interest in Christina's following of Madonna's career was her observation that what she appreciated about Madonna was her omni-presence in all areas of the entertainment industry. Although Madonna was certainly not the first all-around entertainer, or even the first artist to distribute her music (and book) through her own label, she was the first high-profile "artist-as-conglomerate."

It was not Madonna's voice that propelled her to the top of the pop charts and it is not her music that has left an indelible footprint in the pantheon of American pop culture. It was her daring performances and apparently impulsive (but actually quite calculated) pushing of society's buttons, as well as her much-chronicled image as a ball-busting businesswoman, that made her unique in the entertainment industry. Christina wanted a part of that. In fact, Christina grew up in the midst of the first batch of "entertainers" who were *notorious* for their carefully crafted images, as opposed to actual artists who were *famous* for a given talent, such as Barbra Streisand and Frank Sinatra. It was no surprise then, that Christina would later tell the London *Times*[4] that she sought "similar respect as a businesswoman." Despite Christina's admiration for "The Material Girl," her remarkable vocal gifts would assure that, if anything, she would be filling the shoes of Mariah Carey, while fellow Mouseketeer Britney, who, unlike Madonna was not even involved in the production of her music, would be placed by the press in that role.

The New Mickey Mouse Club was a wonderful, family-like atmosphere for Christina. In fact, at the end of each show taping, the whole cast would gather round and sing the show's theme song: "And now it's time to say goodbye/To all our company," they would sing as they all held hands and embraced, "M-I-C, See you real soon! K-E-Y, Why? Because we like you! M-O-U-S-E." After they had sung the lyrics, the melody broke into a fun rap, which the Mouseketeers would cheerfully dance to.

Christina said that being on *The New Mickey Mouse Club* was also comforting because she no longer had to put up with her classmate's jealousy. "It was a really great growing experience for me to be on a show that had so many people who had dreams like I did," she recalled. "I had a hard time at school because a lot of kids didn't share my dream of becoming a recording artist or superstar one day…I wanted to make a record and sing for thousands and whatnot." As a member of the club, Christina was no longer ostracized or picked on for being different. All the kids in *The New Mickey Mouse Club* had dreams similar to hers and were working equally hard toward achieving them.

It was a haven for Christina, who was finally surrounded by like-minded younger people who she could identify with. But it was also disruptive to spend six months in Florida and then pack up and return to Wexford. Christina had to give up some favorite sports, including softball and volleyball, because she could not join any teams during the summer due to her commitment with the Mouseketeers. Christina also acknowledged that being on the show at that particular age had its drawbacks. "I was 12 and 13 at that time," she explained, "It's an awkward age: You're changing…I was trying to get comfortable with the changes and stuff."

"We would always look up to Keri Russell because she was like 16," Christina said, referring to the now-famous television actress. "She had the car. She had the boyfriend. She was more developed. We totally looked up to her as what we wanted to be. Now, of course, that's changed, but at that age, the youngest, you wanted to be older. Aside from that, I had a really great time doing that show."

When she said "we totally looked up to Keri," Christina also meant Britney Spears. She further recalled, "Me and Britney were the youngest, she was like 11; I was 12. It ranged from us to people who were like 18." In fact, they rarely hung out with the older Mouseketeers.

Lindsey Alley, a former Mouseketeer who spent seven seasons on the show and later went on to graduate as a theater major at the University of Missouri, could not remember much about Christina because, understandably, an older teenager would not be hanging out with a 12-year-old. Noted Alley, "If you want me to be perfectly honest, I don't remember many stories about Christina because she was so much younger. Sixteen-year-olds don't really hang out with twelve-year-olds, you know what I mean? She was very sweet and incredibly talented. She was all of like 60 lbs, and had the voice of a seasoned diva."[5] Matt Casella, casting director for *The New Mickey Mouse Club* concurred with Alley. "They'd call her the diva," he said. "They all sort of took a step back and went, oh boy, I'm gonna lose a few solo songs this season."

Shelly would later explain, in light of all the comparisons and pitting of one against the other, "You couldn't separate Britney and Christina." She also told *AllPop*, "They were inseparable on *The New Mickey Mouse Club*. I mean literally. Britney's mom Lynne and I lived at each other's apartments practically with these girls back and forth. They're so alike, personality wise." That was one reason, but the other was that all of the Mouseketeers lived in the same complex, so it would make sense that the two girls would spend a significant amount of time together.

Because of the closeness in their ages, Christina was in fact particularly close to Britney, but it was a friendship that fizzled soon after they left the club. The friendship was rather superficially based on their ages and the relationship between their mothers, and the two girls had not known each other before they were selected for the show. When her hometown paper interviewed Christina, she failed to mention Britney as a particularly close friend, but in one of the many publicity shots taken for the show, Christina is sitting right next to Britney. "As the two youngest cast members, we really bonded," she would explain later. Christina, Britney and Justin Timberlake would get together and the three of them would hang out at Florida's Pleasure Island and dance and dance.[6]

In October 1993, after taping her first season of the show and right before Christina turned thirteen years old, Mike Mendoza wrote about *The New Mickey Mouse Club* in the *Los Angeles Times*:

"More than 15,000 aspiring Mouseketeers auditioned last winter for seven slots on *The New Mickey Mouse Club*, the third spinoff from the original that premiered in 1955. Who would've thought that the '90s version would be such a hit?

Christina Aguilera, Nikki Deloach, T.J. Fantini, Ryan Gosling, Tate Lynche, Britney Spears and Justin Timberlake will join the returning 13 for a sixth season of music and dance performances, comedy skits and guest stars, as well as some more serious subjects. During the season they'll tackle such topics as eating disorders, depression and teen suicide—not the usual Disney fare. Mouseketeer fans seem to love Mouseketeer music, and the new mice on the team are only too happy to provide it. They've just released a debut album that is a mix of R&B, hip-hop, and of course, Disney-style music. Recorded during the show's hiatus, the CD features 12 original songs by 13 club members. A single and a music video are also promised, with a 10-city concert tour scheduled this month to promote the album."

That year, the Mouseketeers also performed concerts throughout the park and enjoyed perks including a "Silver Passport" good for park admission anytime. Apart from the perks, celebrity and artistic education that Christina gained on *The New Mickey Mouse Club* that first season, it was also as a 12-year-old Mouseketeer that she took her first step toward actually obtaining representation for her future career as a recording artist. Ruth Inniss, whom the *New York Beacon* had described as an "independent public relations whiz"[7] and who was then, coincidentally, working as an RCA talent scout, happened to be in the Disney studios, and she came upon the young performer. Inniss was in Orlando doing publicity for the female R&B singing group, SWV, who was in fact a musical guest on *The New Mickey Mouse Club* during the same season that Christina joined the show.

While she wandered the studios, Inniss heard Christina singing and asked to speak to her mother. Shelly recalled wondering what trouble Christina had gotten herself into and admitted, "I'm the mom!" Quite the opposite had happened. Christina's voice had impressed the savvy publicity woman to such an extent, that she explained to Shelly that she could help the girl with her singing career. They agreed to stay in touch and speak again once Christina's contract with Disney was over.[8] In an MTV interview, Shelly admitted that a talent scout who was representing an R&B girl group had approached her when Christina was on *The New Mickey Mouse Club*, and had offered to represent her daughter. Shelly did not name this talent scout and did not explain what, if any, role the woman had on Christina's career. Regardless, Christina had taken one more step toward her life-long dream, and she had done it all on her own by way of her incredible voice.

On December 16, Christina-the-Mouseketeer was one of the performers at a Christmas show and dance sponsored by WWSW radio in Pittsburgh. The show was a fundraiser to start a college trust fund that would benefit the children of Jay Weiss, a local man who had been killed while delivering pizza in September. Even though she was not yet thirteen years old, Christina already understood that her celebrity was a powerful weapon that could be used to help other people.[9] In fact, she had already decided that if she did become famous, she wanted to help out other children involved in abusive situations.

Right before she took off for Orlando for a second time in May 1994, the *Post Gazette* interviewed Christina. "It's really fun," she told a reporter when questioned about what it was like to be a Mouseketeer. "All of us together—we're like a big family. We fight like brothers and sisters sometimes, but then we make up and we work very well together." When asked if she thought of what she did as a job, Christina shrieked "No! It's a vacation, I can't wait to go." She then added, "You have to be having fun to be able to do something like this for eight hours." As far as Christina's real family, although it might have appeared that her overwhelming success and talent overshadowed the rest of her siblings' accomplishments, Shelly took pains to make Rachel and her stepchildren feel valued and important. An avidly involved parent, Shelly would organize parties for them for no particular reason, something many who live in their old block found amusing. She also nurtured Rachel's artistic leanings, although they were geared toward painting. In turn, Rachel was very supportive of her big sister and later said that she had no doubt that Christina would one day make it as a singer.

For Christina, and the rest of the Mouseketeers, 1994 was a busy year. Most shows were filmed in sequence in front of a live audience, which was a change from the previous arrangement where the shows were filmed in parts. The Mouseketeers also appeared in parades and made appearances in the Magic Kingdom, Epcot Center and the MGM Studio. According to Ruth Inniss, it was in February of 1994 that Shelly finally contacted her about Christina's singing career. The women agreed that Inniss would act as Christina's manager. They further specifically agreed that upon Christina's obtaining a recording contract, Inniss would act as her manager in all phases of advancing and developing her career, and receive a standard manager's commission.[10]

On December 18, 1994 Christina turned fourteen. The family followed the usual ritual of letting the birthday girl pick the place to eat dinner. When she blew out the candles in her birthday cake, her wish was the same one she had been hoping for and asking for every year since she was six years old. She wished she would become "a star." Sooner than she expected, the dream would be coming true.[11]

FOUR
The Demo Tape

By the time Christina left *The New Mickey Mouse Club*, she was no longer enrolled in school. "She never went to high school, she graduated from home schooling," Shelly explained. "I began home schooling her in 8th grade so she could freely travel."[1]

Christina recalled that after taping her second season of *The New Mickey Mouse Club* in 1994 (which aired in 1995), she abruptly learned that it would also be her last season with the show. As the Mouseketeers were all preparing to go back and start taping again, they received a letter in the mail that explained that they wouldn't be taping anymore.[2] After that, all of the cast members "went back to our own home towns, went back to our own schools. Britney and I kept in touch in the early years because we were both trying to get record deals. I knew she was in Philly doing demos and I was working with a couple of producers out of New Jersey."[3]

Christina did not rest on her laurels. She was determined to have an album out before she had graduated from high school. She taped the final season of *The New Mickey Mouse Club* in 1994, and by early 1995, the independent and determined teenager hooked up with New Jersey-based producers Robert Alleca and Michael Brown.[4] Although a business listing could not be located for the apparently now defunct business endeavor, Brown and Alleca were the founders of BAM (presumably Brown Alleca Music) Records, which was an independent company based in the basement of, reportedly, Robert Alleca's home. Christina even befriended Alleca's wife, Sheila. "Thank you for making me so comfortable away from home," she later wrote, "and introducing me to calamari." Although Christina has not explained how she made the connection with the producers, it would appear to have been the work of Ruth Inniss. According to Inniss, Shelly called her for help once Christina's contract with the Walt Disney Company lapsed.

The fact that Michael Brown and Bob Alleca were credited as working on keyboards, drum programming and mixing, as well as being "producers" on R&B girl-group SWV's "It's About Time" album, adds much weight to Ruth Inniss' claims. As established previously, Inniss was representing SWV when she walked into Christina's life off *The New Mickey Mouse Club* set. It seems reasonable to assume that Inniss would recommend or suggest the people who had worked on her former clients' album to Christina and her mom, and thus was able to help them make the connection to BAM.

Brown and Allecca gave Christina the offer to use their studios but they agreed that they would never release the demos commercially. She recorded eleven songs, which her lawyer later described as "rough and unfinished"[5] in BAM's basement studios. Even back then, the producers and Christina apparently saw the potential in having the half-Latin singer vocalize in Spanish. Thus, one of the songs, an up-beat dance track titled "Just Be Free" was also recorded in Spanish, bringing the total recorded songs to twelve. Most of the original songs were up-beat dance mixes, and some of them were ballads designed to showcase Christina's voice. According to the record company that later released the recordings, Christina co-wrote each of the songs.

Those early tapes, made simply to get her foot in the door as Christina put it, already demonstrated Christina's raw vocal agility, despite the dull quality of the song lyrics. Christina's hunger for success actually comes through in the songs, as she sings her heart out with strained emotion, trying to sound as if she is letting all her inhibitions run free. If she did in fact co-write the songs, then they were also a demonstration of Christina's songwriting dexterity, because although the album's lyrics could be called unoriginal and perhaps even cheesy, it could not be said that they were not catchy. Not bad for a fourteen-year-old. More importantly though, Christina's songwriting proved to be an early sign of the intense artistic involvement that the singer would have in every single endeavor she decided to embark on during her career. She was already showing, at fourteen, that she was first and foremost a talented musician and artist. Years later, after Christina had gotten her foot in the door by way of a multi-platinum selling album, those early recordings which she had only intended for use as demos, a fact she had made clear to the producers, would come back to haunt her. As it was, the demos were not particularly helpful for Ruth Inniss. That same year, several labels, including RCA, passed on the opportunity to sign Christina. The resurgence of pop music in radio play and album sales was not even dimly visible at that point. Discouraged but not defeated, Christina left for Japan to jump-start her career on distant shores.

By 1995, Christina got the opportunity to travel overseas to further hone her musical skills. That year, she performed in places as far flung as Tokyo, Japan and Brasov, Romania, where she represented the United States at the Golden Slag Festival alongside Sheryl Crow and Diana Ross. She always kept her eye on the same goal. "I always wanted to have my own album recorded and released before I graduated high school," Christina explained. She recorded a concert in Los Angeles that was broadcast in Japan by FM Osaka.[6] While in Japan, thanks to the efforts of her demo producer Michael Brown, Christina was able to record a hit duet and a video with one of that country's most famous pop stars, Keizo Nakanishi. "He was very popular at the time and was looking for an American girl who could sing with him," Christina later explained matter-of-factly. "So, I got the job."[7] The single was released in Japan on the Pioneer Records label and Christina performed two concerts with Nakanishi at Tokyo's NHK Hall.

When one listens to the song, it becomes clear why Christina considered it a "job." In fact, the pop tune was even of a worse quality than the catchy demo songs she had previously recorded. The upbeat pop confection titled "All I Wanna Do" had an unoriginal chorus ("All I wanna do every day and night/Love you forever/ Wanna wrap my arms around you/All I wanna do is to hold you tight/Hold you forever/And never never let you go"), a disastrous production and did not highlight Christina's vocal abilities. Regardless, compared to Nakanishi's quavering vocals and broken English her voice sounded breathtaking. If anything, the experience gave Christina just a savory enough taste of fame, with perks such as a video shoot and concerts, to make her even hungrier for success in the music industry.

Her success overseas continued unabated, with appearances in a number of high-profile music events as well as a tour. She kept videos of all her appearances, which she later put together into one package that she would present to her manager along with her musical demo tapes. Christina knew that her friends' mothers did not think that her traveling schedule and freedom were appropriate for somebody her age. She appreciated the fact that her own mother, as Delcie Fidler had before her, understood how important her career was and did not attempt to stop her. "A lot of my friends' moms would always be, like, 'Aren't you scared to let your daughter go and do this? Don't you even care?' But she's been so courageous in giving me the freedom to go out and do this. A lot of other mothers wouldn't allow their children to do it out of fear or out of not wanting to cut the apron strings."[8]

FIVE
The Mysterious Management Deal

The Christina Aguilera story presented by the media entirely glosses over Christina's life after she left *The New Mickey Mouse Club*. There is not one article that, in chronicling the rise of Christina, explains or even mentions, where or how she produced her demo tapes, or how the connection between Christina and her management came about.

According to the myth perpetuated by countless publications and the fluff biographies written about her, she was "discovered" after she left *The New Mickey Mouse Club*. By whom or where were not parts of the equation. The *San Diego Tribune* later reported: "High-powered manager Steve Kurtz discovered her as a Mouseketeer and offered to shepherd her career." *The Washington Post* noted, "A year earlier, she'd caught the ear of Ron Fair, a senior vice president at RCA who would sign Aguilera and become her executive producer." Who was it then? Steve Kurtz or Ron Fair? The *Los Angeles Times* pointed out, with slightly more clarity, "While working as a Mouseketeer, Aguilera caught the attention of Steve Kurtz, who asked to be Aguilera's manager and who sent a tape of the little girl with star power to RCA Records—with a note that RCA A&R director Ron Fair still has on his wall."[1]

Jackie Robb, who wrote a short biography of Christina in 1999 was even more vague, breathlessly announcing in a tone more suited for a fanzine: "Before 1999, fans of Christina followed her rise to fame first as a Mouseketeer, then as a movie soundtrack singer in the movie *Mulan*. It was Christina's magnificent voice you heard when the poignant ballad 'Reflection' played as the credits rolled. But what you probably didn't know is this— the same week Christina was recording 'Reflection,' she was also offered a record deal with RCA Records."[2]

Writing in her daughter's website, Shelly Kearns, who is usually very thorough when answering fan questions, was equally vague when discussing Christina's "discovery": "Then at age 11, she was on MMC, which was aired on Disney channel alone. After that, she landed a lead song on the *Mulan* soundtrack, and was signed to RCA records all in the same week. The rest is history."[3] The rest may be history, but exactly how did the record contract come about? Christina herself has been oddly evasive; but then again, because the press simply reported as fact that she was "discovered" by her manager, they never really confronted her with the "missing years" of her meteoric rise to superstardom. However, when MTV asked pointedly: "Tell us how you landed a record deal", Christina replied, in a similar fashion as her mother, and the same way Jackie Robb later described it (probably from Christina's own mouth): "I landed a record deal simultaneously as I landed the *Mulan* soundtrack. I had just turned seventeen years old and during the same week, I just landed both. I recorded the *Mulan* soundtrack first and then a few months later I was out in L.A. doing the record for about six months."[4]

In fact, according to Ruth Inniss, in 1995 when Christina was fourteen years old, she set up a meeting between Christina, her mother and Normand Kurtz. Kurtz was a powerful and well-known music industry lawyer, who headed Dartmouth Management Co. and the Dartmouth Record Co. The savvy businessman in him knew that Christina was uniquely talented and he consulted his son, manager Steve Kurtz, about this new, up-and-coming vocalist. According to Inniss, she had only set up the meeting with Kurtz so that he could offer some pointers and help her steer the teenager's career.[5] Perhaps they could even co-manage Christina. However, in a highly unethical move that Inniss would later attempt to reverse, Normand Kurtz handed over representation of the budding singer to his son Steve, who headed Marquee Management Co. The younger Kurtz took on the representation of Christina.

In the liner notes for her album, Christina duly noted, regarding the elder Kurtz: "You are the one who started it all and believed in me from the beginning. Thanks for keeping your promise that all this would happen, just as I dreamed." There was no mention of Ruth Inniss. Christina has never commented on the allegations herself, which is in line with what she once told an interviewer when commenting on her reaction to heated discussions: "I'm like the peacemaker, you know what I mean? That's what I believe in, or what I should believe in. I think finding a common ground because after a while, I do want to just settle an argument and just do the right thing."[6]

Although Steve Kurtz would later deny ever having met Inniss; neither he, nor Christina, nor her mother would ever provide an alternate scenario for how they came to meet. In fact, Steve Kurtz was not lying when he said that *he* had never met Ruth Inniss. It was his father, Normand who had the initial meeting with Inniss and Christina. On the other hand, Normand's passing along of Christina to his son, who later enlisted Normand's help in managing her, was a distasteful and possibly illegal tactic to cut Inniss from her client. (The fact that Kurtz rebuffed this author's attempts to set the record straight by answering a number of straightforward questions adds weight to Inniss' claims. It would appear that after the negative publicity that descended on Kurtz following Christina's lawsuit, he would have had nothing to lose by explaining what the situation had been; unless he had something to hide. In fact, it was only after the second time that the author called his offices, and mentioned "Ruth Inniss" in a set of questions he left for him, that Kurtz said, through the assistant, that he would not cooperate and he was "not going to change his mind on that.")[7]

Apparently forgetting or conveniently ignoring the verbal agreement she had previously struck with Ruth Inniss, Shelly allowed Christina to sign into contract with Kurtz. It is impossible to know exactly how involved Christina was in the entire process. If she was, in fact, entirely aware of what was going on, then she was already demonstrating a canny mind and businesswoman practicality that would serve her well in dealing with management problems and the administrative aspect of her career. Although musicians are usually associated with free-spirited natures that suggest a lack of interest in the business aspect of their careers, it was the harmonious dichotomy of Christina-the-artist with Christina-the-businesswoman that allowed her to further her own career so quickly. However, Shelly's role in molding her daughter's career cannot simply be described as important, it was essential. Without her support, there would have been no career—certainly not so early in Christina's life.

The Ruth Inniss fiasco is a story as old as show business itself. The potential help that Inniss could offer Christina had reached its limit, and Christina needed to move on to a more powerful manager. The agreement with Kurtz gave him the right to collect a maximum of 20 percent of any commissionable income he obtained for Christina for a potentially indefinite time and a minimum of four years. Part of the contract allowed Kurtz to use other management professionals to help manage Christina. According to Christina, this would come at no extra cost to her. Eventually, he would enlist the help of his father and a co-manager; Katrina Sirdofsky, in managing the burgeoning career of one of pop's most promising new voices.[8] Christina would later complain that Steven Kurtz had unduly influenced the attorney who had drawn up the contract.

Soon after Kurtz signed her, he was going to the Grammys. "I was like 15 or 16 years old and he came back and he framed his Grammy ticket and it was like 'Wow!' to me," Christina remembered. "On the ticket he wrote, 'One day you'll be holding the same ticket as a nominee for Best New Artist.'" He could not have known what prophetic quality his words would take.

In fact, by the time Christina had turned 15, she was busy nursing a crush on Red Hot Chili Peppers guitarist David Navarro. "I used to sleep with the inside cover of their CD every night underneath my pillow," Christina recalled. "For Halloween, I seriously carved a Dave Navarro pumpkin. I was hard-core. I was a fan, hard-core fan, whatever you want to call it."[9] This crush is important because it is a demonstration of Christina's diverse musical tastes and influences. She may have admired Mariah's vocal gymnastics, Janet Jackson's videos and Madonna's showmanship; but she also enjoyed plain old rock.

Soon after she had obtained her demo deal, Christina "heard this girl had signed with Jive—I was being shopped there, too—and my gosh, it was Britney. And I thought, 'my gosh, we're both going for the same thing.' It was cool to me that we were both doing it, but never would I have imagined what was to follow."[10] In fact, Larry Rudolph, one of the most powerful show business lawyers, had signed on a 15-year-old Britney for representation and had found a home for her talent at Jive Records. Soon, the label would own not only the Britney Spears juggernaut, but also the Backstreet Boys, 'N Sync, and a significant piece of the booming teen pop entertainment industry pie, a segment of the marketplace it would become irreversibly identified with.

In the midst of all this, Steven Kurtz was not exactly lying back. By December of 1997, he was already shopping Christina at a number of record labels. Soon after he signed her, he wrote a note to the Senior Vice President of Artists and Repertoire (A&R) for the RCA record label, Ron Fair. The curious note, which Ron Fair has kept on his wall, read: "To Ron Fair, RE: Christina Aguilera, She's 16, lives in Pittsburgh, has star quality," and had an analysis of each of the songs on the demo tapes. Kurtz followed up the analyses with a cryptic, "Any interest? Call me."[11]

The distinctive, self-assured voice of a then 14-year-old Christina definitely caught the ear of Ron Fair. He heard the rough demo and thought, "Excellent singing but the material was not really strong."[12] Quite ironically, this was the same complaint that critics would have about Christina's debut album, which Fair himself would executive-produce.

Despite the poor quality of the songs, Fair was so intrigued by the young vocalist that he decided to call Christina for a meeting. He recalls: "Then I took a meeting with Christina and said, 'Okay, sing!' It was in a very, very small office, with three or four people crammed into it, but she basically got into that performance zone and sang acappella, with a complete sense of self-possession, with perfect intonation. She was very determined and extremely professional. From a musical point of view, her chops were way beyond her years and it was obvious that she had the potential to become a major vocalist."[13]

Like the fairy tale story of Mariah Carey's signing by Sony Records chief Tommy Mottola, the story has gained mythical proportions. At another time, Fair remembered telling Christina, "So sing for me." And Christina recalls, "He totally put me on the spot," but Fair recalled that "She was very much in her own zone, tremendously cute," and as soon as Christina was done with her improvised performance, he decided to sign her to RCA Records.[14] The rest, of course, would become part of show business history.

"I went to my boss," Fair explained, referring to RCA head Bob Jamieson, "and said, 'This girl's the bomb! Let's sign her.'" After getting the go-ahead, he recalled: "I started off by offering her, what I call a garden variety demo deal."[15] One can imagine that Christina may have been somewhat disappointed, because she had already done the demo thing and probably felt she was past that. Bob Jamieson, the President of RCA, was delighted. Just four years ago, he had accepted to head a record label that was, according to *Business Week* magazine, "left for dead with a corporate parent that few took seriously."

When Jamieson, a New Jersey native, who had spent much of his early career at the Columbia and Polygram labels, arrived in mid-1995, parent company Bertelsmann (BMG) had acquired RCA from the General Electric Company in 1986. Since then, a succession of management shifts had failed to get the label on track. In early 1995, BMG hired entertainment executive Strauss Zelnick to revive BMG's North American music business. At that point, Jamieson was heading operations for BMG Canada. When Zelnick offered him the RCA post, Jamieson turned to Jack Rovner, whom he had worked with at Columbia Records in the 1980s (nurturing top acts including Bruce Springsteen) to be his second in command. It was under Jamieson's command that RCA grew to account for just over 10% of BMG's overall $4.6 billion in revenue.[16]

Despite its small size, RCA's push to reestablish itself as a major player was considered critical for its parent company BMG

The Mysterious Management Deal

Entertainment. BMG includes more than 200 labels around the world, but its biggest label is Arista, home of such artists as Whitney Houston, TLC, and Kenny G. While BMG was on the rise at the time Christina signed on to RCA, all was not well at the label. legendary producer Clive Davis who headed Arista Records and made a star of Whitney Houston, would soon leave and form his own label, J Records, which he used to groom and launch the career of multi-platinum-selling Alicia Keys, the most successful female teen act since Britney and Christina. With Jamieson's new management and some lucky breaks, RCA was slowly crawling back into the Top 10.

One thing that could help the label would be to claim a piece of the teen pop pie, before it became impossible to cut into. A multi-platinum-selling album from a multi-talented teen pop diva would be very helpful in getting the label back on top.

It is not surprising that in the midst of this climate Christina did not have to wait for long to obtain her desired album deal. In fact, Ron Fair recalled that soon after he signed her to the demo deal, "a buddy of mine called from Disney," looking for a very particular young vocalist who could actually belt out, not just sing in falsetto, a high E above middle C. The note was required to sing the theme song for the destined-to-be-a-hit animated Disney movie, *Mulan*. The soaring ballad titled "Reflection," dealt with a young girl who is confused about her identity. More importantly, the song was a perfect match for Christina's vocals.

Christina locked herself in her bathroom and once again sang her heart out to a karaoke tape of Whitney Houston's "I Wanna Run To You," a hit single from her *Bodyguard* movie soundtrack, which included the high E that the Disney producers needed for their own song. Christina recalled feeling "so cheesy and so tinny." She recorded it in her bathroom, right by the shower stall. "It was the closest thing I had to get the sound of a microphone. I was like, 'I don't know what to do!' Since it's not like in a recording studio where you can do take after take, if you're halfway through a song and you mess up you have to stop, rewind, and play it all over again. So I must have been up until like four in the morning trying to get the perfect recording. It was crazy."[17] The excitement that the young singer must have felt as she hit the desired note must have been as powerful as her own voice. Christina later recalled calmly: "I had to prove that I could sing this note and I did." She explained that people later called it the "note that changed my life." It remains quite clear that even if she had not gotten the opportunity to sing that song, Christina was destined to take off.

Christina's "I Wanna Run To You" demo was rushed to Disney. They flew her to Los Angeles, she sang the song a couple times, and within 48 hours of the initial call, Disney officials were telling her, "Congratulations, you got the deal." It could not have hurt that the teenager had already been a part of the Disney family and, in fact, had only recently been released from the five year contract she had signed with Disney. It took about a week to record the song. Because she had to sing so "belty" for so long, she explained to the *Pittsburgh Post-Gazette*, "After singing and singing and singing and singing, it just gets so tiresome."

She was scheduled to fly home the day after the recording ended and Christina was exhausted and glad to be taking a small break. When she heard that a 90-piece orchestra would be arriving to record the accompaniment for the song, she begged to stay and hear it. "It's enough to bring tears to your eyes, hearing a 90-piece orchestra playing your song," she later recalled. "It was amazing."[18]

That same week, RCA Records signed her to an actual album contract, under the tutelage of Steven Kurtz. Christina was 17 years old when she signed the contract, and she was in fact under Kurtz's representation, but later, the signing would come under close scrutiny as a result of Christina's complaints regarding her manager's behavior. In reporting the signing of Christina by RCA, the *Pittsburgh Post-Gazette* noted, "RCA wants her to record her first full, solo album by September, before the *Mulan* hype ends." They further noted that Christina "and her managers are already choosing songs for the pop/R&B-style album in the vein of Mariah Carey or Whitney Houston. The album is expected to be released in January." The timing was curious, because Britney's album was scheduled for release that same month. While Britney's *...Baby One More Time* was in fact released that January, Christina's debut would be inexplicably delayed for almost seven months.

SIX

The Teen Pop Machine

Disney's *Mulan* premiered in June 1998, and "Reflection," as expected, turned into a Top 15 Adult Contemporary single and became Christina's first charting American hit. The single did not come with instant celebrity, however, as it was not the personality behind the song but the song itself that mattered to audiences, and more importantly, to Disney's marketing department. One review of the *Mulan* soundtrack called the music "predictable, the lyrics less than smart," but pointed out that "Broadway's Lea Salonga and popster Christina Aguilera do fine with their respective versions of 'Reflection.'" The song's role in Christina's career had more to do with exposing the talented young vocalist to the producers and writers that would later help make her debut album a multi-platinum smash. Christina performed the song live on "CBS This Morning" and the "Donnie & Marie Show" two shows that certainly did not target the teen demographic that Christina wanted to break into. The single went on to garner a Golden Globe Nomination for Best Original Song in a Motion Picture and it got Christina the attention of some of the best writers and producers in the industry.

Diane Warren, one of the most diverse, well-known and consistent hit-makers in the music industry, actually heard Christina that morning, and turned around to see her on the television. "Who is that?" she wondered immediately. She was taken aback when she saw such a polished, self-assured 17-year-old singing the song so early in the morning. Her performance is the real thing, she recalled thinking. Christina's look at the time was rather dowdy. She had short hair, but cropped in a layered fashion that would have been more appropriate for an older woman. She was wearing demure black pants and a blouse and was light years away from the sexy, belly-baring, self-possessed superstar she would later become. She did, however, exhibit her trademark mannerisms as she performed the song.

After the success of "Reflection," RCA groomed Christina for almost a year. The label spent $1 million on writers, producers and voice lessons, all of which Christina embraced. "I was never trained enough to know when is too much, what's going to blow my voice out," she candidly admitted. "Since then, I fell in love with technique, how to make your range go even farther, how to place notes, all these things I never knew about, rather than just singing and listening to my favorite vocalists and going on instinct. I never would have been able to hit the notes I'm hitting now a couple of years ago."[1] Christina, not surprisingly, was turning out to be a very dedicated young professional and she promptly became involved in developing her vocal technique. She would later explain during an Internet chat, "I do work with a vocal coach now out of New York. He helps me…I try to do exercises for 45 minutes a day. There is a tape that I exercise to."[2]

RCA wanted Christina's debut to be a wonderful introduction of a singer who they believed would be their own Barbra Streisand, but they were also anxious over competition from the Jive label and tried to speed up the production. One of the producers who worked on her album, Eric Foster White, recalled that right before Christina put out her album: "The Backstreet Boys were already out there, Britney was definitely happening…" Christina's own competitive streak would sometimes, inevitably, surface as she was working on her own album and watched her fellow Mouseketeers getting their share of attention as they performed on television shows. "I would watch 'Total Request Live' and see all their videos and go, 'I can't wait till I'm a part of that,'" Christina recalled candidly.[3]

Actually, "Total Request Live" was yet another chess piece aligning just in time for Christina and it would play a big part in her career. The highest-rated show on MTV owed its popularity to its affable host, latter-day Dick Clark, Carson Daly. The charismatic, 27-year-old enjoyed instant rapport with teenagers all over the country—eventually one million of them—with his Average Joe demeanor and thousand-watt smile. *People* magazine named him the Sexiest Television Personality, and Liz Smith breathlessly described his "big, soulful blue eyes and an ingratiating smile: handsome but not model-stunning."

The rise of "Total Request Live" was in itself a result of MTV's change of direction in programming. Critics complained that the secret of the network's success was the result of a Faustian bargain through which the station sacrificed its initial credibility to cater to teens' most immediate and banal tastes. That was nothing new. "Since its inception in 1981, MTV's been able to jump from trend to trend—be it early-'80s new wave, late-'80s hair metal or early-'90s grunge and gangsta rap—and reinvent itself for each era," explained an article in *Newsweek*.

"MTV's last big moment of reinvention came with the advent of the Backstreet Boys. It was 1996, and the station was in a ratings slump because grunge had finally hit the skids and hip-hop had yet to take over as a dominant ratings force. "I remember going to a meeting that year where they told us we were going after cutting-edge, freethinking, revolutionary minds," says [Tabitha] Soren, who helped build MTV's credibility in the early '90s by producing smart, in-depth documentaries and covering the 1992 presidential elections. "But six months later we were told, 'Forget all that. Thirteen-year-olds are buying records. Britney Spears is gonna be the hottest thing since sliced bread. That's gonna be our base.' It was just this total flip." It's a turn of events that even the 19-year-old singer still finds hard to believe. "Oh, my goodness," says Spears. "I owe a lot of my success to MTV. I was really a nobody and they were playing my video like I was the most popular thing in the world. It was really, really sweet."

And it was sweet for the struggling music channel as well. The synergy experienced between Spears and MTV had only occurred in the '80s as the rise of Madonna coincided with the rise of the struggling new music channel. According to *The New York Times*, the audience of one million viewers, mostly teenagers, was "For advertisers in search of record-buying, movie-going, clothes-shopping, trend setting and trend-following youth... the bomb. For record companies, it is nuclear."

"Total Request Live, TRL," made its debut on September 14, 1998. It followed another Daly project MTV had titled "The Carson Daly Show," which, in turn, had followed "MTV Live" and a later show titled "Request." "Total Request Live" was a fusion of the concept of video requests and live television. It would turn into quite a lucrative franchise for MTV and the young host, and included interviews with the hottest musicians on the scene and would later expand into television and film actors. Daly explained: "About a year and a half ago, [MTV] opened the Times Square studios," which was all part of a "face lift, and I came on the first year of that face lift. This has been a remarkable year for MTV, with the largest audience it's ever had. I know my fellow hosts know their music and are passionate about it. We're paid to be a liaison, to be part of the pop culture—not to spend three hours in makeup being a star, as some of our predecessors apparently did."

Regarding the rise of the teen pop industry, Daly told *Newsweek*: "Once you make music your business, there's no room for a polarized philosophy. I don't have time to be opinionated. I have a show to host and produce. It's like I'm a bartender: someone wants a Zima, and I might think it's kind of an iffy drink, but you know what? I'm gonna give it to him in a cold glass and hope he gives me a nice tip."

Entertainment Weekly described the hour-long show thus:

> Fans phone and e-mail in their votes for their favorite current videos, which are then compiled into a Top 10 list; the fun here is in trying to keep your fave act prominent, and to savor the suspense as Daly unveils the day's tally...the

videos aren't simply broadcast— they're decorated with all sorts of techno-doodads. Along the bottom of the screen runs a crawl containing e-mailed comments from viewers. As Korn's "Make Me Bad" unspools with black-and-white menace, Myra from Texas writes, "That video kicks hardcore butt!" Meanwhile, outside MTV's Times Square studio in New York City, a gaggle of kids crowd around a camera and microphone to put in their 2 cents as their images are projected onto the lower corners of a video.

By November 1998, just one month after the debut of "TRL," which was desperately looking for new teen stars to feature on an entire hour, *Business Wire* was reporting:

> "Jive Recording artist Britney Spears hasn't just been making ripples since her radio debut a few weeks back... she's making tidal waves. With her first single '...Baby One More Time' causing a major commotion in Top 40 and Pop radio (it was the No. 1 Most Added Single in its first week on R&R's Pop/CHR chart, beating out other first weekers such as Alanis Morissette, U2, Bryan Adams and Goo Goo Dolls), she's currently sitting pretty at No. 12 with a bullet at *R&R's Pop/CHR* chart and No. 16 on *Billboard Monitor's CHR* chart. With all this radio support, '...Baby One More Time' finds itself sitting pretty in the No. 17 slot on *Billboard's Hot 100* chart.

Soon after, The Minneapolis *Star Tribune* wrote, in a similar vein:

> "At age 13, LeAnn Rimes conquered the country charts. At 15, Brandy rocketed up the R&B charts. Now comes Louisiana's Britney Spears, who turned 17 this month as her debut single, '...Baby One More Time,' landed at No. 8 on *Billboard's Pop* chart."

By December 1998, the *Atlanta Journal Constitution* was writing of Britney:

> "High-profile teen stars LeAnn Rimes, Brandy and Monica hammered their pop music elders when it came to selling singles this year. Now they're being chased by another teen, Britney Spears, whose debut single '...Baby One More Time' has sales of more than 500,000 copies. The '98 leader is Rimes, whose 'How Do I Live' racked up sales of 3 million copies, while Brandy and Monica's 'This Boy Is Mine,' included on both artist's million-selling albums, has sales of 2 million. Spears, who celebrated her 17th birthday recently on the day her single moved into *Billboard's Top 10* (it's currently No. 5), will release her debut album '...Baby One More Time' on Jan. 12 on the Jive label."

Nothing breeds imitation like success. Just as Debbie led to Tiffany and the Backstreet Boys led to 'N Sync, Britney's success was paving the way for Christina. (Not surprisingly, soon after Christina's appearance on the scene, Columbia Records launched Mariah Carey-clone Jessica Simpson and the Epic label came out with 15-year-old Mandy Moore, both of whom failed to achieve the success of the first two stars. Less than a year after the teen pop divas appeared, the "hot property" in the music business became young— as in pre-teen—male vocalists. Backstreet Boy Nick Carter's youngest brother, Aaron Carter became pop's young prodigy, and his platinum album and string of Top 10 hits led to rap/hip-hop youngster Lil' Bow Wow, whose No. 1 album on *Billboard's R&B/Hip-Hop* album led to country music's Billy Gilman, who enjoyed similar success.)

As the teen pop craze picked up momentum and the stars in the constellation of the entertainment industry appeared to be aligning almost magically for Christina's debut, RCA Records executives were salivating over the success that they felt their own teen diva would achieve. They wanted to strike while the iron was hot and Christina herself wanted to see her name in lights, right next to the names of the peers she had worked so hard with. "But," Christina explained, "I was still in the recording studio. I had to work on my patience a little at that point."[4] Working on her patience was turning out to be an arduous task. Christina later recalled how, "all of a sudden I see little Brit-Brit as Britney Spears—the new pop sensation—and I was like, 'Wow! This is crazy!'" When Britney's album came out in January, Christina rushed out to buy her own copy, and then went back to the studio to continue laboring on her own record.[5]

Much of the delay with Christina's album had to do with choosing the right material. "When I met her, she was a world-class singer, but hadn't really formed opinions about what style she wanted to sing or what her direction should be," Ron Fair explained. It was understandable. Christina was an 18-year-old with a golden voice to match her marketable golden mane, but she did not have a true understanding of demographics, marketing or the importance of the bottom line in a record label that was still struggling. Her artistic direction was also very much in the air. "She was very much a raw talent, so building a collection of songs that would become her first album was a time-consuming process. We wanted to find the ones that could knock the door down and put her up there."[6]

They decided that the lead single would be the last song they actually received, a frothy, slightly suggestive dance track titled "Genie In A Bottle." Originally, "Genie In A Bottle" was not a track that Christina wanted included in the album. "To tell you the truth…I don't know, maybe I shouldn't say this, but I really didn't want 'Genie In A Bottle' to be my first single," Christina later told *MTV News*. In fact, Christina was almost done recording the full album. They were looking for possible singles for release when, all of a sudden, a song landed in Ron Fair's office.

"He called me up and told me that there was this amazing song," Christina recalled. "He said that it had good potential and thought it would be a smash. So, I heard it, but I actually wasn't too crazy about it." She reconsidered, "thinking all songs sound weird in the demo stage, but once I got to the mike and worked on it, it became something else, and I'm really proud of the results."

Christina trusted the instincts of Ron Fair; the man who had set everything in motion by pitching her talents to his boss. She would later write, "I can't forget to express the greatest appreciation of all to the best A&R man in the world, Ron Fair, for putting forth so much time and dedication into this record. I see you as a musical genius. I have learned and grown so much from your advice and example."

It was not surprising that Christina would heed his advice. When she relented, the pop/R&B confection was titled, rather obscurely, "If You Wanna Be With Me." It would seem a wonderful publicity strategy to select "Genie In A Bottle" as a title because unlike the other unimaginative title, "Genie In A Bottle" produced an Arabian vibe which was carried over to the promotion of the album, and inspired new fashion trends with beads and other Middle Eastern fashions.

The song was produced by ex-System member David Frank and Steve Kipner. Initially, Christina said that she had not written any lyrics for her album. She explained, "basically, [I did no writing], because there wasn't enough time as we didn't want a long gap between the release of the *Mulan* soundtrack and my album."[7] Curiously, as she distanced herself more and more from the album, she started taking more and more credit for her writing. After the success of "Genie In A Bottle," she explained that she had participated in writing a small part of the song's hook. "In 'Genie In A Bottle,' the only writing thing I think I got in there was the little hook, 'I'm a Genie In A Bottle, baby,' so that little 'Come, come, come on in,' that was my whole little thing, my little hook-y thing in there."

Even later, Christina claimed that she had also been involved in the song's production. "I was a little unhappy with the rough beginnings of the song, so I put my own flavor into it," she said. "Before that, it was too much keyed into the pop sound that was happening at the time, which often has no soul." However, "I put some ad-libs into it, spiced it up, and the R&B drum pattern changed it." Finally, two years after the making of her album, she told *Time* magazine: "I actually had some contribution in the writing on my first album. But I was so new and green, I was like, 'Oh I'm just having fun in the studio.' I didn't know I should have a credit, so I kind of got cheated."[8]

Actually, this early involvement in songwriting (and production) would prove to be just a small step in Christina's ever-increasing involvement in her career, and more importantly, her artistry. If the pop industry was moving toward packaging young singers and selling them as products, it is admirable that this was one young singer who would not yield so easily. She understood that because this was her first album and the record company needed to recoup on the investment, they would have to play it safe. However, Christina would later take creative risks that even some of the most established artists in the pop world tend to keep away from, and the risks paid off. She had important roles in the writing of the remixes that made hits of "What A Girl Wants" and "Come On Over."

Songwriting was something that came naturally to her and she thoroughly enjoyed it. "Everything inspires me to write songs from the railing I'm leaning on to the clouds in the sky, people in my life, dust on the ground. Everything inspires me." She later added "It is always fun for me to write because anything is possible."

Steve Kipner, who co-wrote "Genie In A Bottle" later said he was impressed by Christina during recording because she did not need coaching to improvise complex R&B lines, a skill he generally saw only in older artists. "She's internalized all the riffs from Chaka Khan to Etta James to Mariah and made them her own," Kipner later told the *Los Angeles Times*.

"Christina was just 18 and she needed to connect with her audience and there was never any question that that was the way to do it," Ron Fair explained with typical sympathy for the teenager's reservations about the sexy pop song. "In our business, it's more important to start off with a number one record on a debut act than it is to start off with a great song. But it's still great sugar candy."[9] Sugar candy that would effectively compete with, and clobber, Britney Spear's "...Baby One More Time," which had already topped the charts by the time they decided that "Genie In A Bottle" would be the first single.

Christina did not want to compete with Britney simply because she was never a pop lover. She wanted to give her music an R&B edge. Voicing the same complaint that her idol Mariah Carey expressed years after her debut album came out, Christina explained: "I was held back a lot from doing more R&B ad-libbing. They clearly wanted to make a fresh-sounding young pop record and that's not always the direction I wanted to go in. Sometimes they didn't get it, didn't want to hear me out because of my age, and that was a little bit frustrating."[10] Eventually, she planned on being quite involved in the writing and production process. "But I want to write more about experiences I've gone through," she later said. "I've gone through bad situations. I come from a divorced home. I've been around abuse. I've lived a different life, been on the outside." She later said that *Christina Aguilera* was the most "pop" album she would ever record.[11]

"What A Girl Wants" was actually one of the first songs they chose for the album and that Christina recorded. It was produced by Guy Roche who had worked with R&B teen vocalists Brandy and Aaliyah, and with superstars of the magnitude of Cher, Dru Hill and K-Ci & Jo Jo. "I was thrilled to work with so many great writers and producers on my album," Christina said later.

"Blessed" was penned and produced by Travon Potts who had previously co-written teenage R&B vocalist Monica's chart-topping "Angel of Mine." Meanwhile, Carl Sturken and Evan Rogers who had worked with such successful "boy bands" as 'N Sync and Boyzone (The Brand New Heavies) contributed a pair of tracks; the soul-flavored, mid-tempo "Love For All Seasons" and the upbeat pop ditty "Love Will Find A Way." According to her website, Christina "was particularly proud of the album's ballads." A rather interesting concept because there was only one truly new ballad on the album: "Obvious," a tune written by newcomer Heather Holly.

The biggest indication that RCA was as anxious as Christina about getting her record out quickly and capitalizing on the building momentum for teen pop, was the fact that they included two previously recorded ballads on the record. In their haste to get Christina's album out they included her previously released adult contemporary hit, the Matthew Wilder-produced "Reflection."

Furthermore, RCA had to select a song written by Diane Warren for Christina to sing. Diane Warren was and still is one of the most consistent hit-makers in the industry and is particularly well known for her chart-topping ballads. She has written songs for superstar divas like Barbra Streisand, Bette Midler, Mariah Carey, Celine Dion and Cher; male artists of the stature of Bon Jovi and Elton John; successful teenage acts including the Backstreet Boys, Destiny's Child, and Enrique Iglesias; and Latin legends as diverse as Julio Iglesias, Chayanne and Alejandro Fernandez. In short, it was certainly not Warren's track record that made the selection of a song penned by her a dubious move.

The remarkable thing was that the label was in such a hurry that Warren did not even have time to pen a new ballad for Christina (she did contribute the mid-tempo "Somebody's Somebody," even though upbeat songs are not Warren's forte). Thus, they simply asked Diane's permission for Christina to record "I Turn To You"; a rather insipid ballad previously performed by male pop group All 4 One that had gotten nowhere. Christina's soaring vocals just barely managed to save the dull song and even then, it would become Christina's lowest-charting single.

As far as Christina's debut album goes, it is a testament to her vocal ability, and her label's marketing strategy, that it enjoyed such overwhelming success.

SEVEN
The Selling of Christina

By the time RCA was ready to launch Christina's album, she had not only blossomed professionally, but physically. Although she was a petite thing; just five feet two inches tall, the girl with the powerhouse pipes had a firm abdomen, a minuscule waist, bright blonde hair (which she dyed several shades lighter with a number of hair products), and huge blue eyes (which she accentuated with colored contact lenses that deepened their blue hue). For one, Christina preferred her hair curly, but she deferred to the record company and had it straightened. "Unfortunately, pop is often about eye-candy," she later explained knowingly. "My record company told me to have straight hair even though I prefer it curly." In fact, most fans and even other artists commented that they did not like Christina's curly hair.

"She has an incredible voice and presence," Bob Jamieson said in an interview. "You know immediately that she's a star. She has that X factor." According to him, "We worked on her clothes, her makeup, her hair. The main thing, we helped her find the material." However, neither Christina nor, apparently, her record label, had picked out a defined style for the young singer to stick to, because she was widely criticized in the fashion press for some of her more outrageous choices. Although Christina would later become quite comfortable around Jamieson (she would even affectionately call him "the big guy"), initially she was somewhat intimidated by all the older men who were marketing her as a teen pin-up. "It can be hard to be eighteen and be in this business," she later said. "Your album is huge, and these people twenty years your senior are seeing you as a product. That can be scary. I just wanted to make music, and all of a sudden it was all about this package—what your look is going to be. All these decisions are being made for you."[1]

The record company publicity department was not able to talk her into dropping her last name. According to Christina, she was proud of her Latin heritage and because of this she decided to keep her surname, despite its phonetic complexity for the average American. By this point, however, she had made it clear to RCA that she planned on recording a Spanish-language album. "A lot of people wanna perceive [me] as a little white girl, trying to sound however, I'm just singing, like, what feels natural to me and what's most comfortable. And I'm not completely white. I am half Hispanic, half American-Irish. My father is from Ecuador, South America, so I am proud of my Latin roots," Christina told MTV in late June. "I'd like to get the Spanish community involved as well, being that my last name is Aguilera, and record a Spanish album one day and release it. That is really important to me."

Thus, despite Christina's story about her last name, it would seem unlikely that the record company would have made her drop what amounted to a legitimate passport into the Latin music world. Ron Fair inadvertently added weight to Christina's story, because he seemed genuinely uncomfortable with Christina being labeled a Latin artist. "She's of Latin descent, yes," Fair said, and added, attempting to downplay her heritage, "But I think she represents millions of kids across America who are of Hispanic descent but are completely American. She's got the pipes to be the next Barbra Streisand or Celine Dion, and that, to us, is really all that matters."[2] Even the pictures that eventually made Christina's album cover suggest a whiteness that is almost luminescent because light is being reflected on her face and blonde locks. (Actually, when Christina first saw the proofs for the cover picture, she exclaimed, "Wow...look how dark my eyes look here. Almost black!") It is no wonder that Christina felt that "once I signed the deal that I had become a product that needed to be sold. You have to be a certain way, look a certain way. All I want is to stay honest and sincere, I never want to give out a fake vibe."[3] In fact, at certain moments it seemed like Christina was getting caught up in the hype.

In May, right before her hectic schedule caught up with her, Christina wanted to have a little fun. She called her friend, Marcy and told her, "Let's just have fun with this. Set me up with a really cute blind date." But then, a "friend" of hers, who was actually a former boyfriend she broke up with soon after the release of the album was hurt because he wanted to go with her, so she ended up "going with two dates."[4] In fact, Shelly Kearns herself later said that Christina had gone with a "guy from Quigley," as reported in the *Post-Gazette*. It appeared that Christina wanted to downplay the boy's importance in her life, and certainly stop short of calling him her boyfriend (this despite the fact that in her album liner notes she had written, "To Chris (My B.B.Y.) You've been so amazing in being there for me since day one. I know it's not easy to deal with my schedule and all its demands, but you never fail in giving me 'what a girl wants' whether I'm home or away. Xoxo"), probably because the record company wanted to depict her as "available." Could it be that an 18-year-old pin-up could not be tied down because it would destroy the fantasy? Christina was practical enough to understand this, despite her later claim that although she had to deal with "time differences, international dilemmas, problems, connections, things like that…it's just a matter of really…taking time out for friends. Even if it's two minutes, just to call and check in and say hey and see how everybody is and getting back to them as much as possible. It's always been really important to me, especially now in my life, when there's so many fake aspects of the business and superficial people trying to get at you for superficial reasons, it's so important to keep those old friends…"[5]

Regardless, Christina leapt at the chance of attending her "friend's" prom on May 14 in Quigley. Her previous experience with school had not exactly been stellar, and she thought it would be fun and even interesting to see what a prom, one of the things she had missed out on because of her career choice, would be like.

When she arrived at the Sheraton Inn, Warrendale, much to her disappointment, Christina realized that things hadn't changed. She met with frosty glares from some of the other girls and only two girls came up to talk to her. Privately, they had been telling their boyfriends, "If you talk to her, I'll kill you." "It would've been fun if they hadn't done that," Christina remarked. In what must have been even more hurtful, the promgoers all left the dance floor when the DJ started playing "Genie In A Bottle." "It was kind of sad," Christina recalled, "all I want to do is be normal. But really, it's other people who won't let me be that way."[6]

Shelly Kearns explained the situation thus: "She attended her friend's senior prom and when 'Genie In A Bottle' came on, the girls there, true to form, grabbed their dates' arms and yanked them off the dance floor."[7] It was after the prom incident, which Christina repeated ad-nauseam (in a noble attempt to assure her young fans that her life had been anything but perfect), that a former classmate from North Allegheny High School pointed out, "Everyone here at N[orth] A[llegheny] supports her and is excited for her recent recognition. Yes, I've met her, and one of my good friends still keeps in contact with her." She further cast doubt on Christina's claims of ostracism, when she explained, "We supported her, and when she says things like this, which are blatantly false, it concerns me." Although it turned out to be a mistake on the part of the publication, which stated that Christina had attended a prom in North Allegheny when she had in fact been at a prom in Quigley, the girl's claims of supporting Christina were clearly at odds with Christina's numerous statements about her classmates' jealousy.

One day in the summer of 1999, Christina was taking a break from recording and the rest of the activities pertaining to her record release. She wanted to do something fun and get out of the Upper West Side apartment she was keeping in Manhattan. She decided to go for a stroll at the Virgin Megastore in New York City's Times Square. As she meandered through the store and looked through the different album racks, checking out the latest releases and probably dreaming about the moment she would see her own album in the store, she heard a commotion. She turned around and saw a guy running around with a Kangol cap on and a tumult of people behind him. *Who is that guy, and why is there so much commotion surrounding him?* Christina wondered. There were fans screaming hysterically all around him. Christina was informed that the young man was Limp Bizkit frontman Fred Durst. One of her friends loved Durst's music and had made Christina get into it as well. Ever the devoted fan, Christina decided to go ask for his autograph. By the time she approached him, however, he was running away from the crowd. Christina's jacket caught his eye, and he turned around and said, "That's a really cute jacket." He could not have known that soon he would be seeing a lot more of Christina and that they would become really good "friends."[8]

Although her personal life was somewhat unfulfilling, Christina's professional career as a singer was about to take off. It all started with the proper marketing platform. In order to get Christina's name out there in a short period of time, the Internet was to play a huge role. Britney Spears spent almost a year touring malls all around the country before the release of her hit single. Christina did not have to submit herself to such a tour, because RCA understood the power of Internet marketing, and, to be fair, Britney had, in many ways, paved the way for her. RCA hired the New York-based company, Electric Artists, to handle Christina's Internet "buzz," and they handled it quite effectively. Nick Cucci, Marketing Vice President for RCA, later told *The Wall Street Journal,* "Internet marketing is no longer 'Oh, let's make sure we have a website.'"

In promoting Christina, Electric Artists bypassed banner ads and websites in favor of postings on message boards where teens who might like her music would hang out online. The problem for the company was to find a way to market to Christina's audience without letting on that they were being marketed to. Electric Artists hired a team of cyber-surfers to find the online places teens typically hang out, like clothing site Alloy.com and hip teen site gurl.com. The team also hit up America Online, asking them to do features on Christina. First, the company started talking up her single before it was released and encouraged teens to listen to it and request it on radio stations and MTV. From there, they moved on to up selling the fans to buy the CD. Fans didn't know whether they were talking to a real person who just happened to like Christina Aguilera, or a "hired gun" talking up the singer in the hopes of grabbing a few more fans.

In the industry, this type of marketing is called *viral marketing*, which springs from the concept of "tell two friends and they'll tell two friends and so on and so on and so on." "We'd come back in a couple of days, and we'd hear people talking about the artist," said Ken Krasner, head of Electric Artists. "It's kids marketing to each other. We call it *viral marketing*." The company also hired Christina's biggest online fans to keep promoting her work on the Internet in exchange for free concert tickets and other goodies. "We didn't break Christina," Krasner admitted, "but we helped accelerate the process by putting the music in the hands of kids and watching them talk about it."[9] Christina's official website was designed and written for her teenage fans, and it included an appeal to keep requesting Christina's video for "Genie In A Bottle." It also included pictures, news, video and music clips. Later they included a highly popular Rumor Mill section, where Christina's mother, who presided over the website, answered questions from fans. Although the questions posed were answered honestly, they tended to shy away from the more controversial aspects of Christina's career, and feigned ignorance over the legitimacy of comments allegedly made by other performers about her.

In June, RCA showcased Christina in New York, Los Angeles, Toronto, Las Vegas, and Minneapolis. Aimed primarily at BMG staffers, as well as local radio and retail representatives, the gatherings had her performing the album with only piano backing. In the audience, MTV's Ananda Lewis was quite taken aback when Christina began to sing. She could not believe that the sultry voice was coming from a teenager. But the teenager's record company knew where her strength lay. Christina did several dates of the Lilith Fair tour, which showed her performing with only piano accompaniment as well. Nick Cucci explained that, although the album was put together mostly for the teen-age market, it "skewed smartly" with bluesy cuts toward an older audience also. Etta James' "At Last" was a favorite performance cover for Christina, yet another indication that her appeal was not limited to toddlers but rather aimed at teenagers 18 and above. Christina did nothing to sway this image, stating on one occasion that she would like to be seen as "a pop girl with an edge." If there were any doubters, she quickly added that she liked "a bit of toughness with my girliness."

In her appearances, Christina enjoyed performing with a live band. "I want the kids to see a side of me that they haven't seen yet," she told MTV. "'Genie In A Bottle' will be done differently, sometimes. We'll put some cool Arabian intonations into the whole vibe of it, to get people into a Middle Eastern mood. And then, of course, I can also do my piano ballads that couldn't be on the record, such as the Etta James song that I love to cover, 'At Last.'" One thing that must be noted is that Christina's penchant for live performance was genuine. Her experience with *The New Mickey Mouse Club* had left Christina in a love affair with the stage, and she enjoyed improvising with her voice, mainly because she actually had the range to do it. She added, "Certain people want to see me as solely a pop act, but there are many different sides to Christina Aguilera besides the pop girl."

Nick Cucci agreed. "I think we've done Christina fairly uniquely in that we knew that she would appeal to teens, but we also knew that she was much more than just a teen artist." In fact, the showcase gatherings were similar to the invitation-only soirees that had been used to expose Mariah Carey in the past. "I've worked with Mariah, Whitney, and Toni Braxton, and Christina is in that league," RCA executive and Bob Jamieson's right hand, Jack Rovner told *Billboard*. (Christina later reciprocated, thanking Rovner for his "vision and leadership."[10]) Ron Fair told *The New York Times* that Christina was "our Streisand," a comment the newspaper termed part of "the hyperinflation of the business."

The first batch of articles that came out regarding Christina outlined the major accomplishments that had led to her success. All of them dedicated a big chunk of the article to superficially discussing her time at *The New Mickey Mouse Club*. Inevitably, this led to the Britney comparisons, and most of the articles were annoyingly titled: "Move Over Britney Spears." The similarities were obvious; both were young, petite, pretty girls who liked to wear short tops that showed their abdomen. Both were putting out pop records. Even if they had not worked together during their *Mickey Mouse Club* days, the press would probably have thrown them into the same category because they were, by all appearances, targeting similar audiences. Christina soon grew weary of the comparisons, and although she was very diplomatic at the beginning, in the end, some of her weariness started surfacing, based on the fact that, unlike Britney, she felt she actually had a powerful voice.

"We do have a history together," Christina explained patiently. "We were on *The New Mickey Mouse Club*. She and I were the youngest of the cast members, so we were sort of like the babies, so we instantly bonded." But, she added, "Now it's kind of crazy how people put so much pressure on the competition between us. People want to compare me with her, because I am the new one, like here's another one who also shows her tummy'…it's kind of crazy!"

At first, she was quite philosophical about it. "Everybody gets compared to someone," she said during one of her first promotional trips. "But we are two very different artists. The way we approach what we do vocally and the way we approach music in general—it's coming from two completely different areas." Christina was preaching to deaf ears.

But as the rumors that they were actually involved in some kind of unseemly rivalry ("people think we catfight too!" she told one publication) grew more and more, Christina wanted to set the record straight. "It hurts my feelings, all the backbiting, and I'm sure it hurts her, too. There is NO competition, we're both good in our own way. When her album came out, I went straight to the record store to buy it. I wanted to support her,"[11] she added, "I seriously was the first in line to buy it. I mean I wanted to support her because she's my friend and I'm sure she did the same thing when my album came out." Christina should not have been so trusting. Britney wasn't exactly falling over herself to talk about Christina. Fully embracing the concept of "Out of sight, out of mind," she barely mentioned the superior singer when questioned on the successful fates of former Mickey Mouse Club members. "Yeah, Felicity, J.C. and Justin. Ryan Gosling, he's on Nickelodeon right now, doing the new Hercules. And, um, I think that's it," Britney said. Finally, as an afterthought she added.

"And Christina Agulularia [sic], she's signed to RCA now and her album should be coming out pretty soon." (She had also bought Fred Durst's C.D. When MTV questioned, "What's in your Walkman right now?" in July, Christina explained, "The new Limp Bizkit CD. I like Fred Durst, and I love that band.")

She also insisted that the similarities were superficial, and that the comparisons were not accurate. "Well I think it's unfair for any debut artist...people always want to compare the new person to whoever they think is quite similar, and I can see the similarities. We're around the same age, we have similar music types..."

The only time that Christina would ever come close to suggesting that she felt she had the better voice was when she lightly hinted at it by way of explaining, rather wishfully it would turn out, that people would differentiate them "once my album is released...I mean, I'm a ballad singer as well. I think people will get to see that Britney and I are very much two different artists, two different styles, two different sounds. I think people will see that more and more." She was rightfully concerned that people would fail to notice her extraordinary vocals by lumping her into the same "teen queen" category, so she herself pointed out: "We both have our own music style, but I have other vocal possibilities, a bit like Mariah Carey."[12] The implication, of course, was that Britney did not. Once again, Christina's career was eerily similar to Mariah Carey's, who was initially bombarded by articles claiming she was imitating Whitney Houston, who had preceded her own appearance on the pop scene by a couple of years. In fact, Christina was happy to be placed in the same category as both of the older divas. She told the MTV Radio Network, "I've actually been compared recently to singers that I look up to, like Mariah Carey and Whitney Houston, so that has been really amazing."

After Jessica Simpson and Mandy Moore jumped on the scene, (the closest either one of them ever got to a hit was Simpson's top 3 ballad, "I Wanna Love You Forever" and her sophomore album, *Irresistible*, which debuted at No. 6 on *Billboard*) they too were thrown into the same category.

Once, when Christina was at a record store, she was eavesdropping on a conversation between a coterie of girls eyeing Hoku's single

"Another Dumb Blonde." Hoku was yet another pop star who was launched during the pop craze, but she achieved even less success than Moore and Simpson. Christina thought the girls had seen Mandy Moore's album and chirped, "Another dumb blond!" Upset at the categorization, Christina thought to herself: "Oh, that's nice! We're all lumped into one category." She was about to sneak out when she realized that "Dumb Blonde" was part of the song's title. Later, the girls saw her and asked for an autograph.[13]

When she was asked about them, Christina made a perceptive statement that highlighted her maturity: "I have met all three [Spears, Moore, and Simpson], actually. I think they're all really sweet girls, talented in their own different ways." Jessica Simpson would not reciprocate with equally kind words. "They all have differences, and so do I. So I think that the comparisons, you know—I think they're all really talented artists, but the only thing is, you know, whenever you overlook everybody for being the same thing, that's what bothered me a little bit, you know? I mean, we all have our differences, different styles in live performances, you know? So it's all different things. Whenever you get lazy and put it all together, then it's not cool."[14] In a sense, that's exactly what it was. Lazy journalism.

Christina's dealing with journalists was still light-years away from the demanding diva she would later become, sending out editors to fetch her food and beverages. At a photo shoot in an austere Hollywood Hills mansion for *Mademoiselle* magazine, Alisa Valdes-Rodriguez, a writer for the *Los Angeles Times* observed, "Aguilera appears observant, quiet and more than a little overwhelmed by all of the commotion being made about her. When a call comes for Aguilera from her manager, he screams the good news that she has just been booked on 'The Tonight Show' for August 27. Aguilera smiles politely then asks, 'Which one is that?'

She's not kidding; she really doesn't know. It's not because she never watches TV, but because she's young. Really young."

When she did appear on "The Tonight Show," she was awed at meeting Jay Leno. Christina was in the upstairs part of the studio getting her hair done, when Jay walked in and said "Oh, it's nice to meet you," and, Christina exclaimed: "Oh my God. It's Jay Leno!"

Although she would still be young countless magazine covers later, Christina became shrewder in handling the press and was very involved in the way she wanted to come off in pictures and text.

Christina Aguilera: A Star is Made

EIGHT
Pop! Goes the Genie

On June 22, "Genie In A Bottle" was officially released nationwide. Christina later recalled the thrill she felt when she was driving in her car with her mother and her sister and she heard the song on the radio for the first time. It was one of the most exciting moments of her life. The song quickly jumped onto the *Billboard Hot 100* and, in three weeks, had cracked the Top 5. Diane Martel, who had previously directed Mariah Carey's "Dreamlover" video, directed the video for the song. The video was taped in Malibu beach and it featured Christina in a beach house partying with friends; sitting on the house's wooden porch as she sang; lying in the sand wearing shorts and a tied-up belly-baring shirt ("I was out on the sand, greased up in, like, baby oil, in shorts and a little cutoff top," Christina recalled) and on the hood of a car seductively asking the video's male model to "Come, come, come on and let me out."

The lighting of the video prominently featured Christina's golden tresses as her best feature, although the singer herself was rather obscured by the dark shadows, suggesting that the record company still did not know what to do with the popster's image. The choreography featured Christina, wearing orange pants and a beaded blouse, with her dance troop behind her, simulating a genie coming out of a bottle. It was filled with symbolism and her dancing was incredible. Despite the fact that there are scenes in which Christina and friends are gathered around a flaming campfire, she later complained that she had been freezing during the video shoot. Considering what she was wearing, it's not hard to believe her. "God! First of all, I was so cold. I was freezing my butt off," Christina later told *MTV News*. "If you look at the video, I think I did a good job of faking it, of being warm." The comfortable crew members were all wearing heavy coats, hats and scarves around their necks.

Christina was excited over all the attention her song was getting and about the public's quick, positive response to the song, which had a meteoric rise to number one. "It's a dream come true that people are responding in such a positive way to my music," Christina told *Billboard* excitedly. "At first, I was a little afraid that some people might not completely get where I'm coming from particularly with 'Genie In A Bottle.'" As it would turn out, she had reason to be a "little afraid."

Christina was referring to the song's occasionally seductive lyrical tone, which would soon feed the first major backlash of her short career. "Fueled by a chugging groove and richly layered vocals, the tune is punctuated by a breathy command to 'rub me the right way'," explained *Billboard* magazine's Larry Flick. And it was not only the song itself that suggested a mature sexuality. The video, which featured Christina on a car hood seductively asking the male model sitting inside the car to come and let her out, also followed up on the song's sexual overtones. But Christina would deny time and again that the song was truly sexual.

"The song is not about sex," she would patiently explain to one interviewer after another. After the outcry over Britney's over-sexed lyrics and tone, she wanted to avoid comparisons. "It's about self-respect. It's about not giving in to temptation until you're respected."[1]

For its release in Malaysia, however, Christina had to re-record parts of the single, including changing "hormones racing" to "heartbeats racing," and "rub me the right way" to "treat me the right way." Such changes inevitably made the song lose some of its lyric playfulness. (This was hardly unprecedented. Artists constantly re-record songs or remove them from Asian versions of their albums because many Asian countries find American songs, including Ricky Martin's

"She Bangs" and some of Janet Jackson's tracks on "All For You", too provocative.)

The kids-oriented Radio Disney network also refused to play "Genie In A Bottle" due to its "suggestive lyrics." RCA desperately wanted to reach the pre-teen demographic, so they had Christina, David Frank and Steve Kipner record yet another version with more innocent words that started playing on Disney outlets, including L.A.'s KDIS-AM. Some of the revisions regarded the couplet, "You're licking your lips and blowing kisses my way/But that don't mean I'm gonna give it away" which was changed to "You're smiling at me and looking so fine/But that don't mean I'm gonna give you my time." Despite the changes, the mainstream American version remained intact, and the alleged sexual innuendo was heating up the charts. By June 27, the single had climbed to No. 6 on the *Billboard Hot 100*.

People magazine called the single "sexy, pulsating," and another publication called it the "year's frothiest Pop record." *Rolling Stone* praised its "sensually sensible poetry," while Christina's own *Pittsburgh Post Gazette* called it the "steamiest hit of the summer" and "smoldering." Ironically, newspaper of record *New York Times*, was the only publication that actually "got" the song's youthful message: "One of the summer's catchiest singles captures the moment's anxieties about teen-age sex. 'Genie In A Bottle,' sung by the blue-eyed former Mouseketeer Christina Aguilera, is a skittish dance hit propelled by indecision. 'My body's sayin' let's go,' the 18-year-old singer whispers, 'but my heart is saying no.' The chorus then spirals upward, riding bubbly dance beats, as Ms. Aguilera declares herself the kind of genie who appears only when rubbed 'the right way.' This double-entendre, shocking to some, nonetheless expresses a distinctly female sexual need and imagines a self-aware Ms. Aguilera in charge of it."

Christina explained: "If you listen to the words, 'My body's saying let's go but my heart is saying no.' My heart is saying no. So it's really a song about self-respect and treating me the way I want to be treated before I just give my love away to anybody." She did admit that the song was "sexy."[2] She was right. The song could certainly be deemed sexy and suggestive, but in essence, it was not advocating teen sex or promiscuity. "You're licking your lips and blowing kisses my way/but that don't mean I'm going to give it away," Christina purrs, again stating that there will be "no nookie," as she later put it. Mostly, the sensuality came from Christina's own interpretation of the song; the sighs, the oohs, the aahs and the R&B ad-libbing that she had improvised as she tried to give it a uniqueness that would set it apart from other pop songs. "I didn't think that 'Genie In A Bottle' would come across as much as another song might have," she later said. "Being that I've always looked up to great singers like Mariah or whatever, I wanted a 'Vision of Love' type single, one that would really let me let loose."[3] The misunderstanding of the song's message and the outcry over its sexiness could be attributed to Christina herself, and so could its success.

On a more negative note, 80's teen Pop star, Debbie Gibson, said of Christina: "It terrifies me to hear an 18-year-old sing 'come on in, let me out,' with some conviction." Her suggestion that the song was actually alluding to the sexual act was unfounded; the chorus actually said, "come, come, come on and let me out"—of the bottle. The only metaphorically sexual part of the song, if any, was her invitation to "rub me the right way." Gibson would sporadically attack Christina's image, yet she refrained from being negative about Britney. It is interesting that while the press actively fostered a rivalry between Christina and Britney, a complete fabrication that Christina was forced to address on a number of occasions, they failed to pick up on the fact that a feud was in fact brewing between 80s teen queen Gibson and current princess Christina.

Later, Gibson shed more light on the situation, explaining: "I've met a number of the girls. Some of them have been really respectful, but sometimes I get the feeling that they're thinking, 'Yeah, but *we're* doing it now.'"[4] It would appear that Christina fell into the latter category. In an interview with MTV, Gibson explicitly stated that while she believed Britney "knows to a degree that she's playing a role…which I enjoy…she always has a little tongue-in-cheek glint in her eye when she performs"; Christina "lives and breathes the sexual image, which frightens me. I look at her and go, 'Ooh, she's gotten a little ahead of herself.'" (Gibson's success, which culminated with her writing and producing a No. 1 single that spawned two multi-platinum albums, seems rather modest when compared to Christina's. The sales of both of Gibson's albums still did not equal the staggering amount of copies sold by Christina's debut.)

Christina was understandably upset about what she perceived to be a double standard. "If I went out and did what 'N Sync does on stage, with all those pelvic thrusts, I would get lots of bad press," she explained, regarding both her song's lyrics and her performances of it. "I think it's about pulling it off with class, being sexual without being sexually demeaned."[5] If the "Move over Britney Spears" coverage had been annoying, the equally unimaginative "Genie out of her Bottle" coverage, which highlighted the controversy over the song, was less of a pain.

The publicity about the song's lyrics only helped Christina in the end. The song showed no signs of slowing down. By early summer, "Genie In A Bottle" had sold just under 100,000 copies. A huge blip in sales got the song to No. 1 on *Billboard's Single Sales* chart. For the week ending July 4, the song stood at No. 3 on the *Billboard* chart. Two days later it debuted in the Top 10 of TRL. Less than two weeks after its official release, Christina's debut single was two spots shy of being the number one song in the nation. For the week ending July 11 she seemed even closer to that goal, as the song was poised on the brink of reaching pole position. "Genie In A Bottle" was No. 2.

One week later, boosted by strong sales, the song, which was already receiving widespread airplay on the radio, leapt to the top of the *Billboard Hot 100,* knocking down Will Smith's "Wild Wild West," which had just reached pole position the week before. It would never sit on the spot again, as Christina kept her No. 1 standing for five weeks, a significant amount of time considering that it was summer, and hits from Jennifer Lopez, Ricky Martin and a host of other high-profile singers were competing with her. (In fact, in a comparison between Lopez's "If You Had My Love" and "Genie In A Bottle," *The New York Times* opined: "Both the romantic come-on offered by Ms. Lopez and the titillating maybe whispered by Ms. Aguilera as she creeps under the sheets fully clothed, generating sexy but ultimately modest fantasies. The difference between them is a matter of better beats and a real voice, both the property of Ms. Aguilera. Winner: 'Genie In A Bottle.'")

At 18, Christina Aguilera had the number one song in the nation. To those who doubted Christina's staying power and believed she was a Britney wannabe, her incredible chart performance demonstrated that she could easily outshine Britney's "...Baby One More Time," which had only remained at the top spot for two weeks, and would become Britney's sole No. 1 single. By early August, "Genie In A Bottle" had gained Christina her first gold and platinum certifications, and it went on to sell over 1.3 million copies. The video accompanying the single was performing equally well, particularly with the desired teen demographic. It made its debut on the all-important TRL on July 6 at No. 9, peaked at No. 2, and was forcibly retired on October 7, because it had spent more than 65 days in the Top 10 countdown.

Because the video was not half as girlish as Britney's "...Baby One More Time", and because the song had more of an R&B edge to it, Christina's clip also earned active play on VH1 and BET. It became a fixture on TRL after its debut on July 6. Carson Daly later recalled watching the video the day he unveiled it and thinking "This is definitely TRL material."[6]

The success of first single "Genie In A Bottle," which Ron Fair had anxiously awaited and expected, simply set the standard, and certainly raised the bar, on the expectations for the album from which it was culled. The single was *everywhere* that summer. The label's marketing strategy, coupled with the inherent media interest in a second Mouseketeer making it big and the media's frenzied coverage of the teen pop industry, pretty much ensured strong first week sales. Christina would not be disappointed. The album was released, amid a number of album signings and appearances, on August 24. During one hotel stay in Chicago, Christina chided a hotel bellman for not recognizing her. "Are you on vacation?" the man politely asked the petite diva. "I only have the No. 1 single in the country," Christina huffily explained.[7]

She was extremely sweet to her fans though. "I want to thank you all so, so much. I love whenever I do shows in any city and you guys come up to me. And I do apologize if you've come up to me to give me something to sign and a lot of times it's out of my hands and I feel awful if I can't. But I know none of this would be possible without you, so I do appreciate you," Christina told her fans on the day of the record's release. "So I look forward to seeing you all on my tour. And the album is out today, so go out and buy it. Thank you!"

If at first the Britney comparisons had been somewhat to Christina's detriment, once the reviews were in, they uniformly informed the public that this was one Mouseketeer who actually had the chops to go with the marketing. Although they panned the song lyrics, all of them positively highlighted Christina's potential.

In his *Rolling Stone* review of Christina's album, Barry Walters asked the question: "Is there room on the pop charts for one more ex-Mouseketeer?" and answered it himself: "When the results are as sophisticatedly saucy as Christina Aguilera's 'Genie In A Bottle,' pedigree isn't even an issue. A mid-tempo argument for soulful affection weaves rolling Hip-Hop rhythms, hypnotic keyboard countermelodies and sensually sensible poetry into a deftly underplayed performance from an eighteen-year-old bombshell whose greatest assets are her powerhouse pipes."

Walters found much to blame on the album's production ("the usual producer-songwriter suspects clone Monica-Brandy-R. Kelly tunes too closely") and lyrics ("Bubble-brained lyrics give Aguilera little substance to spin into gold") and little fault in Christina's "copious vocal curves and trills." He chastised: "Pop's next *It Girl* deserves to be outfitted in something more flattering than the empress's old clothes."

The Plain Dealer noted, "Unlike Spears or that champion bellybutton flasher, Shania Twain, Aguilera can really sing. She has a rangy R&B voice that is mature in a good way, emotionally knowledgeable rather than just purringly sexual."

The Boston Globe opined: "While the tunes are at times painfully familiar and overtly skewed toward the teen market, Aguilera's singing soars above the fray. Where Spears comes off as a quick study who can mimic serviceable licks and carry a tune, Aguilera is a real singer. Mariah, Whitney, and Celine all come to mind; Aguilera is similarly blessed with the sort of breathtaking elasticity, golden tones, and sheer power that separate the divas from the dabblers."

The Miami Herald was more cynical: "Another veteran of *The New Mickey Mouse Club* with a recording contract. L-o-u-s-y. But at least this one can sing."

The New York Times was very positive about Christina's potential: "Beyond its sleek design, this album hints at a real singer's emergence. She has striking vocal power and range, if not a clue about expressing individuality. Once she has fulfilled the requirements of a teen-age pinup, she may enlist her bold talent to make music as personally nuanced as 'Genie In A Bottle' is serendipitous."

Newsday offered some of the first criticisms of Diane Warren: "Aguilera has the gift of elevating mediocre material into something special. She alone provides the emotive thrust on the now-prerequisite Diane Warren ballad 'I Turn to You.' Yet, she can effortlessly ride the syncopated groove of 'So Emotional.' Her versatility never belies her commitment to the lyrics. The conflicted emotion she brings to a song such as 'Obvious' turns it into a soulful aria. Aguilera is a true talent."

Newsweek gave her album two stars and noted, "At first blush, she's Tiffany to Britney Spears's Debbie Gibson—except she's got quite a voice. Even her sultry, limber soprano, though, can't surmount some of the R&B dreck on her debut."

The Washington Post followed up on the Diane Warren trashing, explaining: "It's a measure of Aguilera's perceived potential that she gets not one, but two songs from hitmaker Diane Warren. The first, 'I Turn to You'…is an inspirational ballad in the tradition of 'How Can I Live Without You' that works despite being built on an astounding accumulation of clichés. Aguilera manages to sing them as though she's never heard them before and also shows vocal restraint rare in someone so young. Alas, Warren proves mortal on 'Somebody's Somebody,' whose up-tempo energies are not really the writer's forte."

"I Turn To You" was the only song that almost every critic found unoriginal: "Anemic", "straight out of the Michael Jackson songbook," "a rip-off of 'Because You Loved Me'" were some of the terms used to describe it. Its flop in terms of chart standings would prove that even Christina's soaring vocals could not save it.

But to prove that there are as many opinions as there are critics, the ever-praising *Billboard* noted: "The self-titled project provides an engaging blend of trend-savvy uptempo ditties and warm ballads produced by such luminaries as Carl Sturken and Evan Rogers, ex-System member David Frank, Stephen Kipner, and Guy Roche."

After the reviews were in, Christina reacted with modesty: "Well, I don't pay much attention to all that. There are a lot of opinions out there. I do want longevity with my career, and it is nice to hear people say flattering things about my voice....I look at performers like Madonna and Janet Jackson, and I know that someday I'd also want to be accomplished on the screen, the studio and the stage. But I guess whatever happens happens."

Actually Christina enjoyed the comparisons and was quite comfortable hitting sky-high notes during her performances—but the remarkable aspect was that she could just as effortlessly belt out a sultry blues song with her lower register. Just as some time after Mariah Carey's debut critics started pointing out that she was overusing her famous upper register, Christina also started to fend off criticism for her vocal gymnastics, which critics felt she was sacrificing in favor of actual emotion. Christina was unaffected. She felt proud that she was able to hit the notes, and they were a part of her own, unique artistry: "Hitting high notes is a part of who I am. I feel liberated when I let my voice soar."

On August 29, five days after the release of her album, music industry bible *Billboard* duly reported: "Christina Aguilera unseats Backstreet Boys and trumps Puff Daddy on this week's *Billboard 200*. The former Mouseketeer debuts at No. 1 with her self-titled RCA album, which logged in sales of 253,000 units, according to *SoundScan*. The triumph makes Aguilera the second alumna of Disney's *The New Mickey Mouse Club* television show to have an album enter the chart this year at No. 1; the first, of course, was Britney Spears."

Christina not only trumped Puff Daddy, she sold almost 50,000 more copies than the bad boy rapper, whose albums were widely expected to surpass the first-week half-million sales of his previous effort.

In a similar track, *MTV News* explained: "Who knew the Mickey Mouse Club would be a launching pad for late-Nineties pop sensations? For the second time this year a former Mouseketeer has hit the No. 1 spot. The self-titled debut from Christina Aguilera, following in the footsteps of Disney alum Britney Spears, sold 252,000 copies for the week ending Aug. 29, according to *SoundScan*."

When Britney made her own debut at No. 1 on the *Billboard 200* albums chart, she sold 120,000 copies of her album, less than half of Christina's initial numbers. Following Christina on the chart that week were Puff Daddy's *Forever* (which sold 205,000 copies); the Backstreet Boys' *Millennium*; Limp Bizkit's *Significant Other*; Mary J. Blige's *Mary*; Britney's ...*Baby One More Time*; Santana's *Supernatural*; Kid Rock's *Devil Without a Cause*; Noreaga's *Melvyn Flynt: Da Hustler*; and Ricky Martin's *Ricky Martin*.

At eighteen years of age, after a decade of struggle and only two months after the release of her number one, platinum-selling single, Christina Aguilera could boast of having the best-selling album in the United States, with her closest competitor 50,000 units away from her. If the frightened little girl in her had ever needed a boost in her confidence, making her debut at the top of the charts must have been immensely comforting. The universal critical acclaim was also exciting and even relieving. Christina had been uncomfortable with the Britney clone claims and she was genuinely worried that her vocal ability would get lost amid all the comparing and poor press coverage. She had broken through the entire buzz, the marketing and the rumors with the one thing that had gotten her so far: her golden voice. Now the excitement was over. After all, as far as the album *and* the single went, there was nowhere to go but down.

NINE

The Seduction of Fame

After the album's No. 1 debut, the record company desperately wanted to keep the buzz about it going. If there is one thing that all record companies are deathly afraid of, it is one-hit wonders. With the release of her second single, Christina would quickly prove not only that she was here to stay, but also that she was a consummate professional and talented musician with her finger carefully positioned on the public pulse. First, there was the record company to please and what the record company wanted was promotion in the teen marketplace. On September 15, Christina made a surprise guest appearance on "Beverly Hills 90210" and sang "Genie In A Bottle" in a bar as the group celebrated David's birthday. Two days later, with her hair done up in an unbecoming perm, wearing an orange blouse and black leather pants, Christina finally performed live on "TRL." She sang the hit that made her a household name and other songs from her self-titled debut album, including "So Emotional." Only 12 days later, she hosted the show, and on October 4, she was guest host again, wearing an original light purple tank top that said *CRL (Christina Request Live)*.

The first time that Christina performed on TRL, host Carson Daly was not on the show. Christina, always the consummate professional, left him a post-it note saying that she was sorry that she hadn't been able to meet him and that she hoped to meet him soon.

"Carson, so sorry I missed you. Next time. Love, Christina." Christina discussed the note on a radio station in Tucson, Arizona, and soon *USA Today* reported it, insinuating that there was something going on between them. The tabloids weren't far off in picking up on the note and even before Christina was a certified celebrity, she had her first encounter with the unfounded rumors about her alleged promiscuity that would soon start to hound her mercilessly. At first, Christina thought, "Wow, I'm cool enough to have gossip said about me." Then it was more like, "Wait a minute, I never said this." The fact that she was on Carson's show on three occasions within a month seemed to add fuel to the rumors, which were entirely untrue. Christina never dated Carson Daly. (On March 1st, however, Madonna was on TRL, joking about Christina with Carson. Rather than simply denying there was anything going on between them, Carson called Madonna a bigmouth. In fact, months later, a "golfing buddy" of Daly's said that Carson confided that he had accidentally pulled out Christina's hair extensions in the middle of "a steamy sex romp." Although Christina did have blond hair extensions at one point, the whole scenario seems rather far-fetched. Later, she did confide that there had been "chemistry" between them.)

That same month Christina made her first appearance on the British television music show, "Top of the Pops" performing her number one single. Curiously, Mariah Carey had recently made an appearance performing her latest No. 1 hit, "Heartbreaker," at the music show and Christina had made a comment about how she would love to meet Mariah. Mariah allegedly told her coterie that she would meet anyone but Christina.

"I don't know what's going on with Mariah?" Christina said when she was told of the affront. "I love her to death. She continues to be a huge inspiration. I know I did want to meet her. For whatever reason, I didn't get to. Maybe in the future." The future would come and go but Christina would not meet Mariah Carey. Christina did admit, "I'm unclear as to what her view is on [meeting me]." Although at the time the allegation was leveled it seemed yet another ridiculous rumor about Carey's allegedly egotistical ways, her decision to drop out of VH1's "Men Strike Back" after Christina became involved in it, a rumor which was also denied, appeared to point to the fact that the younger vocalist might have been making Mariah nervous.

It certainly seemed odd that after all the praise that Christina had heaped on the best-selling female singer of the '90s, Mariah would not reciprocate with a few kind words. After a decade as the undisputed queen of the pop charts (Carey had long since outsold Madonna and outshone her performance on the charts; she had more number one singles and weeks at number one than any other female artist, which prompted *Billboard*'s "Artist of the Decade" designation), Mariah was about to get a run for her money. Although she probably viewed Britney as a Madonna wannabe (she did in fact deign to take a picture with Britney), the comparisons with Christina struck close to home because it appeared Miss Aguilera was positioning herself as the "New Mariah Carey,"[1] and, at 29 years of age, Mariah still had a long career ahead of her. As things would turn out, Mariah had reason to be concerned.

The sales of her 1999 album, *Rainbow*, which came out just weeks after Christina's, were considerably lower than those of her previous album. In fact, sales in the United States had been declining almost by half: 10 million copies for *Daydream*, 5 million for *Butterfly* and 2.9 million for *Rainbow*. Although many speculated that Christina and Britney were stealing Carey's fans (a famously rabid bunch which Mariah playfully calls her "Lambs"), it was in fact the singer's transition from pure pop to music greatly influenced by R&B and entrenched in rap that caused the precipitous decline. The question became, did Mariah understand that, or did she in fact believe that the younger pop stars, mainly Christina, were draining her audience?

Previously, Carey had been involved in a low-profile tangle with her producer, Walter Afanasieff, when he started producing music for Columbia's new pop-diva-in training Samantha Cole. Despite her standing as the best-selling female recording artist, Mariah's deeply rooted insecurities and fierce competitiveness led her to feel threatened by any new artist who might represent competition. Carey biographer Marc Shapiro wrote: "Mariah began to resent the time Walter was taking away from her sessions to work on Cole's album, and she must have felt that Cole was a threat to her status as top dog in the pop world. Resentment turned to jealousy when Walter and Samantha began to date. The tension between Mariah and Walter grew, and she began to challenge openly and uncharacteristically some of Walter's creative choices in the studio. Then, one night while working on her album at the famed Hit Factory Studio, Mariah's emotions exploded. A minor disagreement over the arrangement of a song grew heated and ugly, and Mariah and Walter were soon screaming at each other. The argument spilled out of the studio and into the street where passersby reportedly heard Mariah say some nasty things about Walter dating Samantha." Cole later said: "She [Mariah] is always talking about me. I regret that we can't be friends. There's room for ten more pop divas out there."[2]

If she was so upset over competition from a woman whose career never took off, one can only imagine what it must have felt like to witness the rise of a teenage superstar who sold exactly the same number of copies of her self-titled debut as Mariah did, and would rack up four number one singles before her sophomore album, just like Mariah. There is plenty of evidence to support the allegations of diva dissonance between '90s queen Mariah and current princess Christina, and there is certainly more truth to these rumors than there is to the alleged rivalry between Christina and Britney. In fact, it seems improbable that Christina will be meeting Mariah any time soon. (Having said that, it is important to point out that rivalries between pop stars are an inherent part of pop culture because of the nature of their celebrity. Madonna, for example, has lashed out publicly at Mariah, which prompted the latter to complain: "I loved Madonna's first album even though she's horribly rude about me all the time. Maybe the difference is that my success came out of high school and hers took a little bit longer—I don't know!" Madonna, however, wore a t-shirt that said Britney Spears during one of her concerts in London in 2000.)

In September, Christina attended and was a presenter at the "MTV Video Music Awards" held at the Metropolitan Opera House in New York City. They had been amply promoted on MTV as being on "9.9.99," and Christina's was one of the faces that flashed on the screen when the channel aired its advertisements promoting the show. Wearing a leopard-print jacket, fuchsia blouse and black skirt, she made her first fashion faux-pas. To top it all off, her hair was permed into a nightmare of frizz.

Right before she went on, she was introduced to Tommy Lee. Christina was too shy to say "hi," but he introduced himself to her because he could tell she was embarrassed. "She's cute," he said later. Christina jokingly admitted, "He helped me, he's more experienced than I am…" Together they presented the award for Best Rock Video, which went to the band that, according to Christina, proved that the "rules of rock aren't written in stone." Korn took home the trophy for "Freak On A Leash."

On October 10, less than a month after her performance on "Top of the Pops" Christina added the United Kingdom to her list of conquered countries, as "Genie In A Bottle" debuted at No. 1 on the British singles chart. The song also rose to the top of Austria's singles list and achieved No. 1 placing in Germany, Norway, Spain and Switzerland. On October 18, Christina began a second week at the top of the U.K.'s Singles chart. It was quite a formidable accomplishment considering the fact that most acts quickly tumble down the charts after their debut, because unlike the *Billboard* charts, English charts are based exclusively on single sales, which usually means the single will debut at its peak. Less than two weeks after her spectacular performance, "Genie In A Bottle" moved up to No. 1 on *Music & Media's Eurochart Hot 100 Singles* ranking. By November 8 "Genie In A Bottle" was still No. 1 on the *Eurochart Hot 100* singles. That month, Christina appeared on the cover of *Teen People* magazine.

On a personal front, Christina claimed in interviews that there was nobody special in her life, except for that former boyfriend back home, because she simply did not have time to nurture a relationship. In fact, the only young people that Christina was able to hang out with were her dancers Buddy Mynatt, Nick Aragon, and Jorge Santos. Aragon, a friendly, half-Latin 20-year-old, noted: "We are her sanity. Before she had us, she had to be so old with everybody; it was all business, business, business."[3] Christina enjoyed being a kid when she was fooling around with the dancers, but Nick later said that she never abandoned her amazingly adult work ethic: "I've worked with the Artist and Ricky Martin," he explained, "Christina's the hardest-working person I've ever met. She gets this look on her face, almost like a glare, and I know not to go near her because she's focused." Christina admitted as much, explaining that she never had time for silly romances. "...All my life, my career has been my number one focus, more so than boys ever were. That's the way it's always been, and I really don't want anything to get in the way of that."[4]

There were signs, however, that she was letting her guard down and she was starting to develop something more than a friendship with her dancer Jorge Santos. In November, amid much publicity, Christina performed the National Anthem at the MLS Cup Championship. "New England Revolution" hunk Brian Dunseth, who captained the U.S. Olympic Soccer Team, was quite taken with Christina. So much so that he gave her a Revs shirt as a souvenir of her trip to Foxboro Stadium.

Dunseth probably did not notice the big "love bite" on the back of Christina's neck that her blonde hair extensions were not able to entirely hide. He probably also failed to notice how "friendly" Christina was with Santos, the Puerto Rican dancer whom she was slowly falling in love with.[5] Oddly, nobody in the press ever picked up on Christina's relationship with him, probably because Christina knew that she had to remain single for the sake of appearance. (Perhaps the plethora of acting offers being sent to Christina had some merit behind them.) Almost a year later, Christina was forced to admit: "He was one of the first dancers I hired. We were just together for a while on the road, and eventually we were in Europe when things just kind of erupted between us."[6] Although he was hardly movie star handsome, the young Latino (his birthday was on July 26, 1976) had tanned good looks and stood about five feet seven inches tall.

Christina had previously stated of her ideal man, "I usually don't go for the Brad Pitt, typical gorgeous guy. I go for the cute guy who has more of a rough edge—a little more street." That was an on-target description of Santos, whom the *Boston Herald* described as a "Prince look-alike." The relationship was flourishing at a moment of endless possibility for Christina, and it could not have hurt that, like her, Santos was of Hispanic descent and involved in show business. A female cousin of his, Adrienne, was the token Hispanic of the R&B girl group 3LW (3 Little Women) and he appeared in one of their videos. When Christina told him that she was trying to learn Spanish, Santos gave her the book "Spanish for Gringos." They had much to talk about and much in common. (Christina was also quoted as saying: "I want a bad boy in public, and a pussy cat at home!")

"I would never let a man control my emotions," Christina later sang on her sophomore album. "When he smiles I feel like a little child/When he says I am full blood boricua/Read the tattoo on his arm/He tells me 'Mami, I need ya!'/And my heartbeat pumps so strong/Getting lost in a ritmo/He whispers 'Te quiero' Te quiero/I begin to give in with no hesitation/Can't help my infatuation." Christina was chronicling the emotional rollercoaster that falling in love with Santos must have meant for her. She had usually eschewed any situations in which she could be vulnerable. A romantic relationship placed her in the most vulnerable place she could ever be. Coming to terms with such a predicament would be an important part of her personal growth. Her relationship with Santos suggested that she had closed in on the chasm.

By December, Christina's album was holding strong onto the Top 5, selling over 500,000 copies in one week alone. On December 13, it was certified for sales of 4 million copies by the RIAA. In *Billboard*'s *Year-End* charts, "Genie In A Bottle" was the year's seventh highest-ranking single on the *Hot 100*. In fact, on *Music & Media*'s (Europe's *Billboard*) *Eurochart Hot 100 Singles of the Year*, Christina was two notches higher. Her album managed to sneak into *Billboard*'s Top 20 (despite having been released only three months before) at No. 16 with sales of over 2.5 million copies. The *Billboard* top singles also included Santana, Jennifer Lopez and Ricky Martin. There was widespread talk of a "Latin explosion." It fell to the *Los Angeles Times* to point out:

"The real U.S. Latin explosion of 1999 was led by artists such as Conjunto Primavera, Elvis Crespo, Alejandro Fernandez, Los Tigres del Norte, Charlie Zaa, Los Angeles Azules, Bronco and Marco Antonio Solis—all of whom were certified gold in the U.S. by the RIAA this year, meaning they've sold in excess of 500,000 copies of an album here. (Zaa went platinum, with sales in excess of 1 million.)

Both the Latin explosion (in Spanish) and the Latino explosion (in English) this year are the direct result of a Latino demographic explosion in the U.S. that has been building since the 1970s.

By 1990, the U.S. Census Bureau estimated the nation's Latino population at 22 million, a number equal to the entire U.S. population in 1850. Latinos now number an estimated 31 million and are expected to reach 81 million in the next 50 years.

For population reasons alone, no one in the music industry dares categorize either the emergence of Latinos in English Pop or the growth of music in Spanish as passing trends…Until this year, the major labels had tried to target U.S. Latinos almost exclusively with Spanish-language music—probably a mistake considering that 75% of them were born and raised in the U.S., according to census figures…After this unprecedented year, most labels are actively seeking Latino stars for the mainstream English market, with several set to emerge next year. Miami-based producer/songwriter Rudy Perez says the industry has only now realized there is a huge market for English hits by Latinos.

"It's a totally virgin market, if you can believe that exists in the U.S.," says Perez, who has been asked by several major labels to help find bilingual and bicultural artists such as Martin. "Believe me, I work with all these label presidents. And right now? They know this is what it's all about now."

Just as it had happened when her pop debut came out, the timing was perfect for Christina if she wanted to put out her Spanish album. She had entered the pop arena when teenage singers were at the height of their popularity, right before the market became over-saturated. (The casualties after the wave had passed are too numerous to mention.) Now, she was going to record an album in Spanish at what was the perfect moment for a number of reasons. For one part, there was the exponential growth of the Latin music market, which was in itself a byproduct of the growth of Latin American consumers and the country's acknowledgment of them as an important buying force. However, even more significantly, there had been a rise in profile of this Latin market, which was now getting coverage and attention from the mainstream American press that had previously ignored this music and equated Latin music with Mexican *bandas*. It was a process that had started after the death of Tex-Mex singing sensation Selena, and had climaxed with the rise to stardom of Ricky Martin. RCA wanted to strike while the iron was hot, and they decided to sign one of the hottest producers in the business. The knowledgeable and well-connected Cuban-American producer Rudy Perez, who had worked with countless Latin legends, would be one of the album's main producers.

Christina was excited. "I'm trying to get a Spanish record out in Spain," she explained rather naively at the time. "They're not going to release that Spanish record until I go over there myself and make appearances and whatnot." It appeared odd that Christina said that the album would be released in Spain and not Latin America (although the BMG Latin division did include the markets in Portugal and Spain). She later added, "The Spanish side of me is something I'm really interested in tapping into, and getting to explore. I'm still learning the language to its fullest. But 'Genie In A Bottle' of course will be translated, and 'I Turn To You,' the ballad that will be the third or fourth single, will be translated."[7]

Her work for the Spanish-language album had not actually started, although they began selecting songs, but by January, the wheels had been set in motion and the album would be ready for release later that year. BMG Latin would handle the production and distribution. Christina's statements however, about wanting the album released in Spain and wanting to explore the "Spanish" side of her, as opposed to the Latin or Hispanic side of her, seemed to suggest a disturbing lack of knowledge about her roots. It appeared that Shelly's honest efforts to imbue her daughter with a sense of pride about her background had not been fully assimilated.

In early December Christina took part in the Santa.com Holiday parade in San Francisco. Wearing a long coat with Dalmatian dots on it, she excitedly waved to the crowd from aboard a float as they gathered to watch. The rest of December was all about payback. Christina performed at a number of shows sponsored by the radio stations that had been so receptive to her music. On December 13, she performed for WKTU's "Miracle on 34th Street." The same day, Christina rehearsed with B.B. King for a television special, "Christmas in Washington" at the National Building Museum. The concert, shown on TNT December 12, was a benefit for the Children's National Medical Center and Christina performed for president Bill Clinton.

Later, Christina performed for WFLZ's *Y-2 Concert* in Florida. Almost 15,000 fans gathered to celebrate. She kicked off the show in a silver top and gem studded jeans, with a sequined blue bandana topping off the ensemble. She signed autographs for fans (anointing herself "the genie") and performed a fast, upbeat dance version of "The Christmas Song," which RCA had recently released as a single.

With all her performances for radio stations, Christina was not only giving back. There was much interest on her part in wooing radio programmers. RCA had just released her second single. Just before the barrage of appearances, Christina had been discussing with the label what the next single would be. "You know, some people do want me to stay in that pop scene," Christina explained cryptically. The record label still wanted Christina to exploit the teen pop scene, but, Christina countered, "I want to grow from there. I always want to continue growing and getting to that level of, 'Oh, she's a real singer, a real ballad singer, she can do it.'" Then she admitted: "The next single will be 'What A Girl Wants,' but a totally cool remix of it." The remix played up the funky R&B edge that Christina had imbued the song with. She helped with the writing (the song had a few lyrics that were not included in the original version) and the production, and once again transformed the song into a lightweight but pleasant Pop/R&B confection. When she re-did the song, Christina displayed vocal acrobatics that seemed to mirror Mariah Carey's own vocal styling in her No. 1 1992 single "Emotions," where she started singing in her lower register and carefully scales notes until she reaches the highest echelon of her well-known upper register. When Christina recorded a Spanish version of the song for her eventual Latin album, her scaling carried her from the lowest to the highest notes in her range, replicating exactly, if perhaps somewhat less effectively, what Mariah had done in that song.

The video accompanying the single was directed by Diane Martel (who also directed "Genie In A Bottle") and choreographed by Tina Landon (who worked on Britney's "Oops!...I Did It Again" as well as Ricky Martin's "Livin' La Vida Loca.") For the video, Christina's look was much more defined and the lighting allowed a much clearer view of the superstar. Her bleached-blond hair was sleek, straight and fell on her face at rather severe angles. She was wearing black leather pants that accentuated her generous backside, and a blue (aquamarine) tank top. In the video, Christina arrives at some kind of playroom with a number of her friends, and tells the male model that she has a surprise for him. Then she breaks into song and starts the choreography. The video alternates shots of the dancing with shots of Christina sitting on black speakers singing. A small remix in the middle of the song carried over to the video, which featured Christina lying on a couch in full Victorian garb, tiara and all, being powdered and fussed over by servants. She lifts her fully embroidered skirt flirtatiously, exposing a bony leg wrapped in white stockings.

On December 16, "What A Girl Wants" reached pole position in the all-important *TRL*. Four days later, Christina performed at the *Jingle Ball* for radio station Kiss 108.

The station had previously held a much-promoted contest pitting schools against each other in a test of school spirit. Radio promotions clog the airwaves, but the Christina Aguilera contest run by

WXSS-FM was something different. Students in grades 9 to 12 had until 5 p.m. December 6 to put their name, grade and high school on a 3-by-5 index card and drop it off or mail it to Kiss FM, requesting Christina's presence at their high school. It took 1.6 million index cards for students at Franklin High in Milwaukee to get a visit from Christina. The winner was announced on the December 10 morning show, and Christina performed a concert at the high school on Thursday night, December 16.

As 1,300 teenagers watched, Christina and her three male backup dancers performed "What A Girl Wants," "Genie In A Bottle," and "The Christmas Song." "It was a little shorter than I expected, but it was good. I'm happy," sophomore Andrea Larson said. Nine other schools received trophies for their efforts. It is a testament to Christina's immense popularity that the station eventually received more than 4 million cards, which explains why area retailers were reporting that their stocks of 3-by-5 cards were exhausted.

December was turning out to be quite a sweet month for Christina. Although it is not that unusual for an artist to have two solo singles in the Top 20 of the *Billboard Hot 100*, it is rare for both songs to move up with bullets. In late December, Christina repeated a feat accomplished by artists of the stature of Diana Ross, Linda Ronstadt, and Donna Summer, as her version of "The Christmas Song" took a leap from 44 to 18 on the *Hot 100*, while "What A Girl Wants" advanced from 13 to 11.

Despite the immense popularity of "The Christmas Song" as a cover for the scores of Christmas albums that high-profile artists put out each year, Christina became only the second artist (the first being Nat King Cole) to have a *Billboard Hot 100* hit with the holiday classic. Christina's plethora of appearances during the holiday season had boosted her already comfortable chart standings to incredible new heights. She had quickly proven that she was no two-hit wonder, as "The Christmas Song" marked Christina's third Top-20 hit in less than three months (the song would peak at No. 18). RCA promptly took notice of the singer's popularity and the fact that her melodic voice was ideally suited for powerfully emotional Christmas songs. In less than a year, Christina, like her idol Mariah Carey, would be able to put out her own album of Christmas favorites. RCA Video Productions hastily put together a special video, *Genie Gets Her Wish* for release in the holiday season that featured footage of Christina throughout the year along with the videos for "Genie In A Bottle" and "The Christmas Song." Despite the apparent lack of material, the video topped the *Billboard Home Video* sales chart and obtained platinum certification for sales of 100,000 copies.

But Christina's work was not over, as RCA decided to milk the enthusiastic performer until the last day of the year. It was announced by MTV that Christina would be performing on MTV's live New Year's Eve special. "I'm nervous about what's going to go on that night. Everything's going to be so chaotic," she stated. She quickly added humor to the situation, adding, "My mom already warned me, 'You don't want to go in any elevators.'" The cable channel's studios were one floor above Times Square.

After the whirlwind of promotional appearances, December 31st came quickly for Christina, whose head was still spinning after such an incredible past 6 months. She started out her performance by doing a live version of "Genie In A Bottle," complete with her dancers. She was wearing tight leather pants and her blonde hair, which had been permed to look straight, was also streaked with tiger-like black stripes. Later Christina performed "What A Girl Wants" and excitedly demonstrated her soulful vocal acrobatics at the end of the song. Christina took pictures with her dancers after the show. Jorge Santos, whose curly locks were entirely cropped off, posed for one picture with Christina. She is up against him, with her hand on his chest, and both are smiling for the camera, Santos with a coy grin and Christina displaying her usual exuberance.

Christina helped Carson count down the last ten seconds of the year(what a year it had been) and together with Carson was the first person to be seen by MTV viewers in the year 2000.

TEN
Rumors, Romance & Controversy

On January 1, MTV honored Christina by having her as Carson Daly's very first guest at 12:01 a.m. When the *Billboard* list was unveiled for the week ending January 9, Christina must have been ecstatic. "What A Girl Wants" knocked Santana's "Smooth" off the top spot and became the first new *Billboard Hot 100* No. 1 single of the year. In line with Christina's other notable firsts, her chart-topping feat was the first time in the rock era that a woman obtained the first new No. 1 single of a decade. The single maintained its number one position another week, after which it fell to number two. Regardless, it was Christina's second No. 1 single in a row, and brought her cumulative weeks at the top of the charts to seven. Furthermore, by late February, the single, which like "Genie In A Bottle" reached No. 1 on the single sales chart as well, was certified gold, and went on to sell over 500,000 copies. It must have been especially satisfying to Christina, because she had been more involved with this song than she had been with "Genie In A Bottle."

After the release of "What A Girl Wants," MTV produced a weekend special featuring Christina with her sister, Rachel, and a couple of friends talking about guys, love and a host of other topics that typical teenage girls discuss. It had the atmosphere of a slumber party, with Christina wearing a rhinestone-encrusted head rag, a sleeveless and collarless t-shirt, and informal pants. During the special, Christina picked an Eminem video as one of her Top Ten videos. One of Christina's friends asked her, "So, do you still have a crush on Eminem?" and Christina said, "He's cute and everything, but he's got too many girls after him. Besides, he's married, so I'm going to stay away from that."[1] That part was true, Christina bantered about Eminem being cute, something that the rapper himself would not find amusing. He was also irritated about the fact that she mentioned his marriage, which soon ended in divorce amid allegations of domestic violence.

Following that, a discussion came up about his lyrics, some of which concern domestic violence. Christina said that joking about domestic violence was "not cool." She gave a message to her female fans about not letting the male have too much power in the relationship and that they should not hesitate to get out of such a situation. Considering Christina's own background, her comments were delivered with genuine concern. She later recalled, "I probably said that song ["97 Bonnie and Clyde"] is disgusting. You know what I mean—jeez. Slicing up your baby's mama and stuffing her in a trunk and shoving her in the ocean with your daughter watching. That's disgusting. I'm sorry, but I think the majority of the world thinks that's disgusting."[2]

After the taping and airing of the MTV special, Christina thought nothing more of it. It was fun and had consolidated her status as one of the MTV Generation's most popular stars.

On January 3, the invitations for the 42nd Annual Grammy Award Ceremonies were sent out. Christina would be receiving hers soon. She was busy capping off January with a trip to the Super Bowl. Christina kicked things off at halftime performing a new duet with Enrique Iglesias called "Celebrate the Future Hand in Hand." Although she performed with Enrique, the previous night she had actually been holding hands with Carson Daly. She had spent the night before the Super Bowl in a strip club in Atlanta called Cheetah. One fellow patron claimed that Christina and Carson were given a lap dance at the establishment. Exhibiting the same poor judgment that would get her into trouble with Eminem, Christina felt the need to spill the beans on who else she had seen at the club. Upon being escorted to the VIP room, Christina reported, "Carson's there, and Joey [Fatone] from 'N Sync. That's the shady part nobody says anything about 'N Sync being there; we had 98[degrees], we had a couple of members of Backstreet. I'm totally tattling, but it's the whole double standard." For all her reasons in doing it, Christina still sounded like the first grade tattletale. Perhaps it was not that hard to understand why fellow pop stars would come to have a diminished view of the petite singer.

On Tuesday, January 4, Christina was actually one of the many superstars announcing the 2000 Grammy nominations in a ceremony that began at 8:15 a.m. at the luxurious Beverly Hills Hilton in Beverly Hills, California. On hand were fellow nominee Sarah McLachlan, R&B star Mary J. Blige, and Best New Artist nominee Macy Gray, as well as Dallas Austin, Steven Curtis Chapman, Martina McBride, Carole Bayer Sager, Tom Scott, Latin pop star Thalia, and, coincidentally, Diane Warren.

When the nominations were announced, Christina was "dying. I was shocked. I don't know what was going through my mind, but I wasn't expecting it at all, just because I'd only had one single out…I didn't think that's all it took."[3] She would be up against Macy Gray, Kid Rock and Britney in the Best New Artist category.

Christina was wearing her blue contacts and her perfectly straight, blond hair was dyed several shades lighter, contrasting with her black sweater that was complemented by a leopard-print skirt. She seemed genuinely excited and explained to reporters after the ceremony, "I mean, to be up against, Madonna, Madonna…it's definitely been a great year." She would be competing against the "Material Girl" in the category of Best Female Pop Vocal Performance. Britney and Sarah McLachlan were both nominated as well. McLachlan noted, "She's so mature and so polished at such a young age," and singer Mark McGrath graciously said, "Christina's got a hell of a voice!" Christina saw Chilli of TLC at the announcement of the nominations. "I saw her at the Grammy announcements, [where] she was also an announcer, and she was very cool."[4]

Christina had been taken completely by surprise. It is not that she believed she was not talented enough to get a nomination, but she felt that because she had only come out in August, and had only put out one single, that she would not be nominated. Despite her manager's excitement and his belief that the nomination was in the bag, Christina was reluctant to believe it. "People around me were saying it would happen, but I'd only had one single out."[5] (Technically, by then "What A Girl Wants" had come out as well, but only "Genie In A Bottle" actually fell into the cut-off date for eligibility.)

January also saw the release of the inevitable Christina Aguilera doll. Christina herself was producing the official doll, and she had to pose for side view and back view mug shots. Although the doll was rushed to stores as soon as it was ready, it had in fact been pushed back from a Christmas release date, which would have meant bigger sales. Marketed to the pre-teen crowd, the singing doll was later released in a variety of outfits. "It's weird, looking at it. It's like my Mini-Me," Christina explained, referring to the popular *Austin Powers* movie. "The doll has the outfits I wore in the "Genie In A Bottle" video. It's fun. I do have a lot of really young fans who would enjoy it, and it's collectable."

An editor for Amazon.com described the doll in great detail: "She has a wide smile, layered blonde hair, and the familiar, ultra-thin figure of 11.5-inch fashion dolls (so she can share their clothes and accessories). But this doll has lots of added features packed into her lithe frame. In her back is a battery compartment for four, 1.5-volt AAA batteries (included), with a removable song cartridge that can be replaced with other songs as the star's career continues. On her sides are control switches— one for volume and one to select a 20-second sample or the full version of 'Genie In A Bottle.' The on-off button also serves as Christina's belly button! She's dressed in cropped jeans with a matching jacket, a brown faux-suede halter-top, and brown high-heeled sandals. Four tiny accessories come with the doll, including a hand-held microphone."

"I just crack up about it," Christina said after the doll's release. "It's a trip for me. I cringe a little bit when I see [one of them], because it's not that cute. We're going to try to get it to look a little bit more like me because I'm kind of unhappy about it right now. But I thought it was something cool that young girls and collectors could get into." (According to the *Daily News*, the doll's look was not the only thing that Christina was unhappy about. The paper claimed that the French company that made the dolls designed them so that the chips could be switched among dolls. In other words, a young fan could place a Britney cartridge into Christina and make her sing "...Baby One More Time." According to them, this caused Christina to threaten to pull out of the deal. In fact, the doll included the removable song cartridge.)

In a warm-up before her own tour, which would be sponsored by the Levi Company, Christina toured at selected dates with R&B girl group TLC. She had been pondering whether to actually get involved in a tour before she embarked as headliner on her own summer tour. It would be rather soon, but she decided that it could be productive to be an opening act before carrying all of the weight on her own shoulders. TLC's tour had already started by the time Christina joined. In fact, it was only after a member of her management flew out and checked out the show and decided that the "vibe" was appropriate, that Christina decided to jump on the bandwagon.[6]

By her second show, Christina had still not met any of the members, except for Chilli. She was very welcoming and approached Christina. "We're happy to have you aboard. Are you excited?" she asked the younger diva. "Yes!" Christina replied excitedly.[7] Christina was starting to feel the pressure of being a full-fledged celebrity. "At times, it really is overwhelming," she explained. "I mean, the schedule alone, and the loneliness of it too. You're living out of suitcases, hotel rooms, you know? Different city every day, and it's tough."

The tour took her to Canada, internationally, and major cities like Boston, San Francisco and Los Angeles. In fact, it was during her New York concert appearance that January that Christina finally met with Fausto for the first time in 12 years. "There's always room for forgiveness, he's a part of my life now," Christina later admitted. "It has been interesting getting reacquainted with my father."

Even Shelly later admitted, "I'm also quite impressed with the status of things with her natural father, Fausto. I actually have seen a tremendous amount of healing take place, which is a blessing in itself. He's become very supportive, has made major amends and is quite supportive of her being open with everything in order to help those still in such a situation. Very few abusers come to recognize, admit the gravity of their mistakes and then have the courage to go on to rectify things as he's done—particularly when they've got the entire world watching. That takes a LOT of work. I'm surprised and feel I must hand it to him."[8] Although after their first meeting they kept in touch continuously and later exchanged Christmas presents, Fausto complained that their relationship could have been a lot better.

"It's a fun show," Christina explained. "I got my band out here with me…and also I'm doing something a little unexpected and introducing the kids to Etta James. Doing a cover called 'At Last,'" Christina elaborated, getting pumped up as she always did when talking about the blues legend. "What is cool is that I've done this song as an encore sometimes before, and I was like, 'Your parents might know this, you guys might.' Younger fans don't. But what's cool is that they all really seem to get into it whenever I do it, and they appreciate the realness of it, I think. You know, that I'm just naked out there without anything. No dancers, no band. It's just me and a mic, and it's about being a vocalist."[9] Christina was not even a regular opening act because her fame had soared so high in such a short period of time, that some of the people at the concert were actually there to see Christina and not TLC.

In fact, when Christina canceled her performance for a show in Boston, the gasps of disappointed fans who had paid up to $42.50 for a ticket were clearly audible through the entry area of the Fleet Center as ushers dutifully recited, over and over: "Christina Aguilera will not be appearing tonight." She had been coughing and complaining of a sore throat earlier in the day during a taping with MIX-98.5 DJ John Lander. It was certainly not the first tour appearance that Christina would cancel, either for TLC or for her own summer tour. Apparently, Christina's health was already being compromised her over-booked schedule.

In the midst of the tour dates, Christina co-wrote and recorded a song, "Don't Make Me Love You," that would be included in the soundtrack for the Madonna-Rupert Everett movie, *The Next Best Thing*, that would come out in late February.

She had also started laying out the groundwork for her Spanish-language album. The producer was Rudy Perez, who was fresh from working with gospel princess Jaci Velasquez (who was crossing over into Latin pop) on her Spanish-language album. "It gave me a lot of experience in working with American artists who aren't fluent in Spanish," Perez told *Billboard*. "When Christina came [to me], I had every trick on the book under my belt because I had already experimented with Jaci."[10] Perez translated the lyrics from Christina's debut album, wrote them out phonetically, and devised a system to help her roll the R's. Christina also had a Spanish tutor consistently traveling with her on the road. "Eventually," she explained wishfully. "I'll be able to do [Spanish] interviews on my own."[11] Christina needed to sound fluent in order to convince the Latin market that she was the real thing and all the work in that direction was crucial.

(In fact, by the time the album came out, Christina's Spanish was still not up to par. Although her Spanish sounded virtually perfect on record, she was not able to do any interviews in Spanish, and even during an online chat, when a fan complimented her in Spanish, she replied, graciously but erroneously: "Muchos Gracias!").

The Spanish may have been somewhat less than perfect, but Christina's emotion was genuine. "I understand a lot of Spanish and [singing in it] is an entirely different sensation and vibe for me," she explained. "I feel that it is a language that transmits a lot of passion, much more passion than anything in English. I can definitely feel it. If I didn't feel it, I wouldn't be doing it. But it is something that comes naturally."[12]

Ron Fair explained Rudy Perez's winning technique in the studio to make Christina's Spanish convincing. "The way he made the adaptations, he placed the Spanish vowels and consonants in the same spots they were in the English, and it made a huge difference," he pointed out candidly. "That was probably the major difference."[13] And it was quite an effective difference. By January, BMG Latin released the Spanish version of "Genie In A Bottle," retitled "Genio Atrapado," with a new video shoot, which had better lighting than the first "Genie In A Bottle" video, and brought to light a more sexy and secure Christina vocalizing the song in Spanish.

Although the song did not heat up the Latin charts as "Genie" had (a result of the song's decidedly American Top 40 feel), it did introduce Christina to the Latin market quite effectively and the video received wide airplay on HTV, the most-watched music channel in Latin America. According to Geoff Mayfield, Director of Charts for *Billboard* magazine, the reason for "Genio Atrapado's" failure to chart was "a challenge related more to Spanish radio formats in the U.S. than to the popularity of her songs." Mayfield felt that many of Christina's English-speaking fans would buy the Spanish album, but that the Spanish-language songs would get little airplay on mainstream pop stations, with a few exceptions in cities with large Spanish-speaking populations, such as New York and Los Angeles.

Curiously, MTV Latin America continued airing the English version of her hit, which by then had already plummeted in popularity. Quite ironically, considering the statements he had made regarding Christina's ethnicity when she first came out, it was Ron Fair who spearheaded the release of "Genio Atrapado." (Even before its release as a part of her Latin album, the track came out on the multi-artist compilation, *Latin Latino Éxitos*.)

Rudy Perez adapted all the songs that Christina would use from her debut album, including "Por Siempre Tu," the Spanish version of "I Turn To You." He also wrote most of the new material, including "Si No Te Hubiera Conocido," a duet with up-and-coming Puerto Rican singer Luis Fonsi, a virtual unknown outside the Latin market. Christina told *Billboard*'s Leila Cobo that she had requested him because "we grew up listening to the same things—Brian McKnight and music from Puerto Rico. And he, like I, can incorporate both R&B and Latin." By then, Fonsi had two chart-topping albums under his belt, both of them produced by Perez. His second album, Eterno, achieved a Latin gold certification (100,000 copies sold) within weeks and spawned a No. 1 single on the *Billboard Hot Latin Tracks* chart: "Imagíname Sin Ti."

Fonsi said he felt honored to be asked to duet with Christina. This was one contemporary who had no problems connecting with her. "If you were to have asked me a month before I knew I was going to sing with her, 'Who would you like to sing with, if you could pick a female artist?,' I would have said Christina Aguilera, believe it or not," Fonsi said in a telephone interview with the *Los Angeles Times*.

He had much praise for Christina. "She's young, she is extremely, extremely talented. She has a great control of her voice. She knows her instrument very well, and I really look up to that." Like almost everyone else who met her, Fonsi felt compelled to add: "And for her young age, she's very mature."

Christina recorded the album in Perez's Miami studios during breaks from touring and promoting. She even got a room in Perez's Miami home, and she felt welcome in the Latin warmth and familiarity that was so much a part of his household. Christina really bonded with Perez, and confided in him about her dreams, her background and her father. During one recording session break, she heard Perez playing a standard bolero, "Contigo En La Distancia." "Rudy was sitting there, just playing the guitar," Christina recalled, "and I looked in and I said, 'Rudy, I really love that song. I can really relate to that song.' And he told me, 'That's a bolero.' And after that, I wanted to include it, with my interpretation."[14]

Christina liked the song so much that she recorded it, partly because of a "love thing," she told the *San Diego Tribune*. She failed to note that she meant her "love thing" with Jorge Santos. When her Spanish album was finally released, Christina noted in the credits: "Many kisses and thanks especially to my 'Papi Chulo' for inspiring me to sing 'Contigo En La Distancia.'"

Christina was becoming more and more involved with the production aspect of her albums. "Right now, whenever I go to the recording studio, I'm always soaking in everything. I'm absorbing, I'm learning, I'm getting more familiar with the technical aspect of it," she said. "But I have a great ear; I definitely have an ear for it, and one day I will be producing."[15]

Despite her impossible schedule, in retrospect, Christina was upbeat about the TLC tour. "Touring with TLC was really, really great. That was incredible just because it was my first time living on a tour bus, basically, for that month, playing in huge venues night after night. It was really, really fun for me…That was really incredible, and it was a good learning experience for me to be around the girls, to be on that tour, and good preparation for the tour this summer."

Although her relationship with Jorge Santos was moving along quite merrily, Christina kept stating in interviews that she was not dating. "No time," she told one publication. "It's sort of sad. I see these gorgeous guys in the audience and would love to get to know them. But I'm off to the next airplane." That, and she had a boyfriend traveling with her. In March, she did admit: "My career is my boyfriend. Actually, I fell in love this year for the first time in the midst of all this. I don't know how it happened. It's kind of crazy. It's really, really hard to maintain a relationship being in the spotlight constantly and people are always digging for things, and considering the long-distance factor and how busy I am, it's a strain on any relationship. So we'll see. We'll see what happens in the future."[16]

During the tour dates, she also found time to perform at the American Music Awards. Wearing a tummy-baring bodice with a gown like skirt she performed "I Turn To You," then she stripped away the skirt to dance in slacks during a medley of "What A Girl Wants." Christina felt she had silenced the critics of her "packaged pop" by giving a raw performance, and she perceived this to be a turning point in her career. On February 4, she joined Lou Bega and Carson Daly for the 49th Annual Miss USA Pageant.

On the day of the Grammy Awards ceremony, February 23, Christina was walking on air. "What A Girl Wants" had recently made its debut on the U.K. charts at No. 3.

Once inside the Staples Center, Christina took her seat next to manager Steve Kurtz. When they announced the nominees for Best New Artist, Christina was agitated and nervous. Despite her feelings that it was practically impossible for her to get the Grammy, considering the short amount of time her album had had to register with Grammy voters in comparison with Britney's, there was an inkling of hope. Christina told herself that if she lost, it would not be for a lack of talent, but part of the technicalities of the industry. Sarah McLachlan, Sheryl Crow and Melissa Etheridge all went up to the podium to announce the Grammy for Best New Artist. Christina was at the edge of her seat. "And the Best New Artist is...*Christina Aguilera!*" they shouted in unison.

Christina's knees almost buckled. Once she stood up her knees were quavering. She carefully walked up to the stage, took the statuette, and looked into the audience cheerfully; it was clear that she was extremely emotional. So many years of struggle and hard work stood firmly behind that one moment; it was almost surreal. This was something Christina had been dreaming about since she was eight years old; in fact, Best New Artist was a category that Christina had humbly hoped to be at least nominated for. She did not have a speech planned and even if she had, in the ecstasy of the moment she would have forgotten her words. "Oh my God you guys!" she exclaimed. She quickly thanked her mom and her dad and her fans and walked back to her seat. Once she walked backstage, the handlers took the statuette, thanked Christina and pointed her way back to her seat. "Rip off!" Christina thought as she made her way back.[17] The Grammy would be shipped to her at a later date.

As soon as she sat down, Christina realized that when she had thanked her "Dad," the general public, still in the dark as to most of Christina's life, would assume that she meant her father, whose last name would be Aguilera. Because Christina had been calling Jim her "Dad" since she was 10 years old, it was second nature to her and she had not even thought of clarifying such a thing. She was concerned that the public might have misunderstood. After all the support that Jim had offered her, Christina desperately wanted him to know that she loved him. "He's really been a great dad to her, seeing her through all the rough times growing up and as a teen," Shelly later explained, "She really loves him."[18] The fact that she called him dad, instead of step-dad, was actually a greater testament to that love.

Once she had settled back in her seat, Christina turned and asked Steve Kurtz: "Steve, you don't think people thought I meant my father Fausto, do you? I meant Jim!"[19] It was the only thing that momentarily dampened the moment for Christina, but she had been walking on air ever since her nomination, and now she was even happier. " I didn't expect it whatsoever, just because my album had been out the shortest amount of time out of everyone I was up against,"

Christina later explained, "but I was shocked, completely shocked and overwhelmed. The greatest moment career-wise to date." Christina had previously stated that she would put Steve Kurtz's old Grammy ticket "right next to my Grammy for 'Best New Artist.'"

Upon receiving the actual statuette, it went on her mother's mantle. After the ceremony, Christina stepped inside her black stretch limo and drove off into the night. Still reeling from the excitement, she picked up her cell phone and called Shelly and Carson Daly. Then she turned to the reporter in the car with her. "Did I sound O.K. onstage?" she asked. "I was in shock. I was preparing at that moment to put on my loser face."[20] Christina was all smiles at a post-Grammy party thrown by her record label's parent company, BMG. She had changed into a pair of gold pants and a gold, belly-baring top, Christina was appropriately congratulated, and Bob Jamieson, whom Christina now affectionately called "the big guy" was in attendance at the party thrown for the glittering jewel of his label's roster.

The Grammy win coupled with the success of "What A Girl Wants" propelled Christina's self-titled debut up the charts once again. On March 11, more than five months after its initial release, the album had climbed to No. 3 and had sold 5 million copies in the United States alone. The first pressing of *Christina Aguilera* quickly became a collector's item, because RCA issued new copies of the album that included the remix version of "What a Girl Wants" which was absent from the first pressing. On March 2, after reaching No. 1 on seven separate occasions, the video for "What A Girl Wants" had to be retired from *TRL*. Christina's girl anthem had by then been ingrained into pop culture. (After the release of her second single, most of the articles on Christina were no longer titled "Genie Out of the Bottle" but "What Christina Wants" or "What This Girl Wants"; perhaps Christina's allegations of "lazy journalism" weren't so off-the-mark after all.)

On April 16, the Alma Awards were taped in Pasadena. Christina attended but did not perform. Two days later, VH1 aired a special that had been taped earlier that month, and that had a special impact on Christina's career. It was a response to the "Divas Live" special that the channel had aired previously, featuring such notable female warblers as Aretha Franklin, Celine Dion, Mariah Carey and Shania Twain. This version of the program, titled "Men Strike Back," featured the Backstreet Boys, Sting, Enrique Iglesias and Tom Jones. Christina's forceful performance of "I Turn To You" and "What A Girl Wants" was good enough, but it was her rendition of Etta James' "At Last" that really wowed the public.

Christina came out onstage amid total darkness with a spotlight aimed directly at her, just the way she liked it. She was wearing a black suit and hat and sang with a sultry, energetic voice. VH1's own music critic Michael Hill, who attended the taping of the concert, pointed out: "Young Christina Aguilera has a set of diva's pipes already and can cram more notes into a single line than a trio of Mariahs. Though she delivered her hits, 'I Turn To You' and 'What A Girl Wants,' with great technical prowess, the real surprise of her set was a rendition of the pre-rock'n'roll-era pop standard 'At Last' with a small jazz combo. For a suitably world-weary version of the tune, check out Joni Mitchell's *Both Sides Now* disc, but Aguilera gets points for tackling something so outside the box of teen fodder."

The New York Times did not share this opinion, contrasting Enrique and Christina by noting, "Mr. Iglesias isn't much competition. He's a video-era star best described as a himbo, who poses like a hunk but sings like someone yelping at a karaoke bar. Christina Aguilera, the show's token female singer, has the opposite drawback: a big, agile voice that she shows off compulsively, overloading every line with Mariah Carey-style ornaments. In 'At Last,' she starts oohing and ahing before the first word of the song."

After the taping, Christina met up with Enrique at Nell's, a dance club in Manhattan. They had met previously, of course, during their Superbowl performance and then had caught up a number of times when Christina was recording *Mi Reflejo* in Miami, where Iglesias grew up and keeps an apartment. The Latin music community in Miami is rather tight and most of the musicians know each other, even if there are very defined boundaries between them. It is therefore not surprising that Christina ran into Enrique when she was in Miami working with Rudy Perez, who, coincidentally, had produced a couple of songs for Enrique's father.

Christina's website duly noted, "Christina and Enrique went dancing after the 'Men Strike Back' performance, and ran into each other when they were in Miami the next week." What the website failed to report, but the patrons at a Manhattan club did not, was that Christina and Enrique kissed during their dancing session. Sources explained that the couple showed up at 2 a.m. for "open-mike night" but they ended up openly making out. Initially, they were only dancing, but when they retired to the downstairs dance floor, things heated up.[21]

"They just started going at it," one source said. "They were kissing very deeply, very passionately. They weren't trying to hide it at all." The reason this is shocking is because by this time, Christina was very much involved in her relationship with Jorge Santos. Her website never denied the kissing rumor outright, cryptically pointing out: "But they [Christina and Enrique] were never 'really a couple' and have not had an opportunity to see each other again." Enrique's spokesman noted, "I know that Enrique and Christina have been friends since they performed together at the Super Bowl halftime show. But since I was not at Nell's, I can't confirm or deny what happened." Christina's publicist, Elaine Shock, was equally vague (or feigned ignorance) and only acknowledged: "I know they were dancing, and it could have been very suggestive. I don't know if they were making out. But I do know they didn't go home together." She was still a lady. Perhaps it was acceptable behavior on the part of Santos, as Christina explained that they had a really "cool relationship."[22]

Enrique was not the only "friend" Christina had gone "clubbing" with while she was involved with Santos. She had also accompanied Fred Durst and when they left the club, Durst offered to take Christina to a milkshake place. "Fred and I were actually being cool with each other," Christina later told *Rolling Stone*. "He took me out one time and bought me a milkshake. He was just like, 'I know this bomb-ass place for milkshakes,' after we left this club. He was so cool." Somehow they had reconnected after that one time Christina had seen him at the Virgin Records store. She was certainly a fan of his music, had openly proclaimed she had bought his album, and she enjoyed spending time with him.

Although superficially Durst, the lead singer of the group Limp Bizkit could appear to be Christina's opposite, they actually had much in common. Like Christina, he always felt like an outsider as a child. "I got my feelings hurt a lot. I was the quiet one—always wanted to be the leader of the team, never got picked, you know," he later recalled. "Not a sob story—just, like, that kid." After a stint in the navy, a failed marriage, and fathering a baby daughter, Durst had no real prospects of his own. Like Christina, he grew up to hide his vulnerabilities with a patina of toughness, and on many occasions it made other people antagonistic toward him. In fact, he shoplifted the rest of the band members—guitarist Wes Borland, D.J. Lethal, Sam Rivers and John Otto—from other groups to put together Limp Bizkit. Although he is Lutheran and Christina is proudly Catholic, they both have abiding faiths in God and are deeply spiritual.

Like Christina, he appreciates the art of tattoo and was a former tattoo artist himself. In short, they appeared to have a lot in common and Durst was enamored with the petite singer. In April, Durst told MTV: "For one thing, Christina's amazing, I really like that girl. I think she's an amazing singer. She's gonna have longevity. She's going to be one of those amazing icon women. I'm really attracted to her, I like her, and I've talked to her a couple of times, and that's that. I haven't had any type of relationship with her, or any type of intercourse with her. She's never sucked my dick, she's never sucked Carson's." Although they did not have sex, Durst later admitted that he had kissed Christina.

While her behavior spurred rumors of unrestrained promiscuity, in fact, Christina was simply maturing into her sexual possibilities, which she had previously eschewed in favor of her career. Now that her career was finally on track—blossoming just as she had always planned—she could finally devote herself to nurturing her neglected emotional life. Unfortunately, she was now a celebrity and any of her actions would come under close scrutiny and judgment, particularly by the growing contingent of female detractors who found Christina sluttish and brash.

Christina certainly did not feel a need to oblige and play the virginal, sweet girl. "Everybody just wants to call all these teen idols role models," Christina told Ed Masley. "And it's a little unfair, just because we're all growing up ourselves, and we're all living life for the first time, and we're all just out there doing what we want to do and making music. It's not just a matter of trying to be provocative. I'm just being me." She was only being herself, but it was an identity that the record label had initially attempted to conceal. "I'm being, basically, a 19-year-old girl who is exploring different sides of herself. And getting up there and doing a couple pelvic thrusts, people don't see it as right. But it's basically not my job to parent America."

Ed Masley noted cynically: "And this is the girl who insisted on telling reporters, just last summer, that her sexed-up breakthrough single, 'Genie In A Bottle,' didn't have a thing to do with sex?" Whenever Masley wrote about Christina, there was a not so subtle deprecation in his tone that appeared to suggest he was suspicious of Christina. Asked about his impression of the singer, Masley commented: "I would imagine that I worked whatever impressions I had of Christina into the stories I did at the time."[23] If taken at his word, then his impression of her was rather negative, demonstrating that Christina also had trouble charming at least some of the journalists who were covering her.

Not that she had time to worry. She was only touching down in Pittsburgh for a two-day break from her exhausting schedule. But on March 16, at 9 p.m., Christina was back at Pittsburgh International Airport. Upon her arrival, the word started spreading quickly: Christina Aguilera is at the airport! Sipping a pineapple smoothie and wearing an ankle-length denim skirt, a faded jean jacket, and with her hair carefully mussed up, Christina barely made it to the boarding area before a wave of fans overtook her.

"I ran all the way from the parking lot," one out-of-breath teenage boy told Christina. "You don't understand, my friend is obsessed with you. He, like, cries whenever your song comes on the radio." Exhibiting the coldness that would alienate countless fans, Christina nodded politely and turned to a pony-tailed female fan who looked like she was on the verge of hyperventilating: "You really set the stage for teens," the girl told her. A young mother tried to give Christina her baby to carry and take a picture. "Oh, no," Christina cried, "I'm afraid I'll drop her." As another wave of gung-ho autograph seeking fans approached, Christina's bodyguard quietly sidled up to her and asked, "Would you like me to hold them off?" Like the diva she believed herself to be, Christina replied, "Just for a few seconds, okay?"

Christina was flying to New York, and in the limo ride from La Guardia Airport to her Manhattan hotel, Christina was telling her publicist about "the Eminem drama."[24]

Christina was actually very concerned. Steve Kurtz had been hearing disturbing rumors about the contents of Eminem's newest single, "The Real Slim Shady." Christina herself had been told that it would poke fun at her supposed crushes on Carson and Fred Durst, including vulgar "insinuations" about her. "It's going to be a *TRL* favorite," Christina lamented, shaking her head. "They don't call him Slim Shady for nothing." Kurtz went on the attack, telling MTV that while he didn't care if Eminem parodied Christina's music, he felt that there "is nothing more important to a woman than her honor, and that seems to be what we're dealing with here." He was right. The song, a catchy rap that garnered impressive airplay and propelled Eminem's album to the top of the charts upon release, alluded to Christina performing fellatio on Carson Daly and Fred Durst. Eminem also playfully noted that Christina had infected him with a "V.D."

In his autobiography *Angry Blond*, Eminem recalled working on the hit single:

> Okay, so they made me do the single. Thing was, I had that hook for a minute, but I was nervous about doing anything with it. I didn't even bring it to Dre. He didn't know I had it in store, stockpiled with a bunch of other hooks. See, I write the hooks a lot of times before I write the actual rhyme. So I had this hook, but I asked myself, "Will this work?" It just needed the right beat. Man, we went into the studio about four times trying to come up with one...We had a meeting on Saturday with the label and they asked, "Well, did you come up with anything?" I played them

"The Way I Am" and they said, "It's a great song. It's just not the first song." Originally, they were talking' about "Criminal" being the single, but I told them to let me take this shit ("The Real Slim Shady" instrumental) over the weekend and I'd have the rhyme written by Monday. Then we'd see if it worked. If it didn't, then fuck it. Right around this time was when Will Smith was dissin' gangsta rap and Christina Aguilera was talkin' shit about me on MTV, putting me on blast about being married during a time when I wasn't ready for the public to know that about me yet. So I waited just long enough to get new subject matter to get into. Now I had something to talk about. I came in on Monday, recorded it, and was done. Interscope, obviously, was satisfied. That situation made me value the saying "Things happen for a reason."[25]

At that point, however, Christina was not one hundred percent sure about whether the rumors were true or not. "I started hearing all of this stuff, and I was tired of it," Christina recalled.[26] She contacted Durst and "was like, 'Something is up, he is being shady.'" Fred Durst admitted to Christina that he had been involved in the taping of the video for Eminem's song. At that point, Christina still "hadn't heard much about it, but I knew that he was talking all this bull about me." Christina's stepfather provided her with much needed support at the time. "My stepdad was so cute," Christina later said. "He was all ready to get on a plane and kick Eminem's ass. I was like, 'That's OK, Dad, it's all right.' It's good to have support like that during those times."[27]

The rumors started coming out at least one full month before the song was actually released, and Christina was disgusted. She had finally removed herself from the high school intrigues that had been perpetrated against her by jealous classmates, and now this. "It's disgusting and offensive and above all it's not true," Christina told *MTV News* of the alleged lyrics. She also told *Rolling Stone*, after the video came out, "Fred is crazy. Fred, man, how dumb are you if you're trying to get with somebody and then you are going to appear in a video that flat-out disses her. You know what I mean?" She added, "...if he really did tell Eminem that, none of it is true. Seriously. I haven't spent 'quality time' with either of those two guys."

Durst, on the other hand, told Howard Stern that he kissed Christina and had gone out with her, but that they had not been involved in any sexual activity. However, he was quite candid in admitting that he did want to be involved with her. Furthermore, Durst went on to call Eminem "one of the greatest rappers of all time," adding that Eminem's trashing of Christina was between Eminem and her. "I think she's a really, really talented woman," Durst said. "I think she's an amazing performer and singer. I think she's going to stick around for a long time, but I think what's going on in her life right now is kind of diluted and washed out a little bit...I don't know." Durst continued, "She's young, and something about her drives me crazy about the way she sings and performs and the presence she has. So I was interested in her. She knows that I didn't do anything. Whatever her and Em have issues on—that's their thing."[28]

Eminem himself explained the whole situation to MTV's Kurt Loder: "I met her before, and I had respect for her too," he said of Christina. "When she had her little 'What A Girl Wants' special [on MTV] and it aired...people were telling me about it, like, 'Yo, she put you on blast. She was picking your video apart,' and this and that. So I was like, 'No,' you know? I was like..."Not Christina."

Eminem responded, "I thought she liked me, or whatever. Yeah. So I'm watching her little special, and I'm watching her with her little friends, and she's giggling, and she picked one of my videos for one of her favorite videos or something. And I was like, 'That's cool that she picked my video.' And then after it came off, [she brought up] my marriage. I wasn't trying to make that as public as I could make it. That was my personal business. It's like, as far as my personal business, I tell people what I want them to know."

"She heard a rumor that I was married and then said, 'Yeah, he's cute, but isn't he married, though?' And I was like, 'No, you didn't just say that. You little bitch.' And then she said, 'Yeah, and, and, you know, doesn't he have a song about killing his baby's mother? And I always tell my friends if you're against domestic, you know, I'm so against domestic violence, and if you're in an abusive relationship...' I was like, why does she just pick my video if she's picking it apart? I would rather have had her say nothing about me."

"So, you know, she heard a rumor. She didn't know if I was married or not. She just heard a rumor and then put me on blast in front of a nation of people that might not have known that, and I might not have cared for them to know that. But I figured, 'Well, fuck it. All right. Okay. I'm married. Okay. Whatever. That's cool. But you said something about me, so I'm going to voice some rumors that I heard about you.'"

Loder replied, "Yeah. And who knows, really."

The problem with Christina was that she still did not understand the consequences that her words could have. She may have been in the industry since she was 13, but she had never experienced the full force of a media spotlight aimed directly at her, and the power that it generated greatly excited her. In fact, just two months before the rumors began filtering about the content of Eminem's single, Christina admitted to *The Washington Post's* Richard Harrington "with a mischievous chuckle": "I like to stir things up every once in a while and get a reaction. If I can't really date, at least I can think about it, or think about having crushes. It's just fun, and they never last very long, my crushes. It would be very nice if I could find the time to actually meet some really cool people, get to know them."

Previously, her interviewer for *Rolling Stone* had perceptively noted: "She opens a copy of the music-insider magazine *Hits* and begins leafing through it, stopping at a full-color, full-page photograph of DMX. 'Mmm,' she exclaims. 'He is hot!' It sometimes seems like Christina uses magazine interviews as dating services..." As far as the Carson Daly rumor mill, it was Christina's own mention of the note she had left for the MTV personality after her TRL appearance that had fed the rumors. Later, when the rumors about her own behavior at the Cheetah had surfaced, she had exhibited poor judgment in revealing the names of all the other men who had been present at the strip bar. Christina did not now how to handle her celebrity. Driven by her insecurity, she sought refuge in the attention that her fame could afford her and she stumbled badly.

"Wow, I'm cool enough to have gossip said about me," she had first thought when she heard the rumors regarding her and Carson. Christina loved being a celebrity. She had previously said that she never forgot her neighbor asking her for her autograph at a block party. In an interview right before her album came out, she stated that she longed for the day when she would be recognized on the street and besieged with autograph requests. "When I see all these people screaming and chanting and holding those signs that they made just for me, my eyes light up, and my whole body just lifts, and I just feel in another state," Christina told *The New York Times*. "I feel like I'm floating on air. It's the most incredible feeling, and I've always wanted it."[29]

Despite her success, Christina could still remember the sting she had felt over being rejected by her classmates, which had left lingering doubts inside of her. *Am I really worthy of this admiration?* These feelings of inadequacy were the driving force behind her compulsive perfectionism at such a young age. Her need to control everything was borne out of the fact that when she had witnessed domestic violence at home, she had been an unprotected child unable to do anything to help in a situation where she had absolutely no control. She had felt entirely vulnerable. Christina never wanted to feel that way again. She was not lying when she confessed to the *Times* in '99: "I tend to be a control freak, and I have to be a perfectionist. I think that's what drives me because it gives me control over a situation. I hate feeling vulnerable to this day."

Christina constantly rattled off to-do lists in front of her interviewers and many of them picked up on her controlling nature themselves. "Within seconds of getting on the phone with her, this 19-going-on-30-year-old singer makes it clear who's in charge here, who's running this show," wrote one reporter. "Aguilera has ambitions, an agenda, and a very tight schedule. She rattles off answers with confidence and nary a teen-agey 'um' or misplaced 'like.'"

Although partly it was Christina's adult nature, which occasionally appeared put-on and superficial, that did not allow her to connect with her contemporaries in an uncomplicated fashion, she was also unable to deal with her celebrity and the fact that her words could anger other people. Soon, many of her fellow teen pop stars would be talking about *her* and they did not have kind words.

Did Christina learn her lesson about gossiping? Apparently not. In an interview in September with the *Star-Ledger*, right before her appearance on the "MTV Video Music Awards," Christina promised a "big secret surprise" duet at the Awards, but she refused to reveal her partner. (At one of her concerts, she told her fans that she would be performing "Come On Over" at the Awards and that she had a very special guest planned. "The guest will blow your mind 'cause its so unexpected," she noted cryptically.) "It's safe to assume it won't be Eminem," noted the reporter, "Or maybe that's not a safe assumption. Asked jokingly if she and Eminem would be performing together, she responded, 'You never know.'"[30]

Although the Eminem rumors were a source of concern for Christina, she had other reasons to be excited—and plenty of activities to keep her busy. For the moment she was still in Miami wrapping up the recording sessions for *Mi Reflejo* (My Reflection), the title that had been selected for the Spanish-language album that was scheduled for release in the summer. She also had to record the Christmas album starting in the spring.

After the Eminem video made its debut on MTV's *TRL* on April 27, there was increased publicity that helped Christina in the end, and solidified her standing as a pop-culture figure. Christina said of Eminem, "…I think it was really wrong of him to dis me like that, because all this past year I've been so positive in recognizing his talent. Obviously he overreacted, because what he said wasn't at all in the same league as what you said. I was offended and really disgusted by it. The fact that he is talking about diseases and all that."

However, Christina herself pin-pointed what had provoked Eminem's ire when she commented, "But I see where he's coming from, in the sense that you take this guy who wants to be respected as a serious rap artist, and all of a sudden he is in the world of MTV and *TRL*. I can see where he would get a little mad and want to rebel against the Britney Spears, 'N Sync, Backstreet Boys world of teen music. And if he has to do it that way and be that immature about it, then, fine, be that way."

"You know, it's hard to be in the spotlight," Christina confessed. "You may be having a rough day already, and you come home and turn on the TV, and then you see [the video with] Eminem with that upset look, sitting between Carson Daly and Fred Durst." Unfortunately for Christina, the video proved immensely popular and spent 20 days at the No. 1 spot on TRL. It was forcibly retired after 65 days on the countdown on July 28.

On April 14, Christina traveled to New York's Radio City Music Hall to perform at the Essence Awards. On April 27 and 28, Christina flew to Orlando, Florida to tape a "Disney Summer Jams" special that would air on UPN and included performances by Enrique Iglesias and 98 Degrees. She also attended a high school prom at Greenbrier High School, which was the prize for a "Prom of Your Life" contest Christina had participated in. Christina was actually ill the day of the prom, but she did not want to let down the students and plowed ahead. Although the school's principal later sent Christina a note thanking her for her professionalism and graciousness in complying with all the autograph and picture requests, Dorothy Hatch a writer for the high school's newspaper claimed: "Colin [the contest winner] gave her a rose and she said something like 'Oh, you're the kid who won the contest' and gave him and his friend a CD and that was it." Apparently, Christina and proms don't mix.

Photo Gallery

Christina performs at the Grammy Awards in replacement of Luis Miguel. She lost out on both her nominations for "What A Girl Wants" and Best Latin Pop Album for "Mi Reflejo."

Christina cheerfully opens a Christmas present at home. Already an army brat, the little girl's smile hides the pain and frustration that she feels over her father's violence toward her mother and, occasionally, herself.

Christina and her mother, Shelly, in 1981 during their brief New Jersey intermission after her birth in Staten Island. Fausto Aguilera is out of the picture, and although he will remain with them until Christina is five, she will later block out the Spanish that she learned from him.

Christina (first from left) enjoys some down time off-stage during her first season on the New Mickey Mouse Club. Already close to Britney Spears who was only one year younger than Christina, most of the other children called her "the diva". The two girls would be locked into a rivalry that started during the NMMC.

Teenage Christina as part of the "cheerleader clique". She was a cheerleader for literally two weeks and had to quit because the strict practice schedule was rivaling her music career.

Christina during the hellish years. In elementary school (below) and in Marshall Middle School (left) Christina was subjected to torrents of abuse from her jealous classmates. From slashed tires to having balls thrown at her during physical education class, it would only stop when Shelly decided to home-school Christina after the eighth grade.

Christina Aguilera: A Star is Made

Christina performs at one of the many local talent shows she would win. "She was a little girl with an adult voice," recalled Jude Pohl of the Pittsburgh theater company, Pohl Productions.

Christina surrounded by the men who made her career. On the far right is "the big guy," Bob Jamieson. Initially made uncomfortable by their suggestions, Christina soon learned to play their game.

Christina tapes her Christmas special, "My Reflection." It aired in December on the ABC network and was watched by 8.8 million Americans.

Christina makes her arrival at the first ever Latin Grammy Awards. Although she failed to win her nomination for Best Pop Vocal Performance for "Genio Atrapado," her revealing clothes garnered most of the comments from the press that night.

Christina answers questions during an interview promoting her no. 1 single "Come On Over" in the summer of 2000. She had made peace with her father, racked up three No. 1 singles and sold over six million copies of her album, but she wasn't happy. Tense and physically ill, her personal and professional lives were in shambles as she attempted to sever her relationship with Steven Kurtz.

Three days before the 43rd Grammy Awards ceremony, Christina rehearses her set list with Jorge Santos at her side. Having gone through the trauma of firing her manager and coming into her own as a professional in the industry, Christina found herself relying on Santos more and more.

Christina animatedly performs during her Sears / Levi's tour. Although the tour was greeted warmly by critics and sold well, Christina was being worked to the ground as she recorded "My Kind of Christmas" during the tour stops and promoted "Mi Reflejo."

Christina enjoys one of her few private moments with Jorge Santos at the beach.

Christina recorded the video "Come On Over" in early June, when her relationship with Jorge Santos was privately flourishing despite Christina's repeated pronouncements to the press that she was not seeing anyone. She was already starting to rebel against the image that her record company wanted to keep projecting.

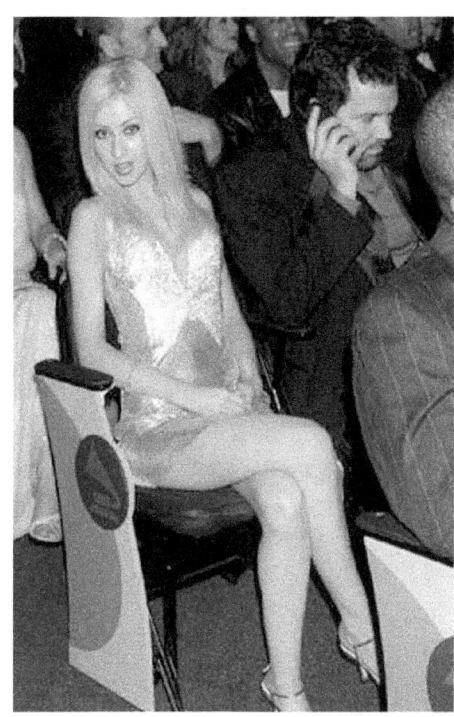

(left) Christina at the 42nd Grammy Awards, where she would win a Grammy for Best New Artist. Steve Kurtz sits beside her, talking on his cell phone. Shelly was unable to attend because she was sick.

(below) Christina winning Grammy as Best New Artist.

Christina lets her guard down in a rare moment during the filming of "Genie In A Bottle" in Malibu Beach. "I was freezing my butt off," Christina said candidly.

Christina proudly shows off her Grammy for Best Pop Collaboration With Vocals, which she won for "Lady Marmalade."

Christina performs "Genie Atrapado" at the Latin Grammy Awards on September 13, 2000. In a news conference the following day she would announce the release of Mi Reflejo with Steven Kurtz at her side. Almost exactly a month later, she fired him.

Christina with Fred Durst, Limp Bizkit frontman.

And with Ananda Lewis during a taping of MTV.

Christina during a taping of MTV and with Destiny's Child.

Christina during a taping of MTV.

Christina with Photographer Extraordinaire, Walik Goshorn.

Christina performs "Infatuation" as part of her set during the closing ceremonies of the Winter Olympic Games on February 24. Christina was almost done recording her sophomore album and she was also done with Jorge Santos.

Christina performs "Nobody Wants To Be Lonely" with Ricky Martin for the British pop music program, Top of the Pops. Ricky approached Christina to help him record a remix of the song, and it shot up the charts worldwide. Unfortunately, Martin's album did not.

A picture from one of Christina's first promotional shots.

Christina Aguilera: A Star is Made

Together at the podium, Christina and Britney Spears introduce Whitney Houston at the MTV Video Music Awards. Ironically, Christina had been forced to perform with Fred Durst at the awards because Britney had already been booked and they wanted something different from Christina.

Christina performs in the Coke commercial that would once again spark rumors of a rivalry with Britney Spears, who did commercials for Pepsi. In fact, Christina's deal with Coke dated back to mid-2000, months before Britney's contract with Pepsi came about.

Christina at her 21st birthday party in the Hollywood nightclub Deep. After blowing out the candles on her enormous birthday cake, "X-tina" said her one wish was for "everyone to get fucked up!"

"X-tina" hangs out during the filming of the Coke commercial in May 2001.

Christina performs at the Caracas Pop Music Festival in Venezuela on January 20, 2001.

ELEVEN
On Tour & In Love

Christina was excited at the prospect of headlining her first tour in the summer. She had been rehearsing intensely, although the best rehearsal had been her stint as tour-opener for TLC. Destiny's Child would be Christina's own opening act for most of her tour dates, an indication of how high she had climbed in so short a time. From opening act to sold out pop phenomenon, with another (multi-platinum, chart-topping) R&B group as her own opening act—in less than 3 months. The singer's jaunt across America and Canada was being co-sponsored by Sears and Levi's.

"It's a partnership in turn. It's good for both of us," Christina said. "They're into supporting music. Levi's did the Lauryn Hill tour. Sears did Backstreet Boys. For me, Sears has even put out Christina Boutiques in their stores, which is a great way for me to be more accessible to my fans. It's all good."[1] Not only would Sears help Christina stage her expensive tour and put her face in TV and print ads, it also created Christina Boutiques in more than 650 Sears stores nationwide fully stocked with her CDs, T-shirts and related merchandise. Even before the end of her first tour, Christina started hinting that she would definitely be changing styles for her sophomore album. When she was asked whether her Levi's sponsorship would preclude any of the collaborations she planned with artists such as DMX, the well-versed businesswoman replied, "Sears is a little straight-laced. But basically, it's a give and take on both parts. And I'm not trying to do anything drastic right now anyway."[2]

Practically speaking, any duet with DMX or other potentially controversial artists wouldn't come until her next album, and by then the sponsorships from Sears and Levi's would be over, she explained. "But even so, I don't know if they would totally object to it," she said. "As long as it was done in good taste and it was fun and cool and something kids would enjoy, it would be OK."

Christina was understandably enthusiastic about the tour because performing live is where she feels most comfortable. "I'm such a lover of live performing," Christina explained. "It's the biggest high in the world to hear, you know, thousands of people sometimes sing back the lyrics of your songs and see their appreciation for your music and what you do." Unlike other divas (i.e. Streisand and Mariah Carey) who have recurring stage fright and limit the number of concerts they give, Christina's upbringing in *The New Mickey Mouse Club* had prepared her for anything. It made the stage a natural setting for her.

"It's going to be exciting to take my full band and my dancers out on the road," she said, "and giving the show an edgy, theatrical vibe. Right now, I'm getting into the creative aspects of planning the show, of covering new ground, doing more blues, soul, and some spectacular choreography." She hyped up the tour through interviews, with the requisite Sears/Levi's logos on a background behind her, explaining that she would sport a new look and that her stage show would be very theatrical. The Levi's sponsorship came at a time when the company was trying to appeal to younger consumers, a large chunk of the marketplace it had been losing during the last couple of years. "We are meeting all our expectations for this turnaround so far," a Levi's executive explained of their sales after Christina had been tied to their image. "I won't be totally satisfied until we are growing again."

When Christina toured with TLC, she seemed to have snuck a peak at their demands for the tour venues. When the contract for her own tour venues was spelled out, her demands, although not outrageous by the standards of the music industry, were anything but modest. In the spirit of full disclosure, some of the more unique conditions are included here:

Christina's dressing room was to "be clean and have a private toilet, washing and shower facilities, hot and cold running water, a large vanity with mirror, clothes rack and extensive lighting (a minimum of 250 watts). In addition, the room should have one (1) large sofa, lounge chairs, two (2) eight (8) foot tables with cloths, plants, flowers and carpet." It also requested a spacious room for the band, for the two back-up female vocalists, and for the four male dancers. They requested a "hospitality room" that included "sofas, chairs, tables for catering and one large color television connected to a cable system, if possible." They also expected a tuning room, a production office, and a management and accounting office.

In a note preceding the list of provisions expected to be offered by the purchasing venue, the contract warned: "Due to the state of our environment, no Styrofoam or plastic goods (cups, plates or utensils) are to be used in the preparation, serving or disposal of the…food, unless specifically ordered by ARTIST representative."

The "food" included: ten bottles of room temperature bottled water "(not Evian)"; full coffee and tea set-up including "real coffee mugs"; "one (1) 6 pack of COKE (Not Pepsi and no diet)"; 4 packs of Carnation instant breakfast, a small container of Nesquick chocolate milk; a pint of organic whole milk; one liter of full fat vanilla soy milk; one package of "Soya Kaas" soy cheese full fat and a bottle of Echinacea capsules. They specifically asked for a small fruit platter of raspberries, blueberries, strawberries, plums and whole bananas "all [of which] must be organic"; a small tray of fresh roasted turkey, chicken and roast beef, "Deli only"; one small veggie tray with carrots, cherry tomatoes, red peppers, cauliflower, celery and Jicama; assorted raw almonds, banana chips and dried cranberries; assorted power bars, Cliff bars and balance bars; a small bottle of "Flintstones" vitamins with extra vitamin C; small bottle of chewable vitamin C tablets; one small cheese platter with Cheddar, Jack, Gouda and Swiss; platter assortment of gums and mints; one (1) roll of APS Film/200 speed exposure; 6 clean large bath towels; display of fork, knives, spoons, plates; a half pint of fat free small curd cottage cheese; one container of "coffee mate non-dairy Creamer"; twelve Solo cups; 4 votive candles with matches; two (2) chicken or turkey club sandwiches (white bread with bacon, lettuce, tomato); and, finally, chocolate chip or Oreo cookies.

One wonders when Christina planned to eat all of the food considering that most of the time she had to leave the tour venue the same night she performed, so that she would be at the next tour stop by the following day. One thing that was notable about the actual contract was that next to Steven Kurtz's name, under the contact information for Marquee management was the name of co-manager Katrina Sirdofsky. According to Christina, Kurtz was paying Sirdofsky $4,000 a week, which was in violation of her contract, because they were in excess of the 20% of Christina's commissionable income that Kurtz was entitled to.

By the time of the start of her tour, Christina's relationship with Jorge Santos had not yet been exposed. The young pop star had enjoyed her quiet down time with Santos in the bus during tour stops without arising much suspicion because he was her dancer. It appeared entirely appropriate for the two to talk and spend time together. In early May, however, while hyping her tour, Christina's management arranged for an interview with *Seventeen* magazine that would be featured in a cover story to hit news stands in July, coinciding with the tour.

Magazine editor Heidi Sherman was selected to interview Christina. Sherman was an expert on teen pop, which she reviewed for Amazon.com (including a later review of *Mi Reflejo*). She also wrote articles for such prestigious publications as *In Style*, *Travel & Leisure*, *Rolling Stone*, *Spin* and *The New York Times*. Sherman went shopping with Christina in New York City, and they did the interview as they looked around. Feeling quite comfortable in such an atmosphere, Christina let her guard down and casually mentioned, allegedly off-the-record, that she was dating Santos and was very much in love with him. What Christina didn't know was that the woman planned to use the little tidbit in her article, for what turned out to be quite a scandalous exclusive and a monster coup for the publication.

After the interview, Christina had to attend a nine-hour cover shoot for the picture that would be featured on the magazine's cover, and other pictures to be laid around the text of the article. As the photographer feverishly snapped his camera, Christina sent several editors out to fetch her chicken nuggets, two big orders of chips, a chocolate shake, two slices of pizza, a mocha coffee and a taco salad. During a break from the shoot she told one editor: "I always had this fantasy of working in a fast-food drive-through for the summer. It seems like a cool job."[3] The resulting pictures were excellent, and a picture of Christina on a motorcycle, clutching a male model (who appears to be Santos, but is not credited anywhere in the magazine) and looking behind her, ended up on the cover. The cover story's publication would see the end of Santos' anonymity.

In mid-May, Christina flew from New York to Canada for promotional appearances. In Canada, "Genie In A Bottle" had already topped the charts and her album had sold 400,000 copies. Ensconced in her hotel suite previous to her performance, she was interviewed by *All Pop's* Stephanie McGrath. Christina explained that her next single would be "Come On Over." "We're going to head back in the studio, give it more of an edge, R&B it up a little, maybe rock it out a little, give it a lot of different new directions and get it out there." Preceding a performance where she played six songs at the Much Music building on Queen Street, Christina held a press conference at the Paramount in Toronto.

There, executives for BMG Music Canada presented her with a four-times platinum award recognizing her sales. For forty-five minutes she fielded questions from reporters as well as contest winners. As usual, at one point the press conference turned to Britney Spears, who had recently released her sophomore album, and Christina was rather forlorn and nostalgic as she explained, "Even watching her in interviews, I find myself missing her lately," she said. "I'm really proud of her, how far she's come and what she's been able to accomplish." She added, "It's cool, she's doing her thing. It's pop music. I don't know. Whenever you bring up Britney, they're two different things, you know what I mean? So I respect her. I just think she's a little more pop-driven."

When posed with a question about Britney's public statements on saving her virginity, Christina took the opportunity to explain her own use of sexual suggestiveness. "I had a good upbringing, I'm very spiritual, and I try my best to follow my heart and my instincts to do the right thing," she said. "But someone somewhere is not going to be happy with whatever I do. You take 'N Sync, you take Backstreet Boys, and they do sexual things. But you take Britney or me for showing some tummy, and *drama*! It's a little unfair. We're artists." (Coincidentally, that month the Backstreet Boys and Christina each took home two trophies at the Blockbuster Entertainment Awards in Los Angeles. Christina won Favorite New Female Artist and Favorite Single for "Genie In A Bottle.")

In fact, the day before her departure for Toronto, Christina was being interviewed for *Rolling Stone* by Neil Strauss and had dined at her favorite restaurant, Houston's. Wearing a black t-shirt that exposed her navel and said "Rockstar" in glittery letters across her chest, Christina cheerfully chatted up the music journalist. "Oooh," she cooed in the interview. "I want a New York boy. There is so much energy here." When asked what "a New York" boy was Christina replied, "A little roughneck. With the bandanna and the cap to the side. You're not going to meet boys like that in L.A."

Christina had recently moved to Los Angeles from the Manhattan apartment she had kept during the recording sessions for her album. "At the moment, I've just moved into my first apartment in L.A. and my free time is spent getting everything from paper towels to ironing board, Q-tips, soap dishes, etc.," she mentioned during an internet chat.[4] Not coincidentally, Jorge Santos would also be moving from New York to Los Angeles, because it would "make work and everything a lot more convenient," his spokesman later said.[5] In fact, they were moving to be closer together as well.

Unlike Heidi Sherman, Strauss would not be able to disclose Christina's relationship with Jorge Santos. Thus, despite the fact that *Seventeen* magazine and *Rolling Stone* both hit the stands in July, only the former would include Christina's confession, while *Rolling Stone* failed to note the irony in Christina's words about wanting a "New York boy."

Christina was set to do the photo shoot for the pictures to be featured on the *Rolling Stone* cover story in June. She would be placed on the cover along with Blink 182, and both Christina and the male group would be wearing beach or surfer-type gear. Her recurring flu caused her to cancel the shoot and reschedule, but Blink 182 went ahead with their own shoot. During her own photo session, Christina took hundreds of pictures wearing a number of outfits, including the beach gear that she had been told Blink 182 would be wearing. It was understood that her pictures would be matched with Blink-182's own photos for the split cover. The man who did Christina's make up for the pictures told her that he was going to be seeing Britney the following week. Christina excitedly gave him her phone number so that he could pass it on to Spears.[6] For unknown reasons, Christina suddenly found herself missing Britney and wanted to talk to her about everything that had happened. The two had not had a lengthy sit-down talk since their days as Mouseketeers. Christina apparently failed to realize that after years of separation, they had drifted apart in many ways.

Christina seemed unaware that she and Britney's paths had diverged wildly, mostly based on their very different upbringings. Christina had blossomed into a liberated and self-confident young woman who was comfortable with her sexuality and felt no need to apologize for her image. Although she had not openly proclaimed her political affiliation, her singing for president Bill Clinton seemed a rather obvious indication of her real views. Almost two years later, Britney expressed her own views, by, among other things, singing for George W. Bush. Bound by her traditions, she is a southern Baptist who preaches about her "values" and her virginity—but she has no qualms about posing in her underwear on the cover of *Rolling Stone*.

The two women clearly had differing ideals and standards, and perhaps nothing illustrated this difference more than the fact that while Britney became well-known for her sex appeal, Christina's voice is usually acknowledged as the reason for her success. Perhaps Christina herself did not understand the sad, but simple, truth: The only reason Britney Spears was, at that point, more successful than her is because Britney came out first, selling a more powerful fantasy: the "All-American girl."

In the spring, Christina headed for more sun in Los Angeles, to work on her Christmas album. On May 6, she was scheduled to record with blues belter and Rock And Roll Hall Of Fame inductee Etta James. The holiday album would be recorded with a 70-piece orchestra. "I'll be doing a duet with Etta James on 'Merry Christmas Baby,'" she perkily explained, "and some new pop Christmas songs with a real R&B edge." Although the latter part of the statement turned out to be true, the former part did not. For unknown reasons, Christina was unable to perform the song with James, but she did end up teaming up with Dr. John for it. The new songs on the album would include "Christmas Time," written by Celebrity Status and Ron Fair— the team behind Christina's "Come On Over"— and "These Are The Special Times" by Diane Warren. "I wanted to bring a real R & B edge to some of these songs," she later explained. "It unleashed the soul in me—it's an all-around feel good album."

In early June she explained, "This week, I'm in Miami recording my Spanish record. Next week, I'm in Los Angeles recording my Christmas record. I'll be in Europe afterwards promoting my new single, 'I Turn To You.' Then I return to the States to open my tour. So it's a pretty crazy schedule that varies day-by-day, second by second. But I wouldn't trade it for anything in the world. I have a blast."

Christina's European promotional appearances were canceled because of her voice problems. She spent a couple of days resting her voice, and Enrique Iglesias sent her flowers. "He's just...he's a wonderful person, really down-to-earth, and for as gorgeous as he is, you wouldn't expect him to be," Christina said. "It's really cool talking to someone like that."[7] Personally, her success in the Latin music world was particularly satisfying for Christina because she had already started her reconciliation with her father. "It's actually getting much better," she said of the relationship. "Just because I'm out on my own, I can see him. I think you can always forgive someone—it's hard to forget—but, I mean, I think it's important to forgive just 'cause I do come from a Catholic background."

On Tour & In Love

In mid-June, Christina's album was still holding on to the Top 25 of the *Billboard 200* albums chart and had gone six times platinum. Although "What A Girl Wants" had winded out of the Top 50 of the *Hot 100* chart, "I Turn To You" had quickly climbed to No. 17 after making its debut on the top portion of the chart.

Although Christina seemed excited over the release of her newest single, mostly because she felt she would finally be taken seriously as a ballad singer and the public would get to see a side of her that they hadn't seen, her third single became her least successful one to date. Christina explained, "My new single is a song called 'I Turn To You.' It's the first ballad I've released, a Diane Warren ballad, and I'm really, really excited about it. It's a song I think that anybody can relate to in any situation. It's about turning to a loved one in your time of need, or the person that has always been there for you or is there for you whenever you need them. It can be love-oriented in the sense that it can be related to a boyfriend, girlfriend, mom, dad, etc."

Maybe so, but the universality of the theme did not translate into a big audience for it. By the time the song reached No. 17 on the chart, what RCA believed to be its airplay-only peak, an enhanced version of the CD single came out. After the release of the commercial single, "I Turn To You" made the Top 5 of the *Billboard Hot 100*, leaping to No. 3 and remaining there for two weeks. For avid chart-watchers, there was an excitement and an indescribable momentum surrounding this single.

If Christina was able to reach No. 1, she would have obtained three consecutive number one singles—quite a remarkable feat that would have left her needing only two more No. 1 singles to match the chart-busting achievement of her idol Mariah. Unfortunately, "I Turn To You" failed to keep Christina's string of No. 1 hits. After spending two weeks at No. 3, fueled by the single sales and held back by rather poor airplay, the single fell to No. 7, and despite the fact that it maintained pole position on the *Billboard Singles Sales* chart for two weeks, it became Christina's first single that failed to obtain any kind of RIAA certification. Furthermore, the video was her first not to be retired from *TRL* and was later selected by MTV as one of the worst videos of the year, and was a selection on the show "When Bad Videos

Happen to Good Artists." That single could be described as Christina's first flop.

The Spanish version of the song, "Por Siempre Tú," which had the same video with small variations and with Christina singing in Spanish, was a similar story. Although unlike "Genio Atrapado," "Por Siempre Tú" managed to chart on the *Billboard Latin Tracks* and even made a short appearance on the chart's Top 10, it was probably because unlike "Genio Atrapado", it had managed to bask in the reflected glory of its American version. It made the Top 5 in Brazil and was the No. 1 tune in Argentina.

In July, Christina received her copy of *Seventeen* magazine. As she skimmed the article, she could not believe what she was reading. "Aguilera bubbles over with giddiness when she talks about her current boyfriend, dancer Jorge Santos. "I actually fell in love for the first time this year," she gushes. "I'm head over heels in love, but it's actually hard with all this travel and my crazy lifestyle." For this chart-topping diva, doing typical dating things with her main squeeze—renting movies, going to dinner, hanging out—is just as exciting as having a number one hit or hosting *TRL*. And, she concedes, "I want to find a guy who's strong enough to deal with a chick like me and a lifestyle like mine. Hopefully I'll find that one day…maybe I already have."

"I freaked out when I saw certain people's names," she later explained. "Certain people's names," meant Jorge Santos. Christina later confided to her friends, "The reporter woman totally ratted me out." The disclosure also ended up, as usual, in England's *The Daily Telegraph*, which pointed out: "Christina Aguilera has found her Genie In A Bottle and he was right there on stage with her. He's Jorge Santos, one of her show's dancers." When the *Rolling Stone* cover story came out, many of Christina's female detractors were shocked to see what she was wearing. Ed Masley noted in the *Post-Gazette*, "she's pictured seductively running her tongue across her lip, her unbuttoned jean-shorts hanging off barely legal hips, bikini string saying: 'Untie me.'" He further noted, "The editors at *Seventeen* reportedly refused to let her show the kind of skin she was hoping to show when she posed for them."

Of course, they did not know the story about Blink 182 sharing the cover with her, but Christina's website explained why she had worn the beach gear and noted, "Christina believes that the top, bikini, and shorts are the kind of clothes the average 19 or 20-year-old girl would wear to the beach during the summer." In fact, Christina never saw any of the photos before the issue hit the newsstands and she would not have any input as to which photos were finally selected by *Rolling Stone*.

She was as surprised as everyone when she saw the picture selected for the cover. "When I first saw it I couldn't believe they chose that shot because it was a shot taken in between shots. I was goofing off in the middle of the shot. I was making a silly face and they just kept it." Just as with the *Seventeen* magazine article, Christina seemed to believe that she had talked too much. "…I read the article and I was throwing out different names here and there and I was like, 'Oh, my God. What are people going to think?' 'Cause I was just speaking my mind. But the whole thing, all in all, I think, is that it shows that I was just being real. It wasn't a posed cover. It wasn't something that I intentionally did on purpose. It's just me being me. And the article, too."

On Sunday, July 2, Christina traveled to the Summerfest in Milwaukee for her tour opener. "Right before I get onstage about five minutes before departing from the dressing room, I gather my band and dancers in my dressing room and we circle holding hands and my bass player leads us in prayer," Christina explained. "That gets us prepped for the show and I'll say my personal prayer, and sometimes I'll lead the prayer. That's the single most important thing I do before getting on-stage."[8]

Christina was confident once she came onstage. "God, you guys, this is my first headlining tour," she told the audience of 17,000 crammed into the Marcus Amphitheater. Though the show lasted just over an hour, including encore, critics pointed out that it struck a nice balance between style and substance. She introduced her cover of R&B diva Etta James' "At Last" by telling the crowd she's "a huge lover of blues."

"Fronting a six-piece band and a dance ensemble of two women and four men, Aguilera emerged atop a runway that spanned the width of the stage wearing a white pantsuit—navel exposed, of course— and sporting multicolored pigtails, presumably hair extensions," one reviewer wrote. "Her dancers, looking like extras in a Gap ad in their white sleeveless tunics and loose khakis, performed acrobatic kicks as Aguilera began with her first hit. She followed quickly with 'Somebody's Somebody,' on which she hit some Mariah Carey-esque high notes, and 'So Emotional,' which got the audience members, most of whom were too young to carry lighters, waving their $5 glow sticks in unison."

Christina made sure the crowd felt a part of the show, frequently turning spotlights on audience members so she could see their signs, which sported pictures of her and slogans such as "We love you" and "Christina: I'm what a girl wants." After 45 minutes, she left the stage to change into a rose-and-burgundy-checkered tank top and sequined denim hip-huggers. She returned singing Free's "All Right Now."

Now that her romance with Jorge Santos had been exposed, Christina felt comfortable enough to hold hands with him during the ballad "Love for All Seasons." (In fact, in one of her concert stops in Puerto Rico, at the Roberto Clemente Colisseum in Hato Rey, Christina excitedly announced that her boyfriend was from Puerto Rico.)

She told the fans how much their letters and cards meant to her and dedicated "I Turn To You" to them. "Thank you! Oh my gosh!" Christina said before dedicating the night's last song, "What A Girl Wants" to all the girls in the crowd. They loved it, too, screaming their approval at an ear-splitting volume. "Girls, I hope you're getting everything you want," she said before leaving the stage for the last time, 70 minutes after she began. The screaming continued until the house lights went off, the cell phones came out, and the glow sticks got stuffed into purses and pockets.

On July 5, Christina performed at the Traverse City Cherry Festival, as part of her tour warm up. Four days later, she traveled to the United Kingdom to appear in the third annual "Party in the Park 2000" festival, which marked Christina's first U.K. live appearance. The concert had set a world record in May by selling out all of its 100,000 tickets in less than seven hours. The event was held in

London's Hyde Park, and all proceeds from the event benefited the Prince's Trust, Prince Charles' charity for young adults. After her performance, Christina was "invited to join His Royal Highness, the Prince of Wales, in the Royal Box."[9]

Two days later, Christina was in Canada, kicking off her tour at the Air Canada Center, where she drew about 13,000 fans. *AllPop* informed its readers: "Dressed all in black, including a tight-fitting T-shirt with 'Rockstar' in silver glitter, the blonde beauty pulled into the Ottawa Westin hotel shortly after noon with a crew of beefy bodyguards." Christina ignored the fans waiting outside the hotel and went straight from the limousine into an elevator that would take her to her hotel room. "She's just tired," tour manager Bobby Herr explained as band members headed out for their afternoon sound check. "She'll probably just get a massage and have a little fast food."[10] Bobby Herr, the man who was handling Christina's tour, was becoming rather close to her. His girlfriend, Kiki Lee Baker was also acquainted with Christina, and they were noticing first-hand that she was being overworked to death during the tour. Later, Christina would come to confide in them and would find their own judgment sounder than Steven Kurtz's.

(Ignoring fans waiting outside hotels seemed to have become Christina's trademark. In July, Ed Masley pointed out in his review of Christina's second concert in Pittsburgh: "Earlier that day, a crowd of 30—professional autograph hounds and hopeful little girls alike—stood waiting outside Aguilera's swanky downtown hotel, many clutching *Rolling Stone* or *Entertainment Weekly* with the singer on the cover. When she finally emerged, a knapsack hanging off her back, a bodyguard hustled her onto the tour bus in the time it took to scribble maybe six or seven autographs, all for the pros at the front of the line. And just like that, the Aguilera tour bus pulled away as irate fathers threatened to wipe up the pavement with autograph dealers in front of police, and dumbstruck mothers held their sobbing daughters to their chests. 'I'm sorry,' said the handler [Bobby Herr]. 'We're already 20 minutes late for sound check.'" What they didn't know was that Christina's over-booked schedule really did not leave her time to sign more autographs or comply with the fans' requests.

Although most of the fault would later fall on Steve Kurtz's doorstep, many of the fans' complaints were directed at Christina's personality.)

The Corel Centre, where the show took place, was half empty when Christina pranced onstage. The official attendance figure was 7,500, but, according to one Pop critic, it looked as if no more than 5,000 people showed up. Even then, the review noted, "Aguilera impresses enthusiastic fans."

The night before her second Canadian appearance at the Winnipeg Arena on July 13, Christina was not sleeping soundly in her hotel room. Her management had contacted Chris Burke-Gaffney, who managed Christina's Canadian opening act, the local duo McMaster & James, because they wanted to know what local studio they should book to work on Christina's Christmas album. Burke-Gaffney recommended Channels Audio & Post-production on Sargent Avenue.

Christina arrived at the studio at 5 p.m. with her full entourage. She did not leave until one in the morning. Local producer and engineer Howard Rissin was hired as assistant engineer for the day. "It was pretty cool," Rissin later remembered. "She showed up with her whole entourage—including a security guy, a personal assistant, and a massage therapist—and then she just sang her ass off till one in the morning."

The evening session consisted of work on an original song called "This Year." "She was just singing vocal parts over, and over, and over—layering, and layering, and layering them," Rissin recalled. "The way they do vocals is pretty laborious, but she worked very hard."

Rissin, who has recorded with some big names in the music business, including K.D. Lang and Roy Orbison, was surprised by Christina's pampering. "I have to admit, I've never seen anyone with a personal masseuse before, and they had limos on the street all night, waiting to take people wherever they wanted to go."

Echoing what almost everyone who works with Christina learns, Rissin explained: "She was pretty focused on the work. We even decorated the studio for Christmas so she could be in the mood to sing a seasonal song. I did manage to get an autograph for my son, though."[11]

He was lucky. A group of fans who were set to meet Christina backstage were left to bite her dust. About two dozen fans were told to be at the Winnipeg Arena at 3:45 p.m. to prepare for a promised 4:15 p.m. meeting. They found themselves waiting until 5 p.m. when Christina made her appearance—which lasted all of three minutes. Wearing a white mid-riff tank top and a purple skirt, she quickly moved down a pre-posed lineup, stopping in front of each group just long enough for a hired photographer to snap a photo.

"She didn't even say, 'Hi,' she just stepped in the middle, and they took a couple of pictures, and that was it," one fan complained. "It's like she had more important things than us—we're the fans. We made her." "She didn't seem like she wanted to be here. She just posed," another fan said. A couple of pre-teen girls fared better. "She said, 'Hi.' I said 'it's nice to meet you,' and she said, 'Thanks.'" These backstage fan encounters were becoming less and less successful and a number of fans were actually turned off by meeting Christina. Unfortunately, the singer was tense and unhappy as a result of her overbooked schedule. After all, she had spent eight consecutive hours in the studio the night before.

Although she tried and managed to keep a smiling face despite the problems, her façade was starting to break.

As if Christina's devastating schedule wasn't enough pressure for her frazzled nerves, on July 19, just two weeks after the kick-off date of her tour, she was slapped with her first public lawsuit. Ruth Inniss had come back from her past to haunt her. In the $7 million suit filed in Manhattan Supreme Court, Inniss alleged that Shelly had agreed to let her manage Christina, but later cut her out of any business dealings and signed on with Steven Kurtz. The suit sought $2 million in damages from Shelly, plus $5 million in compensatory and punitive damages from Steve Kurtz, and his father, Normand Kurtz.

Inniss explained that she initially approached Normand Kurtz to help her manage Christina's career, but was then frozen out of any business dealings. But unlike Inniss, the Kurtzes had mapped out their strategy well in advance. Because *Steve* Kurtz had in fact never met Ruth, he could now deny her charges. Normand, who had been the one initially approached by Inniss, simply refrained from commenting.

Christina and Shelly withheld comment as well, even though they could have easily posted a message on Christina's official website, as they had previously done on countless occasions to refute unfounded rumors. "I've never heard of Ruth Inniss," Kurtz convincingly told reporters. "I've been Christina's manager for three and a half years... and I am not aware of any contributions this woman has ever had concerning Christina's career." He added, "I've never had any dealings with Ruth Inniss regarding Christina Aguilera—ever." Technically, he was not lying.

Michael Steindam, the attorney representing Inniss, said that although she did not have a written contract with Shelly or Normand, there was a promotional video put together by Christina's label which included Shelly referring to Inniss (though not by name) while discussing how her daughter was discovered. The lawsuit received scant attention in the press, and did not generate a backlash for Christina. It soon drifted out of the public arena and it remains unclear whether it was settled out of court.

All the while, Christina was busy working on a new cosmetics and fragrance line for Fetish cosmetics. In mid-January she signed on to be their spokeswoman for a line aimed at young women ages 16 to 22 that included three fragrances, bath and body products, and a complete makeup line all priced under $10. The series of print ads featuring Christina considerably raised her profile among the pre-teen magazine buying crowd. Christina actually chose colors, product formulations, and packaging for Fetish in addition to lending her face to the product. "Christina travels all over the world—she knows what her fans want," explained Bob Bartlett, CEO of New Dana Perfumes Corporation, the company that developed the line. The products would hit stores in January of 2001. "I can bring these amazing trends around the world to teens," Christina said. "I get to give back in my own way. It's cool."[12] (Christina did not renew the contract when it came up for review in 2002.)

As Christina kicked off her tour, the reviews were uniform in their praise of pop's newest critical sensation. "Aguilera proves strength: An expressive voice" (August 11); "Powerful Aguilera show hit with fans" (August 12); "Aguilera wows legion of midriff-baring fans"

(August 17); "Aguilera at home in spotlight" (August 22); "Christina Aguilera proves she has more staying power than most in Detroit"; (August 25); "Critics go for Christina's blonde ambition (August 25). Through her tour, Christina was also trying to build up enthusiasm for the Do Something project she had gotten involved in with her sponsors, Sears and Levis. The premise was rather simple; the program encouraged youngsters to perform volunteer community service. Christina told MTV: "Sears and Levi's and I have agreed it's the best way to get youth involved, because this program actually goes through a whole list of topics you can pick from: domestic violence, child abuse, helping the environment, tutoring, applying yourself in any way possible to help better the community." The singer herself set the example by taking time out of her schedule to visit battered women shelters.

The video for "Come On Over" debuted on *TRL* on August 7 at No. 8. Christina had previously said, "The next [single] will be a new version of 'Come On Over' from my album. The video will be a lot of choreography. You've never seen me dance this fast in your life! (Laughs) It's going to be so tight. A lot of boy/ girl interaction with the dancers. It's probably going to be my favorite video to date. 'Making the Video'—MTV—will be there. It's going to be really, really exciting." Young MTV veteran Paul Hunter directed the video, which featured white backgrounds, colorful clothing, and multiple set changes. This was the first Christina Superstar video. In fact, Christina was comfortable enough during the video's filming in early June, before her relationship with Santos had been in the press, that during one scene where she is wearing a yellow outfit, Jorge is dancing behind her and he suddenly comes up, reaches from behind and as Christina sings looking at him, their faces only inches from each other, he unzips her outfit, revealing a new scene.

The official radio release of "Come on Over [All I Want Is You]" came in August and the upbeat track had a strong debut on the Top 60 of the *Hot 100 Billboard* chart. By its second week, it had cracked the Top 50.

As far as the tour went, of particular importance was the review of Christina's homecoming concert in Pittsburgh on August 27.

Before her concert, Christina was in Cleveland for one day that started with a recording session for the Christmas album in a studio at midnight and ended almost 24 hours later with her performance at the Gund Arena. The Christmas album was still not done, and Christina would drop little tidbits about it as she gave interviews for her tour. In fact, she gave the tidbits as she was actually recording the songs. "You'll even find a little part of my Latin side on that [Christmas] record, too," she told the *Plain Dealer* after the recording session. "'Silent Night' is going to be done in Spanish, just because everyone has heard it in English so many times. I'm giving it my own feel."

Despite the draining schedule, Christina, ever the professional, was pumped up to do her homecoming concert. The next day, she gave a stunning performance. "AGUILERA WOWS 'EM WITH AWE-INSPIRING VOCALS," headlined *Post-Gazette* pop music critic, Ed Masley. He started his review on a somewhat negative note because the previous Monday, Britney, whom Masley called "a ghost from Aguilera's Mouseketeers days" had drawn a crowd of more than 23,000 to a sold-out Post-Gazette Pavilion. He then noted: "Last night, Aguilera, having beaten Spears on Grammy night to walk away with Best New Artist honors, pulled in half that many fans, despite the fact that a portion of the lawn was sold as 'buy one, get one free'—and in her own back yard. As the Battle of the *Mouseketeases* rages on, with Britney's latest effort breaking records every day, it's clear that Wexford's own was born to settle for critical fame in the shadow of Britney's role as America's sweetheart. Not for lack of trying."

Masley described Christina "bumping and grinding her way through the night in only the tightest of low-riding hip-huggers topped by a series of minuscule tops. It was sexy enough to drive home every innuendo of her lyrics. The pre-teens in the audience were loving every minute of it."

According to Masley, "The trouble is, what a girl wants—and desperately, it seems—is to leave her Mouseketeering teenybopper image far behind and position herself as a womanly R&B diva when, in fact, she's better suited to the sticky kids' stuff. As she proved repeatedly last night, she has the voice to be a major force in R&B for years to come. But this could be her only chance to be the second biggest female artist of her generation with the lunchbox set. And judging from the future hits with which she packed her set...the album she's telling reporters she's 'so over' could keep Aguilera in the spotlight for at least another year." Finally he noted, "what separates the *Genie* from the other pop Lolitas of the moment is the voice, an awe-inspiring instrument she uses like a girl who spent her childhood dreaming she could one day be the next Mariah Carey. And today, of course, she is."

Christina brought Shelly and her sisters up to share the stage during her cover of "All Right Now" by Free. She also stopped the show to dedicate "I Turn To You" to Shelly, whom she thanked for cooking her favorite food the previous night and running to the store to buy some Cheetos and Snyder's potato chips, which Christina said she couldn't find outside of Pittsburgh. "All I can say is there's no place like home," she told the crowd. "It felt so good to sleep in my own bed."

A couple of months after the release of Eminem's single, *Hollywood Hamilton's Rhythm Top 30 Countdown* struck back at the rapper on Christina's behalf. "Slim Shady Please Shut Up," a parody of Eminem's song, featured a Christina-impersonating lounge singer responding to Eminem's lyrics.

> "May I have your attention please? Will the Real Slim Shady please shut up? I repeat, Will the Real Slim Shady please shut up?" the song began. Then, the insults flew like pigeons: "...Even his girlfriend's cheating on him/Look at him, walking around living off Dre, acting so cool, but he's really kinda weak though."

In a direct riposte to Eminem's comments, the lyrics went: "As for the question of who came first, Was it Carson Daly or was it Fred Durst? I'm sorry Slim but this is gonna hurt. They both came closer than you ever will jerk." Eminem is described as "a cartoon version of Ricky Schroeder on 'Silver Spoons'" and "nothing but a product hatched to be bought up." Then, the chorus: "You're slim shady/Yes you're the slim shady/You sound like Peter Brady/You get quite irritating/So won't the real Slim Shady please shut up? Please shut up? Please shut up? You're slim shady/Yes you're the slim shady/You sound like Peter Brady/You get quite irritating/So won't the real Slim Shady please shut up? Please shut up? Please shut up?"

Christina heard the song and thought it was "just hilarious. It's so funny. The girl is so white; it's not even funny. I don't know who out there did this, but it's funny and *obviously* it's in support of me. It's very cute, and I appreciate that. It may be on my next record…just kidding." Apparently, Christina failed to appreciate that the girl who sounded so white was impersonating *her*, and had actually convinced more than one radio programmer that she was, in fact, Christina.

TWELVE
Exit Steven Kurtz

As Christina's tour continued, "Come On Over [All I Want Is You]" was rising quickly on the charts, jumping from 26 to 23 just weeks after its release. By late September, it stood as the "Greatest Gainer in Airplay" at number 11. Christina had proved that as far as radio went, she was far from a one-hit wonder. Since the release of her first single, she had enjoyed a warm reception from radio programmers everywhere; and yet it was an odd arrangement. The audience who listened to the remixed version of her songs on the radio were not the same 7 million fans who had bought her album. Christina's audience was shifting as she positioned herself as an older, more mature, artist.

After 54 weeks of release, the album was still poised at No. 21, boosted up there from the 30's by the release of her latest summer ditty. The new album pressings, which included the remixed versions of her No. 1 hits, signaled Christina's incredible artistic growth, even before she had put out her sophomore album. On August 8, "Ven Conmigo [Solamente Tú]," the Spanish-language version of her American hit was unleashed to Latin radio, and was proving equally popular. Finally, one of her Spanish songs that charted on the *Billboard Latin Tracks* was making a heated race to the No. 1 spot.

As Christina had announced, the making of the song's video was made into yet another "Making The Video" special on MTV, a program that had become a true music television staple, but it was also shown on Univision, the most-watched Spanish-language network in American television. "Ven Conmigo [Solamente Tú]" was doing exceptionally well in the charts, in the United States as well as internationally, achieving Top 5 status in the countdowns for Panama, Argentina, Brazil, Venezuela and Ecuador on Latin E! Entertainment Television's "Top E! Music & News" program. The weekend of September 5 could not have been the best one for Christina. She lost her voice and had to cancel her much-awaited concert in Syracuse to close off the state fair. Also, her dancers' tour bus was burglarized in the amount of $1,000. Two Syracuse University students who had been partying with Christina's crewmembers and dancers on the bus while it was parked outside a hotel on campus, stole golf clubs, pyrotechnics and a gym bag. They were later charged with larceny and burglary.

Between the two New Jersey dates for her tour, on Thursday, September 7, Christina attended the MTV Video Music Awards at Radio City Music Hall in New York. She was up for five awards. She was passed over on all of them. During Eminem's presentation he saluted Carson Daly and Fred Durst as he made his way down the aisle of the auditorium and sang "...sit next to Carson Daly and Fred Durst and hear them argue over who she gave head to first." Despite Eminem's comments, Christina gave a show-stopping performance. Wearing a tight red leather suit with her belly exposed, Christina was, in the words of MTV News, "seeking the sublime with her rendition...a performance that was set in decidedly *Arabian Nights*-inspired surroundings, complete with belly dancers and fire-eaters... Aguilera's voice showed little signs of the strain that forced her to cancel a show in Syracuse, New York, over the weekend, and she demonstrably belted out the tune in a manner that left little doubt as to which of the evening's VMA performers were live singers and which were lip-syncers."

Such praise from MTV was not to be taken lightly, particularly when Britney Spears was one of the lip-synching performers. toward the end of her performance, Fred Durst had surprised everyone by walking onstage and rocking the house with Christina. The beat from "Come On Over" had dissolved into rock rhythms and Christina started jumping enthusiastically yelling: "You gotta let it out," as Fred Durst climbed on the stage and sang for less than a minute. When he finished, he quickly dropped his microphone and left as abruptly as he had walked on there. The whole scene was somewhat awkward, but few knew about the turbulence that lurked behind the apparently carefully choreographed appearance. Christina's managers had approached MTV about having her perform during the awards. MTV's position was that one teen pop phenomenon—Britney Spears—was enough, and they would not be able to fit Christina into the set list. According to Fred Durst, however, they offered one caveat. If she was able to do her song with Fred, they would let her play.

Christina herself called Durst.

"Fred, MTV won't let me play the Video Music Awards," she explained. "Will you do a song with me? Will you rap in the middle of my song?"

"Hell no," Durst replied. "I've got an idea though. How about you do your song and I'll come up afterward and do my own thing, a little piece off my new record. I ain't fucking doing no skit with you. I'll come up, size you up and get the hell out. I'll do it as a favor for you because you're so worried that Britney is going to perform and you're not."

The Kurtzes weren't exactly happy about the arrangement. Given Durst's volatile nature, they tended to believe that he would try to sabotage Christina's performance. Durst claimed he did it as a "serious fucking favor because she is so competitive with Britney."

The day of the awards, as Durst and his management team cooled their heels at the rehearsal, Christina just didn't show up. She was fixing her hair.

Durst stormed into her dressing room. "What the fuck are you doing?" he asked indignantly.

"Calm down," Christina replied, trying to soothe him as the make-up artists worked on her hair and extensions.

"No, fuck you! I ain't fucking doing this damn song!" Christina started crying hysterically—freaking out.

"OK, I'll fucking do it." On the stage that day, the two young performing artists played their parts to perfection.

That was not the only surprise Christina had in store for the public, but it would be the most controversial. When she was due to present an award toward the end of the show, Christina walked onstage with quite an eye-popping ensemble that revealed a strap of her thong and exposed most of her legs and abdomen. Even more shockingly, she walked toward the podium holding hands with Britney Spears. Considering the reason she had performed with Durst in the first place, it was rather ironic that she would choose the same Awards to try to downplay the rumors of an alleged rivalry. The two performers joked around at the podium—Christina's mature, diva-like air contrasting with the goofiness that endear so many toward Britney—and they started talking about all the people they had seen that night. Britney mentioned Eminem as one of the people she had met and made a face, which caused Christina to make a face and retort with "Anyway…" In his seat, Eminem was visibly squirming, as he thought they had teamed up to pull a fast one on him.

Together, Britney and Christina introduced Whitney Houston. Britney said that to recognize her, "one only has to listen to her voice." Houston came onstage singing "I Will Always Love You" and presented the Video of the Year award to Eminem.

There was significant controversy over Fred Durst's impromptu appearance in Christina's performance. While some of his fans felt that it suggested an open mind on his part and represented a step toward unity in the pop world, others were outraged over what they believed was a major embarrassment to the rock world. One fan called it "about the worst moment in music this year."

"Fred getting onstage with Christina Aguilera embarrassed us all," Filter frontman Richard Patrick told *MTV News* in the wake of the performance. Fans vented their feelings at MTV.com. One user called Durst a "Pop-lovin' piece of frozen dog shit." Another felt he was "a hypocritical egomaniac."

Almost a month later, on the weekend of October 3, Fred Durst was at a party at the Playboy Mansion. An *MTV News* crew approached him and the reporter asked for his reaction to some of his fans' reactions to his impromptu appearance in Christina's performance at the awards. Why had he done it? "I already told you guys before, I did it all for the nookie, man. That's why I did that with Christina," he explained. "I want that girl, that's that," he continued. "What do you want? I don't want to make music like her. I can't stand that kind of music. People were like, 'What'd you do that for?' What do you think I did that for? It's obvious, isn't it? You know what I mean? So that's the deal. Everybody who was saying that, was wishing they were doing that, too."

The next morning, as MTV aired Durst's comments, Christina was hanging out at her house watching television and was surprised and frustrated. That was the end between Christina and Fred Durst's "friendship." Five days after hearing Durst's comments, an MTV crew caught up with Christina. "You *wish* you got some nookie from it," Christina responded to a camera crew after she caught his explanation on-air. "He got no nookie. That did not happen, OK?" Christina explained. She made the comments with what could have been termed a "mischievous chuckle" and she did not sound very convincing. "I just want to clear the table right there, and the thing with Carson too. Eminem's whole song did not happen, OK?" she said between giggles. "It just didn't, but it's some really crazy stuff that people want to insinuate and people want to say, and it is hurtful."

In retrospect, Christina said, "I'm always getting these calculated answers from people around me, like, 'OK, say this,' and, 'Make sure you don't say anything too mean,' and I saw other people get dissed and they giggled and laughed it off. But mine was harsh," she said in a girlish tone regarding Durst's comments. "It was just coming off of the Eminem [dis]. With the things he was saying—no female should be talked about like that. I'm not gonna laugh it off and say 'Ha ha, it's a funny song, hee hee.'" Christina's girlish giggles, which kept interjecting her speech, suggested that she did not feel as strongly about it as she was attempting to portray. "That's just not gonna fly with me, so I just had to speak my peace. I had to be honest about it and speak for all women. It's like the girl who, you know, the guy boasts the next day at school about getting laid or something, when it totally didn't happen, and the girl's all meek about it," she explains. "Screw that! I'm not trying to be meek about it. If I have something to say about it and someone offends me, then I'm gonna say it. And it was just like, yeah, I have no problem with it."[1]

Durst later reflected, in an interview with *Playboy* magazine: "I did her a fucking favor, and all I got was a bunch of shit. Fans were like, 'What the fuck did you do that for?' Afterward she was on MTV going 'The worst thing that happened to me in 2000 was Fred Durst called me so many times I had to stop answering my phone.' That's bullshit, man. Fucking bullshit."

Finally, Durst joined the long list of Christina Aguilera bashers. "She's an ungrateful, spoiled-rotten fucking asshole who has an amazing fucking talent....She's talented, but she doesn't see what's in front of her because she's so young and dumb. And it makes me think, What the fuck was I thinking? But I did it, and I know that I have good karma coming. Fuck her, man. I don't respect her."

During a 9-day period in mid-September, Christina canceled three tour dates. There were reports of tonsillitis; however, there were also behind-the-scenes management problems causing the shuffling dates. *The Boston Herald* chastised: "perhaps Aguilera's handlers should have planned her schedule more carefully. And they certainly ought to show more respect for her mostly young followers and consider the ramifications of last-minute cancellations." In fact, there was significant chaos at the Tweeter Center that Saturday night as Christina's young fans frantically tried to call their parents who had just dropped them off while other concertgoers who were still arriving were met with a traffic jam of people trying to leave. The later arrivals were being detoured out of the way as police directed four lanes of traffic out of the crowded parking lot, and an outbound traffic jam rapidly formed on Interstate 495.

"I think she should apologize. It's very rude what she did," a 12-year-old girl told the *Herald*. "It was 15 minutes before the show. The lady at the concession stand told us. I thought she was joking." Like most of the pre-teen audience, she had been dropped off an hour earlier by her parents and had to call them at a nearby restaurant by walkie-talkie.

The mother of a 10-year-old girl felt similarly after having waited seven hours to get good seats. "It's the first time she's ever got to go to a concert and she's very disappointed," she said of the little girl, "How do you explain this to a little girl? She's very upset." The only explanation was Christina's recurring throat problems.

The writer for the *Herald* noted, "It...seems rather suspect that each time Aguilera has been 'instructed by doctors' to take a hiatus, that rest affects her concert schedule but she's able to do national TV broadcasts, such as last week's 'MTV Awards' and tonight's 'Latin Grammys'."

Christina felt like she didn't have time to breathe. In the middle of a grueling tour schedule, she had been recording and promoting her Latin album, and recording her Christmas album. She later explained, "It wouldn't have been as bad if I wouldn't have had to record the Christmas album as I toured. Basically, for that album, every free day between shows I had to be in the recording studio, so I had no free days for week and weeks in a row and it was just crazy..."[2] Christina told countless publications that she felt that she had no downtime, but always punctuated her comments with a positive comment noting that when she looked back, she would be proud of everything she had accomplished. "At this point, we have one more Christmas song left to record," she told one interviewer, as her publicist was bursting on the line to declare the interview over. "We've done it while on tour, here and there, all over—in Toronto, Chicago, L.A.

Trying to get two albums out and tour at the same time has been kind of crazy and exhausting. But I know I'll look back and say I accomplished a lot. Both show different sides of me, and show how I've evolved as a vocalist in the last two years."

In truth, however, things were spinning out of control. Christina was supposed to meet a young contest-winner backstage after one of her shows. But the fan's mother complained in an e-mail to the Artist Direct website, that Christina was not nice to her young son; in fact, she left him in tears. Shelly explained, "Christina has days where she's no more than a rag doll, yanked and pulled, poked and prodded, put on a virtual assembly line of over a hundred people a day, each of which have their own personal expectations of what she should or shouldn't do...as if they are God themselves." Christina's hectic schedule, now coupled with the Ruth Inniss lawsuit, had finally gotten to her. The fact that she would have been rude to a fan—again—suggests that she was under serious strain. Not only because her fans are of particular importance to her, but because she would never let her façade break down in front of a complete stranger.[3]

Amid all the tension, it is not surprising that Christina's first tour saw the beginning of the end of her relationship with Steve Kurtz. "I went through a period when I was touring when I was so unhappy," Christina explained cryptically. "A lot of people couldn't see it because great things were happening to me. But I was really being overworked." Overworked was an understatement. The 19-year-old had to keep up with the tour's grueling schedule, do interviews while on the road, and record the Christmas album in the one-day intervals between some of the tour stops. There was literally no downtime. "I'd have really unhealthy people around me who were doing damaging things, and nobody knew this," Christina said. It is obvious that the "really unhealthy people" referred to Steve Kurtz. There were frequent arguments and voice tones rose quickly. "I think a lot of people heard about public arguments sometimes."[4] Christina was certainly not a meek little girl who did not understand what was happening. She was a young woman very much in control of her affairs who knew that she was in an unhealthy situation, but her inexperience precluded her from actually saying "This is too much" and taking the time off. Even Bob Jamieson, "the big guy" said of her, "She's a strong woman who has opinions, and she'll express those opinions. This is not a woman that's gonna sit in a corner and do what people tell her to do." Christina had not kept entirely quiet about the situation. Although she did not want a scandal in the papers, she had been confiding in Fred Durst, who witnessed her over-booked schedule first-hand. "Her managers suck," he said later, "They treat her like shit. She's in the wrong world." Christina was probably already toying with the idea of switching managers. In the end, her new management would come up with a complicated ploy to sever her ties from the Kurtzes without incurring any financial penalties.

Although there were many reasons to keep Christina happy, the teenager was tense. However, if there was one skill she had perfected by now, it was the ability to slap a smile on her face regardless of other circumstances in her life. That month, "Genio Atrapado" was nominated for a Latin Grammy for Best Female Pop Vocal Performance. Christina was the only artist nominated who recorded in English and in Spanish. Other nominees included Colombian Pop/Rock star Shakira (who Christina later said was her ideal duet partner), Mariah Carey's then-beau Luis Miguel, rock band Maná, and Santana.

Christina's Spanish album was released amid heavy publicity in the Hispanic market on September 12 as a joint effort between RCA Records and its Latin sister company, BMG U.S. Latin. The labels shipped half a million copies, a large number for a Latin record, but a low number for an English-language pop star of Christina's stature. (To put the number into perspective, consider that the biggest-selling album of Paulina Rubio's entire career sold 500,000 copies in the U.S. and that the biggest selling Latin female recording artist, Shakira, sold less than 500,000 copies of her MTV Unplugged in the U.S.) In fact, Christina's crossover was the first time a major American star had decided to strut her stuff in the Latin market; and Christina's pioneering efforts were paying off. For one, the release of "Come On Over [All I Want Is You]"in Spanish, "Ven Conmigo [Solamente Tú]" was preceded by a Coca-Cola media blitz, which played the Spanish song in commercials airing all over Latin America, featuring Christina during her tour. This was a wonderful publicity strategy that the record label was banking on—for free.

The beverage company rarely relied on celebrities, much less Hispanic ones, to hawk its products. In fact, the last celebrity spokeswoman used by Coke in the Latin market had been Tejano star Selena, but it had been a low-profile campaign pretty much limited to Texas and Mexico. (It would be almost an entire year before Coke decided to produce some ads for the American market). The release of her Latin album was followed by the opening of her website in Spanish.

"We see Christina Aguilera's career as a twofold career," Rodolfo Lopez, BMG's Vice-President for the Latin region told *Billboard*. Their Spanish-language market encompassed the U.S. Latin market, Latin America, Spain, and Portugal. "There's the English-speaking market and a parallel career as a Latin icon—because I do believe she'll become a Latin icon, no doubt about it."

Christina was particularly excited with this release. It would set her apart from her competition and establish her as one of the first bi-lingual American divas. "This Latin album is not a second album; it's a first record in itself," Christina said. "Before I had even recorded my debut album, I had asked to do the Spanish album." By this point, Christina was already starting to show some signs of exhaustion as a result of her schedule. Wanting to know whether they were becoming apparent to interviewers, this author contacted *Billboard*'s Leila Cobo. How was Christina as an interview subject? According to Cobo, "She was very skinny, prettier than in photos (no make up), seemed smart enough and organized enough. Very concerned about the photos that were being taken because she was tired. I think she'd come from a tour bus from Washington that day…"[5] (She later added, "she didn't sound rehearsed at all. She was very spontaneous."[6])

Her hard work was paying off, however. According to *Billboard*, Christina was not slated to be "a Latin icon in the traditional sense of the word. All the tracks on the Spanish album…have an R&B sensibility and vocal flair not heard in standard Latin pop. If she plays her cards right, the blond, blue-eyed Aguilera could become a flagbearer for a new generation of Latin Pop artists."[7] Steve Kurtz concurred excitedly: "It's never been done before," he told the *Los Angeles Times*. "But Christina wanted to do it. She's wanted to do a Spanish record since I met her, since before the English one came out."[8]

Music critic Christopher John Farley noted in *Time* magazine: "[Christina's] bare waist—so thin you'd think it could fit between two parentheses—looks too tiny to support the strong, soulful melismata that flow from her lips." His review of *Mi Reflejo* was nothing less than a restrained rave: "With this new CD she sets off in search of her Spanish heritage, a modern-day answer to the Spanish explorers of centuries past. The conquistadors were seeking a new world; Aguilera is searching for her roots…The collection offers Aguilera stylistic challenges. Confronted with the bolero standard 'Contigo En La Distancia,' she lends the song nuanced passion. And on 'Cuando No

Es Contigo,' a hard-salsa number co-produced by Sergio George, Aguilera confidently charges through tempo changes. It's a Latin implosion, and we listen, impressed, as she finds new fires within."

Entertainment Weekly's David Browne was not won over by the album and was rather sarcastic in his review titled, "Spanish Flaw; Aguilera goes Latin, but something gets lost in the translation." He wrote, speaking in Christina's "voice": "[I need to] Thank my producer for those diction lessons! For about half the album, I had to sing my hits, like 'I Turn To You' and 'Genie In A Bottle,' in this other language. I thought it would be easy—Ecuadorian, remember?—but geez, he had to write everything out for me phonetically! I'm a hard worker, though. And I showed him that no matter how many foreign words I had to learn, I can still hit tons of unnecessary high notes. Wait'll Mariah hears me on 'El Beso Del Final' (that means 'The Final Kiss,' you guys)! She'll have one of those midlife crises!" *Newsday's* "Sonidos Latinos" section reviewed the album, highlighting "Her soulful voice has nicely matured since her maiden album. There's more passion and showmanship in these renditions."

The *New York Post* predicted that *Mi Reflejo* would be "a major contender at next year's Latin Grammys" and announced: "No other artist has realized English to Spanish crossover dreams with this kind of grace." Writing for Amazon.com, Heidi Sherman (who had exposed Christina's affair with Jorge Santos) noted: "To prove her staying power and worth, she does serious vocal acrobatics with so much confidence and clarity on *Mi Reflejo*, you'll forget that five of these songs are old, that all are translated into a language other than her native tongue, and that she's a modest 19 years old."

Billboard's Leila Cobo believed, "What makes Aguilera's effort commendable is not the occasional salsa beat or the use of acoustic guitars now heard in every album by a Latin artist. Instead, Aguilera breaks rank by virtue of her magnificent voice and by refusing to leave behind her R&B inflections, which give a distinct flavor to every song on the disc, including those that have been specifically tailored for the Latin market." In the end, however, *Mi Reflejo* simply was what it was. Although Christina and her management wanted to portray the album as a pioneering Latin pop record that was somehow greater than the sum of its parts, in fact, the Spanish vocals amid Top-40 instrumentation in the translated songs enjoyed no such synergy and did not fit in nicely with the traditionally Latin boleros and salsa.

Regardless, on September 30, *Mi Reflejo* made its debut on the *Billboard Latin 50 Albums* chart at pole position. Despite albums from Luis Miguel and a plethora of other high profile, established Latin artists, Christina would hold on to the position for 19 straight weeks. She would only be toppled by the king of rancheras, Vicente Fernandez. On the *Billboard 200*, the album debuted at No. 27, falling to 42 by the following week.

Although many critics accused Christina of jumping on the Latin music boom, Ramiro Burr, a respected music critic for the *San Antonio Express-News* who has written about Latin music for ten years, did not join the fray. Burr admitted that when he heard Christina was doing an all-Spanish disc, he was suspicious that she was simply jumping on the bandwagon. "I think that, yes, if one wanted to be a cynic, they could say she was out to make money strictly off the bandwagon," Burr explained. "But she's got so much versatility, power, soul and flavour, she could be singing in French and have the same appeal. I think this is a great record."

The first ever Latin Grammys were held on September 13. Christina arrived with Jorge Santos in tow, wearing a slinky, metallic bandeau top (so small that it looked like a bandanna that she had tied around her breasts), and a long skirt held up by tiny straps made of silver chains with a sky-high slit that exposed her entire leg and partly exhibited her thong strap. It was her first public appearance with Santos and she made quite an impression on the red carpet. Christina's attire, along with Shakira's and Latin rocker Alejandra Guzman's, garnered most of the attention—and comments—that evening. The Grammys had been mired in controversy, because most people felt the awards were a playground for the Estefans. Many winners and telecast performers were familiar names, and the perception that commercial music was favored at the expense of distinctive Mexican styles such as norteño and Tejano caused some grumbling leading into the awards.

The largest Latin record label in the USA, Fonovisa, boycotted the awards. Mariachi star Pepe Aguilar, nominated for Best Ranchero Performance, also refused to attend. Emilio Estefan, who was at the heart of the dispute, sought to downplay what had been said about his influence. "Before people talk, they should get educated. I was very disappointed about that...I hope these awards will unite people." He failed to note that he was nominated for six awards for his work as a producer for various artists. Four Mexican artists from Fonovisa, including Los Tigres Del Norte, Los Temerarios, Los Palominos, and Banda El Recodo, refused to accept their awards.

For her performance, Christina wore a bright red miniskirt with a matching long sleeved halter-top. She performed a pairing of "Contigo En La Distancia" and a salsa version of "Genio Atrapado." She was passed over on Female Pop Vocal Performance in favor of Colombian Pop/Rock star Shakira. The day after the Grammy Awards, Christina convened the Spanish-language press to introduce *Mi Reflejo*.

During the press conference, she spoke entirely in English and in retrospect, it seems odd that the tension between her and Steven Kurtz was certainly not in evidence. In fact, when Christina replied to a question of whether she planned to include the Spanish version of her hits in her concert set for the remaining dates in her tour, she explained that she would in the future, when playing Latin America and areas of the United States with significant Latin populations, then she turned to Kurtz and asked, "Like the West Coast, you think? How about Miami?"[9] (Rather revealingly however, where Christina had previously thanked Kurtz effusively in the album liner notes for her debut, he received no such mention in the notes for *Mi Reflejo*.)

When asked about the apparently exploitative nature of the album, and her desire to conquer the Latin market, Christina retorted, "I'm not sure I'm trying to conquer anything. This is a love of mine, and whoever wants to come on board and enjoy this different side of me can come along with me for the ride."

Christina also raved about Pop/Rock rival Shakira, a Colombian singer who would successfully cross over into the American market one year later. Despite Shakira beating her out for Best Pop Vocal Performance By a Female, Christina said that Shakira "gets up there and she rocks it." Shakira's performance at the Latin Grammys had a similar effect on her career as Ricky Martin's Grammy performance had on his in '99. Previously, Rudy Perez had explained of Christina: "She started visiting all these Latin American countries and listening to Latin American singers, like Shakira. She's a big Shakira fan," he explained. "She heard the passion and romantic melodies and just fell in love with it all." (In fact, for Christina's sophomore album she hooked up with producer Glen Ballard, after he produced some of the songs on Shakira's crossover effort.)

Christina felt like a pioneer in the Latin music industry. "I think we've definitely covered new ground," she told reporters, "because I was very interested in, or influenced by, Soul and R&B, as well; and I wanted to keep some of that in there, too. So it was kind of cool mixing certain R&B, soul flavors with a Latin sense in some songs. I think you heard that on a song like 'Contigo,' and certain things like 'Falsas Esperanzas,' too. I think we've covered new ground there, and that, I'm proud of."

After the press conference was over, Perez noted hyperbolically: "I think Latin music's changed forever."

On September 17, Christina visited the Ecuadorian Embassy. By then, she had reconnected with Fausto and had decided to make peace with him. He had even complimented her on her Spanish. "You were singing in Spanish, and you sound so fluent," he told her.[10] Rudy Perez, whom Christina grew very close to during the recording of her album, felt that "one of the reasons she did this was for her grandparents and father." In that sense, the comment from her father had a special significance for Christina. At the embassy, she signed autographs and posed for pictures with young children from Ecuador.

The raves for Christina's concerts kept coming. "This teen Pop diva keeps it real" (September 23); "Christina Aguilera comes to sing and puts music first" (September 27); "Christina Aguilera is what Houston teenyboppers want" (October 2). For the week ending October 1, as Christina was on tour and her Latin album spent its fourth week at pole position on the *Latin 50* chart, she ousted Madonna's "Music" from the No. 1 spot of the *Billboard Hot 100*. "Come On Over" vaulted to pole position. That same week, "Ven

Conmigo [Solamente Tú]" ascended to the No. 1 spot on the *Hot Latin Tracks* chart.

Before *Mi Reflejo* was released, the Managing Editor of BMG U.S. Latin, Francisco Villanueva had said: "[Christina] must demonstrate that young Latinos, born and raised here, have their own way of making music in Spanish." He had also predicted, "She will make history."

That week, Christina became the first female artist to top *Billboard*'s *Hot Latin Tracks* chart and the *Hot 100* chart at the same time. She was able to hold onto what *Billboard* termed her "triple crown" for two weeks, the time that "Ven Conmigo" spent at the top of the charts before being pummeled by Oscar De La Hoya's "Ven a Mi," which had also been produced by Rudy Perez. "Come On Over" remained in place for four weeks, becoming Christina's second most successful single after "Genie In A Bottle" and bringing her cumulative weeks at the top of the chart to eleven.

For once, Christina's life was perfect. Her father was back in her life, she was getting rave reviews for her shows, and her singles and albums were doing better than even the record company had dared to dream. Christina was at the peak of her career. Unfortunately, she could barely bask in the excitement, for she was trying to sort out her problems with Steve Kurtz. In fact, the week after her record-setting achievement occurred, she ended her professional relationship with her manager. On October 2, Kurtz received a short, two-sentence letter and a brief phone call from Christina's lawyer telling him that his services were being terminated. Five days later, Christina performed at Tiger Jam III at the Mandalay Bay Events Centre in Las Vegas. The concert also featured English singer, Seal and Country Music Princess LeAnn Rimes. The proceeds would benefit the Tiger Woods Foundation that supports different children's charities.

On October 13, Christina's lawyer, Daniel M. Petrocelli, filed a lawsuit in California Superior Court in Los Angeles against Marquee Entertainment, Kurtz and co-manager Katrina Sirdofsky individually, alleging fraud and breach of fiduciary duty and seeking a rescission of Christina's March 1999 management contract. Christina had gotten the best attorney money could buy. Petrocelli was lead council in the multi-million dollar wrongful-death suit Fred Goldman successfully pursued against O.J. Simpson. The lawsuit also sought general and punitive damages, plus all monies Kurtz and Sirdofsky received under the contract. Christina's initial agreement with Kurtz had outlined an arrangement in which any assistance Kurtz received from other people in managing her would be rendered at no additional cost to her. The lawsuit contended that, despite that arrangement, Kurtz was paying associate Katrina Sirdofsky, $4,000 per week from Christina's coffers in addition to his own 20 percent commission.

Specifically, the lawsuit acused Kurtz of having "improper, undue, and inappropriate influence over [Christina's] professional activities." The lawsuit also contended that Kurtz hired Sirdofsky and his father, Normand as "management professionals" he could work with. Ruth Inniss' previous claims appeared to have some foundation after all. Christina claimed that she was 17 when she signed with Kurtz (a fact he would dispute) and that Kurtz had undue influence over the attorney who drew up her contract and made repeated misrepresentations during their dealings.

Petrocelli also filed with the California Labor Commission seeking to void Christina's contract. However, there was a contradiction within the lawsuit itself because it accused Kurtz of "inducing" Christina to sign a written agreement in 1999 that established him as her exclusive personal manager. In 1999, Christina was 18 years old, not 17, so there was no valid reason to find the contract void, especially because Christina had been aided by independent counsel at the time she had signed the contract. On the other hand, it seemed strange that Christina would have signed her contract with Kurtz in 1999, when she in fact started recording her album and recorded the *Mulan* soundtrack in 1998 and both were deals struck under the tutelage of Steve Kurtz. A paragraph toward the end of the lawsuit summarized: "The true facts are that Kurtz did not place [Christina's] interest above his own; did not act fairly and honestly in protecting [Aguilera's] rights and interests; did not advise [Christina] independently of his own interests; took actions which inured to his own benefit; and took actions adverse to [Christina's] interests."

After the filing, quite conveniently, Kurtz and Sirdofsky could not be reached for comment. In the absence of Christina's attorney, an assistant directed calls from frantic journalists to her "new manager" Irving Azoff, who could not be reached either. The 54-year-old Azoff had made his name as the brash manager of acts like the Eagles and Steely Dan in the 1980's. He got his start more than 30 years ago managing bands at the University of Illinois, and he battled record companies on behalf of his rock-n-roll acts. Later, he became a record executive himself, heading the MCA Music Entertainment Group in the mid 1980's and producing movies, including *Urban Cowboy*, starring John Travolta. Azoff, described by *The New York Times* as "alternately charming and abrasive" never left the management business, but as a result of the fickle industry he moved in, he found his artist stable dwindling over the years.

In his 1990 best-seller *Hit Men: Power Brokers & Fast Money Inside the Music Business*, a controversial exposé of the men who inhabited the higher levels during the early days of the music business, author Fredric Dannen described Azoff as "one of the most loathed men in the music business" whose friends called here the "poison Dwarf." It was a reference to Azoff's petite stature (five feet three inches) and forceful personality.

At the time he took Christina on, he was planning a comeback in the form of a new approach to doing business in the music world. "You need a company, not a manager these days," he told *The New York Times*. "You need clout."

Azoff could have used some clout himself. At the time, he was only managing Don Henley of the Eagles and, rather interestingly considering Steve Kurtz's later accusations, the English singer, Seal.

Azoff later explained, "When I first met Christina, she had the most badly planned, overbooked schedule I've seen in my 30 years in the business. She was getting chest infections and throat infections. Labels and managers don't know how to say no, and these kids are getting burned out—just like the young tennis stars used to. It's a matter of whether they break physically or mentally."

On October 14, sparks flew as Steven Kurtz jumped to protect his personal reputation. Kurtz called the action "false and defamatory and inaccurate." Kurtz explained that the agreement, signed in March 1999, had a minimum duration of four years. He further clarified that Christina was over 18 and aided by independent counsel when she signed it. He told *Billboard Bulletin*, "This is a transparent attempt to avoid her contractual obligations to me." Kurtz complained that he had received no prior notice of any of the items in Christina's complaint, when in fact he had been notified on October 2 that the lawsuit was being filed.

"I am very disappointed that Christina would wrongfully attempt to terminate our management contract when, during its term and under my management, she was awarded the Grammy for Best New Artist, each of her singles and albums achieved the number one position on the *Billboard* charts, she sold over 10 million records and had a successful headlining tour," Kurtz wrote in a prepared statement he released on the 18th.

In a phone interview with *Live Daily*, he also expressed concern about information that Christina was 17 when she signed the agreement. "The way the complaint is written is very misleading, so I wouldn't be surprised if someone was misled to believe that…she was 17 [when she signed the management agreement]."

According to Kurtz, he had acted in a completely ethical manner. "I worked with her for a couple of years, I waited until she was of majority [age and] got her own counsel, and then I negotiated a standard management agreement." In fact, it was under Kurtz's tutelage that Christina had landed the *Mulan* soundtrack when she was only 17.

Kurtz added in his prepared statement that he hoped "Christina will question the motives of those persons who have encouraged her to pursue this baseless litigation and isolated her from those who have contributed to her success." However, he noted, "if Christina chooses to ignore the truth and her own better instincts, and continues to dishonor my years of hard work and devotion to her very rewarding and successful career, I am ready, willing, and able to protect my rights and to seek redress for any damage to my professional reputation. In the interim, I continue to wish for Christina the nearly unparalleled critical, popular and financial success she has achieved during the time that I have represented her."

"Obviously I'm disappointed and disgusted. I put my entire career behind Christina," Kurtz later told *Teen People*. "What's so upsetting is that if people like Christina keep doing this to people like me there won't be any more people like Christina." [11]

For once, Christina's off-stage behavior was threatening to upstage her musical success. Her tour had continued, along with the positive reviews, unabated: "Teen diva ready for transformation" (October 13); "Teen star Christina Aguilera exudes confidence in Concord" (October 17); "Christina Aguilera, Destiny's Child take Calif. by storm" (October 20); "Polished Aguilera gives fans what they want and more" (October 20); "Aguilera delivers for teen crowd" (October 22), and, finally: "Christina Aguilera in Hawaii" (October 23).

A week after the flare-up and two days after the closing date of her tour in Hawaii, on October 24, RCA released *My Kind Of Christmas*. It was Christina's third album in just over a year, and featured her shifting styles throughout, "from hip-hop influenced pop on 'Christmas Time' and 'This Year,' to a soaring rendition of '(Have Yourself A) Merry Little Christmas' backed by a 70-piece orchestra," noted *Billboard*.

Christina had also recorded two videos from the album. One for "The Christmas Song (Chestnuts Roasting on an Open Fire)," which had actually been done the previous year after the song was released as a single. The other video was for "Merry Christmas Baby," her duet with Dr. John. The video for "The Christmas Song" was included on the enhanced CD release of the album, which had two different covers. Although Christina was already omnipresent, she promoted her latest release with appearances on several television shows, including "The Rosie O'Donnell Show," "The Tonight Show With Jay Leno," and "Good Morning America." Furthermore, she had signed on with ABC to produce a Christmas special that would air in early December. She would perform many of the songs on the album as well as material from her other two albums and would include special guest appearances.

The album debuted at No. 38 on the pop chart, but peaked at No. 28, and tumbled down after achieving platinum certification. On the *Holiday Albums* chart, however, it reached pole position, and kept it on and off until January. Christina had thus established a perfect track record; her first album had made its debut at No. 1 on the *Billboard 200*, her Latin album made its debut at No. 1 on the *Billboard Latin 50*, and her Christmas album had reached No. 1 on the *Holiday Albums* chart. Coupled with her three No. 1 singles, it was an enviable track record by any standard. Despite her thriving career and her relationship with Jorge Santos, Christina was exhausted. She still felt that while Kurtz might have been an effective manager, his behavior had been exploitative and he had not been looking out for her best interest in a genuine fashion.

In late October, Christina canceled several concert appearances, including a radio festival in Chicago (the annual Boo-Bash) on October 27 and a private Disney Channel event in New York that Saturday, as she fell ill along with nine other members of her tour entourage. RCA Records publicist Pamela Murphy explained that Christina had been diagnosed with a viral syndrome associated with exudative tonsillitis by doctors in Hawaii, where she had been holed up since wrapping up her fall tour following her October 21 show in Honolulu. On October 27, Steven Kurtz slapped Christina with a counter-suit in District Court in New York City.

In his suit Kurtz alleged that Christina had violated the terms of their March 1999 management agreement by prematurely and inappropriately terminating his services the previous month. The suit also named Christina's assistant tour manager, Kiki Lee Baker and entertainment manager Irving Azoff.

Kurtz' suit sought over $1 million for services already rendered, $50,000 for a loan he claimed to have made to fund Christina's fan club, punitive damages and reimbursement for the legal fees associated with the lawsuit.

Mainly, the suit targeted Baker, who was basically charged with orchestrating Kurtz's firing. Kurtz alleged Baker purposely sabotaged his relationship with Christina to "deflect attention from herself." The suit claimed that this was done after Kurtz learned of Baker's alleged mishandling of Christina's money, which is described in the suit as Baker's failure to account for over $180,000 of Christina's tour money and the "inappropriate" wiring of $15,000 to a bank account in the names of both Baker and Bobby Herr. Herr is described in the suit as Baker's boyfriend and Christina's tour manager. In fact, a quick look at Christina's 2000 Tour Rider revealed that B&K Production was handling Christina's tour, and Bobby Herr was listed as the main contact in the contract.

According to the suit, Baker had formerly been employed by Seal, an English artist who had enjoyed some success in the United States after his single "Kiss From A Rose," featured on the *Batman* soundtrack, reached No. 4 on the *Billboard Singles* chart. The lawsuit noted that Christina had performed at "a charity event" in Las Vegas on October 7 where Seal also performed. Kurtz was referring to the Tiger Jam III concert where Christina had performed five days after he received the telephone call from her attorney explaining that his services were no longer needed. According to Kurtz, however, Kiki Lee Baker urged Christina to terminate her contract with him no later than October 2nd because "Baker did not want Kurtz to meet Seal and/or learn the true reasons behind the termination of Baker's employment with Seal."

Due to Seal's rather low profile in the United States, there are virtually no articles dealing with his tour that discussed any problems it might have had in detail. However, Gareth Edwards, an English fan and Seal expert who has run a website dedicated to the singer since 1994, did recall there were problems with Seal's "Human Being 1999" tour, which caused it to shut down prematurely. "I don't know exactly what happened, but Seal's 'Human Being 1999' tour was cut short," Edwards explained. "There was a 6 week tour followed by a 2 week break. The intention was for the tour to continue on to Chicago, Minneapolis, Milwaukee, Rosemont and Cleveland. However, during that break it was decided that the tour as it stood could not continue. It was suggested that Seal might continue with a new, cut down band that could also provide backing vocals. Tony Levin, bassist for the tour, reported this via his diary page at www.papabear.com. Who made the decision and for what reason is not clear, though it was suggested that there were issues with the promotion of the tour and with his management."

Frantic reporters could not locate Baker and were unable to obtain any comments. Kurtz also pointed out that by representing Christina, Irving Azoff was violating the terms of his agreement with her. The suit noted that Kurtz had notified Azoff of that fact earlier the previous month but Azoff disregarded the information.

On October 30, Shelly posted the following message on her Artists Direct message board: "Right now, Christina is ill. She was so overworked, and now has a touch of tonsillitis. I spoke to her last night and she's starting to feel better. I told her about everyone's concern. She'd like me to tell you all thank you so much, and that she sends her love." Christina was certainly ill, but part of the reason for the cancellations was that she was finally taking a much-deserved momentary break after more than a year of non-stop work. Her frenzied schedule had certainly borne fruit: she had obtained three more No. 1 singles, her album had entered seven times platinum territory, her sold-out tour had received steadily raving reviews and now she had released her Christmas album which would soon climb the *Holiday Albums* chart to achieve the top spot, and be certified platinum for shipment of more than one million copies.

THIRTEEN
Her Kind of Christmas

The reviews for the Christmas album were decidedly mixed, but all agreed on one thing: Christina had to rein in her vocals. Reviewing the album for *University Wire*, Jimmy Zha noted, "...Like her musical (and apparently stylistic) hero, Mariah Carey, Christina does have some vocal chops. They are displayed prominently in 'Have Yourself a Merry Little Christmas' and 'Merry Christmas, Baby,' two soulful ballads, which are all that a Christmas album can really offer anyway." On the other hand, "other danceable songs like 'The Christmas Song' become overwhelmingly kitschy, even for a Christmas album. Of course the question is why a Christmas album has to be slightly cheap at all, but the best poor Christina can do is offer up an album that is not entirely cheesy."

People magazine had an almost opposite opinion. The review started out cynically ("In a time when musical careers often flame out in a year or two, it's best to be prolific. Taking that idea to heart, Aguilera releases this set of 11 holiday songs....") and pointed out that while she "duets with Dr. John for the jazz-infused 'Merry Christmas, Baby' and sets 'The Christmas Song' to a kickin' dance beat," "she falters on new cuts such as Diane Warren's painful 'These Are the Special Times' and 'Christmas Time,' credited to a production team called Celebrity Status/Ron Fair." The "bottom line," wrote Sona Charaipotra: "Still a little green."

The *Atlanta Journal Constitution* negatively highlighted Christina's vocal acrobatics: "This collection of hip-pumping Christmas tunes doesn't deviate one bit from the young singer's overdone, "Barbra-meets-Mariah" vocal undulations. Aguilera can make the words 'In Excelsius Deo' last longer than Christmas Eve with the in-laws."

On the other hand, writing for the *Evening Mail*, Andy Coleman called her album "a stylish and soulful collection of traditional carols, Christmas classics, and new material."

Entertainment Weekly noted dryly, "It was originally reported that Aguilera would sing a duet of 'Merry Christmas, Baby' on this album with Etta James, one of her heroines. The blues legend is mysteriously absent from the finished track, but Aguilera oversings so wildly that there wouldn't have been enough oxygen in the booth to sustain another life form." The review was a definite put down, and ended with "All I want for Christmas is for Christina to calm down."

Christina had saturated the airwaves to such an extent that she had to lower her profile, ever so slightly in November. She filmed her Christmas special that would air in December and attended a number of awards ceremonies. Christina also spoke to *Access Hollywood* about her relationship with Jorge. It had, by now, lasted for almost a year. "Over the past year, I did fall in love for the first time," she said, "and that's been a crazy thing along with winning the Grammy, singing to the president, and all these crazy things that have happened in the whirlwind journey that I've been on career-wise."

It was clear that, if only for a moment, Christina's priorities had changed. Whereas before she had put her career first and foremost, she was finally learning that it was important to make time for her love life. It was a process that included overcoming her profound fear of placing herself in a situation where she could be easily hurt. "I think falling in love tops everything in such an emotional craziness," she said. "Relationships are funny, weird, and hard, but I've had a lot of fun and we'll see where it goes." She admitted that the fact that Santos was her dancer could be an awkward situation. "Working with someone that you really care about and love can be a little crazy sometimes. But it's comforting to have someone next to you when you need them the most to cheer you up," she told the television program.

Although she did not comment on it at the time, later Christina would admit that the overwhelming gap between their economic positions and celebrity was not easy on Santos' ego. Furthermore, her worldwide superstardom was another obstacle in their attempts to lead a normal relationship. "Being in a relationship means more pressure because everybody wants to know, and if you go out, you have to worry about photographers. I'm not going to allow that to get in the way of the kind of life I want to lead or what I do."

And she did not. Santos was her escort at the Radio Music Awards in Las Vegas on November 4, and was with her at the taping of her ABC Christmas special on November 7 and 8. For the special, Christina taped carefully choreographed performances of "Genie In A Bottle," "What A Girl Wants," and "Come On Over (All I Want Is You)." She included "Falsas Esperanzas," a danceable, upbeat salsa confection from *Mi Reflejo* to plug her album to her American audience. She also sang "My Reflection," "All Right Now," and performed and dedicated "I Turn To You" to Shelly. Christina also taped an interview that would be interspersed between her performances when the special actually aired. She talked about her motivations and inspirations in conversational asides. A children's choir was brought onstage to accompany Christina as she sang "Climb Every Mountain."

The special was taped in two days to accommodate some of the guest stars. Brian McKnight joined her for a duet of "Have Yourself a Merry Little Christmas." For what would be the final performance when the special aired, Christina changed into a slinky red elf outfit and performed "My Kind of Christmas," featuring a brief appearance by pint-size, 13-year-old rapper Lil' Bow Wow.

Keeping up with the promotion for the Spanish-language markets, in mid-November Christina was scheduled to perform in Mexico City, a place where *Mi Reflejo* had sold an overwhelming 90,000 copies. On November 17, Christina's record company released a statement that read: "Christina Aguilera was given medical attention in Mexico City and requires complete rest." Christina made her way home to New York that Friday to rest and recover.

Because of Christina's edgy image, there was a certain air about her that rubbed some people the wrong way. At times, her airy manner seemed to strike others as being rude, showy and superficial. But, it appeared to be something more than that. Christina had problems with her classmates because they found her arrogant. Although many of her close friends understandably defended her, the truth is that the number of people speaking out against her was growing as fast as her bank account. First, it had been Deborah Gibson's comments about Christina's inappropriate use of her sexuality. Then, it had been Mariah refusing to acknowledge her. Finally, Shirley Manson, of the alt-rock band Garbage, wrote in her website about seeing footage of a "cheap imitation of 'In Bed with Madonna'" with the "tiny Christina" backstage before her presentation, surrounded by a circle of "true and lasting 'friends'" which prompted her to comment: "Why don't you make an effort to be a better person, Christina? Maybe that might bring you a little closer to God, because there is a strong rumor from numerous and credible sources that you are a stuck-up bitch."

It seems odd that so many older members of the artistic community would lash out against Christina. Perhaps there was something behind those allegations about Christina's arrogance, as many fans had found out during the back stage meet and greets. Soon, Courtney Love would join the fray, but not before the phenomenon then moved on to teen contemporaries. While Britney mainly tried to ignore Christina, two other teen acts joined the "lets-bash-Christina" bandwagon.

Jessica Simpson, the 19-year-old artist that Columbia Records was trying to sell as the new Mariah Carey, had reason to be jealous of Christina. But her words, spoken on the record, cannot be denied. Like Deborah Gibson, Jessica had only positive things to say about Britney ("[she's] a great friend of mine. We are very, very cool with each other"), but nothing good to say about Christina. "Christina and I talk, and I think she's a great person underneath the façade. She is very big right now; she definitely knows she has sold eight million records and I don't really like that in people," she candidly expressed to *FHM* magazine.

"I don't think you should act like that. I don't think you should block the hall. It's important to stay normal, but people lose their heads in this business. They lose who they are as people. I knew Christina before her stuff came out and she's a great girl, but BOOM! she hit so fast and some people just can't handle it. She is one of them. She has lost sight of herself, but she's young and it will pass. I hope it will anyway, because she is hurting herself." (Although Simpson later claimed, rather lamely, that the reporter had moved her words around to make the interview sound more dramatic, in a previous interview she had asserted that Christina was "all about the fame.")

Jessica Simpson was not the only teen artist with negative comments about Christina.

The members of Westlife, a boy band that became a pop phenomenon in England (and, ironically enough, was founded by Ronan Keating, a former English boy band member himself), were also upset with Christina. Kian Egan, lead vocalist, took a swipe at her, claiming she was the "nastiest" and "ugliest" person he had ever met. Reportedly, Egan was upset at Christina because she had his bandmate, Mark Feehily moved from a table in a club she wanted to sit at. "We don't like her," the band told an English publication. "She's a horrible person. She's a snot."

Kian said: "Christina is a real bitch. We don't get on with her for the simple reason that we met her in a club one night. She asked one of her security to have us moved so she could sit down."

"You know you have to leave now because this is her table," the security guard told the astonished band member, who refused to budge. "She came across very arrogant," Kian added. "Westlife would never behave like that."[1]

Apparently, it was grade school all over again. Christina was still unable to connect with her contemporaries, or anyone who came in contact with her it seemed. She was badly losing the popularity contest, and for someone who badly craved acceptance and adulation, they must have been trying times. Jorge Santos was one of the few people who came out in Christina's defense, observing in *Teen People* magazine: "People think she's mean, but she's not. She handles her business, and she's gone this far being the way she is because she has to be. You have to get your job done, and you have to get it done the right way. If you have to be strict about it, you have to be strict." He added, "She's just a regular 19-year-old girl who's trying to have fun with her life. She's going through the same things, except she's going through them in front of cameras and on TV." [2]

And the cameras and television were equally harsh judges. *People* magazine named Christina one of the worst dressed women of the year (Britney was one of the best dressed). Mr. Blackwell bestowed her with the same dishonor. Christina had previously explained that she "loves to shop" and was certainly not averse to embracing a trend or two. She was very much a clotheshorse. According to her stylist, she favored head rags— with rhinestones or without—and hip-huggers, sequined tank tops, along with low-riding pants with the waistband of her men's Calvin Klein briefs peeking out. It might have been original and fun, but it wasn't elegant.

"She's all over the map," her stylist, Stephanie Wolf, explained, adding that Bebe and Miu Miu were frequent destinations for Christina. "She dresses like a 19-year-old." The fashion critics were unimpressed. Christina replied with her customary honesty: "OK, did they say I am the worst dressed?" she asked an interviewer. "All I have to say is that I've seen those magazines before, and I've seen some of the things they pick for best dressed, and it's the most boring, unexperimental thing out there. It's very conservative, and that's not what I am."[3] Although Simpson's comments that Christina had lost sight of herself might ring true to casual observers of Christina's career, and would seem even truer when viewed under the light of her transformation in 2001, in fact, Christina was simply breaking through her record company's carefully constructed image and exposing her true self.

In December, Christina recorded a video that represented two firsts. It was the first original video off *Mi Reflejo*, and it was the video for her first original ballad. Rudy Perez had written the song, "Pero Me Acuerdo de Tí," especially for her. It was a beautiful song with simple arrangements that showcased Christina's voice more than any other song in any of her albums did. In the *Billboard Year-End* charts *Mi Reflejo* came in at No. 5, despite logging in nine weeks at No. 1, more than any other release. In fact, it would climb three positions to No. 2 by the following year, when it logged an additional ten weeks on the top spot.

On December 6, Christina attended the Billboard Awards. The awards themselves are hardly surprising, because they are determined by the magazine's year-end chart listings, which are based on a combination of record sales and radio airplay. Although Destiny's Child beat Christina for Artist of the Year, and *Hot 100 Singles* Artist of the Year and Faith Hill beat Christina out for *Hot 100 Singles* Female Artist of the Year, Christina got the all-encompassing Female Artist of the Year.

Christina went up to the podium, and in her excitement, addressed all of the year's most controversial issues. "Thank you so much. God, well, this would not happen without my fans," she said. "So first and foremost, thank you so much." She also pointed out: "I have such an incredible team of people behind me now. I couldn't do anything without you guys." The "now" was referring to the fact that she felt Kurtz had been an ineffective manager previously. She thanked her "Dad, of course" and "sister Rachel" and her "little brother" and she left no doubt as to whom she had sided with after Steven Kurtz's lawsuit when she said, "Kiki Lee Baker, thank you so much." She was open about her love for Jorge Santos when she exclaimed, "My whole band, dancers, Georgey, I love you. Thank you so much." Finally, the last snipe at Kurtz: "Irving Azoff, thank you for showing me what true management is. Thank you for the support and getting me through hard times. Thank you so much, everybody."

Actually, that month, producer David Foster met with Irving Azoff to discuss the possibility that Christina would appear at the 2002 Salt Lake City Winter Olympic Games. Foster felt that Christina was the only young vocalist who could pull off the arrangements of the official Olympic anthem. Azoff was already starting to orchestrate the massive publicity campaign that would be put into high gear for the release of her sophomore album.

On December 8, Christina's "My Reflection" aired on ABC. *USA Today* gave the special two stars and pointed out: "There's a little bit about Christmas: 'My Reflection' is really about, well, Christina, and it seems that the holiday cheer is thrown in just to make it timely." The reviewer noted that while "There is no faulting the singer for the clinical precision with which she pulls it all off...they also are lacking in genuine passion, and at no point do you feel that she is straying an inch from the script." The reviewer felt that viewing the special was like "looking at a beautifully packaged gift that doesn't live up to its promise once the ribbons and bows are stripped away."

The Pittsburgh *Post-Gazette*'s Ed Masley felt that the special was just right, exactly what one should expect from a teen pop diva. "The first half-hour of the first Christina Aguilera network special should do much to push the singer's debut album ever closer to sales of 10 million. It's cute as a button. It's sexy. It frontloads all the hits. It's different enough from Aguilera's summer tour to keep it fresh (with dancers dressed like extras from a Merchant-Ivory film in a smile-inducing introduction to 'What A Girl Wants'). It's soulful in the way a Whitney Houston performance is soulful. And every song is introduced the way an old-school Tony Bennett-era entertainer would have done it, with class and an air of sincerity. Essentially, it's everything a girl (or boy) could want in an Aguilera special." The review ended with: "Aguilera comes out promising 'an hour of good cheer and hot music to heat up your holidays' and then delivers more than half that. Plus, it gives the folks who wouldn't pay to see her live a chance to witness Aguilera grinding her hips through a cover of 'All Right Now' by Free without changing the gender. Kinky."

The special, which was watched by 8.8 million viewers, was released as a DVD and VHS tape and, like her previous video, topped the *Billboard Home Video* sales list. Exactly one week after the airing of the Christmas special, RCA certified Christina's debut album for sales of eight million copies.

Looking back on the year 2000, Christina finally acknowledged that the rumor mill had gotten out of hand. "The rumors this year, they've been really, really crazy about who I've been linked to," she said during an internet chat. She told another interviewer, "There has been gossip, lies, tabloids in the last year. The most important thing is to know that anything you see me do or say is from the heart and it is real. I want that to come across in my live shows, interviews. There is so much superficial stuff in the business anyway. I turn my nose up at it. I'm not into that scene. I want everything I put out to be real. That's what I'd want everyone to know. When you see me—know that it's real!"

The Britney comparisons had not ended, but after more than a year of the pop industry churning out mediocre produce, the "lazy journalists" had gotten their act together and were more perceptive and well informed in their comparisons. The latter fact mattered little to Christina, who was upset at the treatment that her fellow Mouseketeer had been getting in the press. One article was particularly hurtful. "It just ripped Britney to shreds," Christina recalled. "It said, 'One Grammy for her and none for her. This for her, that for her. This is her strong point. This is her weak point.' It is sad to pit two young girls against each other over and over. I just broke down and started crying one night about that article because of how mean it was, just to talk about, 'Oh, [Britney's] Madonna without the brain.' That is so mean, and it's, like, shut up, already!"[4]

The article Christina was referring to appeared in the Minneapolis *Star Tribune* in August. There was a list comparing both singers:

Christina vs. Britney
Albums sold in United States
Christina Aguilera: 7 million
Britany Spears: 17 million

Albums released
Christina Aguilera: 1 (with 2 coming this fall)
Britany Spears: 2

No. 1 songs
Christina Aguilera: 2
Britany Spears: 1

Signature song
Christina Aguilera: "What A Girl Wants"
Britany Spears: "…Baby One More Time"

Revealing lyric
Christina Aguilera: "Whatever makes me happy sets you free."
Britany Spears: "You think that I'm sent from above/ I'm not that innocent."

Grammys
Christina Aguilera: 1
Britany Spears: 0

"Star Search" results
Christina Aguilera: At age 8, lost on first appearance singing "Greatest Love Of All."
Britany Spears: At age 10, won the first round, lost the second.

Internet hits
Christina Aguilera: 85,500
Britany Spears: 387,000

Web sites that slam them
Christina Aguilera: 5
Britany Spears: 182

Tour sponsors
Christina Aguilera: Levi's & Sears
Britany Spears: Got milk? campaign

Voice in concert
Christina Aguilera: Big and soulful.
Britany Spears: Who knows? She lip-synchs.

Stage presence
Christina Aguilera: Can dance and sing at the same time.
Britany Spears: Has more ambitious choreography, but vocals are prerecorded.

Most memorable stage outfit
Christina Aguilera: Leather hip huggers with a blue-and-white diamond pattern and blue halter top.
Britany Spears: Plaid schoolgirl skirt, white blouse and knee-highs—torn off to reveal a leather miniskirt, red top and black boots.

Reminiscent of
Christina Aguilera: Cher with a good voice.
Britany Spears: Madonna without the smarts.

Sex appeal
Christina Aguilera: Her lyrics suggest more than her stage movements do.
Britany Spears: Plays it to the hilt in concert (pole dance, girl-in-uniform bit, etc.).

Boyfriend
Christina Aguilera: Jorge Santos, a dancer in her show.
Britany Spears: 'N Sync's Justin Timberlake, if you believe the rumors.

Navel
Christina Aguilera: Still unpierced.
Britany Spears: Pierced and bejeweled.

Typical fans
Christina Aguilera: Girls who just wanna have fun.
Britany Spears: Excitable girls and excited frat boys.

The lazy journalist not only misspelled Britney's name, but failed to note how the 5'8" raven-haired, dark-eyed Cher was similar to the 5'2" blonde and blue-eyed Christina. By mid-December, Christina was already pumped up about starting work on the new album. "I'm getting many, many ideas for the next record," Christina told MTV from New York. "I can't wait to sink my teeth into it and really get going on it, because it's going to be a whole different project. I'm really excited to get into it." Nothing had changed. After her brief rest, Christina was once again the compulsively hard-working professional.

Even rap impresario Puffy Combs, a.k.a. P. Diddy, called Christina because he seemed interested in collaborating with her. He knew that Christina was looking to change directions, from pop to R&B, and wanted to help. He had previously helped Mariah Carey go from her 1995 No. 1 single "Fantasy," pure pop at its best, to 1997's "Honey," a pleasantly laid-bare R&B confection that made its debut on the *Billboard Hot 100* at No. 1. "[I'll have] a lot of different collaborations," Christina elaborated, "I'm going to be working with a lot of people…I'd love to be working with Timbaland too, and a lot of different producers." Christina announced plans to release the album in spring or summer, and said that she wanted to do a world tour.

Christina said she would take January off, probably in a sun-drenched locale, such as Jamaica or Puerto Rico, the native land of Jorge Santos. "This has caught me by surprise/Should I let him take me to Puerto Rico/I can't hold back no more/Let's go tonight," Christina later sang on one of the songs for her sophomore album. Undoubtedly, the relationship had turned serious. In fact, Christina's lyrics had evolved from "Hormones racin' at the speed of light/But that don't mean it's gotta be tonight" to "I can't hold back no more/Let's go tonight."

FOURTEEN
Seizing Control

As things turned out, Christina's wishes for vacation time were just that. Wishes. Ricky Martin called in December because he wanted to collaborate with Christina on the English version of his new single, "Nobody Wants To Be Lonely." "He asked me to come aboard," Christina explained later, "It's pretty exciting." "Lonely" would be released as a remixed version of the original ballad album track. Columbia had released Martin's sophomore English-language album, *Sound Loaded,* amid minimum publicity. Apparently, they believed that after investing $10 million in crossing him over into the American market, his second album should have been able to stand on its own. They were wrong. The record made its debut in the Top 5 of the pop chart, but failed to achieve the No. 1 spot that his self-titled effort did. Furthermore, after its debut, the album tumbled out of the *Billboard 200* with stunning rapidity, certainly failing to achieve the 7 million sales of *Ricky Martin*.

In the same vein, his first single off the album, a rip-off "Livin' La Vida Loca" titled, "She Bangs" only managed to climb to No. 9 on the *Hot 100*. It appeared that the Ricky-Martin mania that had so gripped the United States in 1999 was over. The album was falling off the charts and Ricky desperately needed a hit that would catapult him back to the top. Christina's radio performance up to that point had been nothing short of extraordinary and he decided that a collaboration could only benefit both of them. "Christina and I feel very comfortable together, we have a beautiful chemistry," Martin told HTV.

Christina clicked with Ricky. She thought he was one of the sweetest men she had ever met and that he was quite a gentleman. The making of the video for the song was aired on MTV and HTV. "We're in this labyrinth," Christina explained, "we barely come together...basically the title says it all." Christina was quick to add, "We're not portraying lovers." *Billboard* noted breathlessly, "Just as the paint is drying on the numerals 2001, the year's first event record—and perhaps the first real contender to displace Destiny's Child from the top of *The Billboard Hot 100*—is poised to react at radio with the gusto of a red-hot volcano. Mercy—red-hot, indeed. The combination of two of pop music's most sexually charged performers, combined with a song drenched in sensuality and a feel-good vibe that's as contagious as kissing, makes for an instantaneously impact-worthy top 40 smasheroo that will have the nation swaying in unified abandon."[1]

The song was unleashed to radio in mid-January and Martin's instincts proved correct. The song made its debut at No. 66 and by January 25 it became the fastest growing track at radio, moving up 32 spots to the 34th position. Curiously, while the English version stalled at No. 13, Ricky's solo Spanish version went to No. 1 for two weeks on the *Billboard Latin Tracks.*

On January 20, Christina performed at the Caracas Pop Music Festival in Venezuela. Sting and Sheryl Crow had been two previous performers at the biggest music festival in the South American country's history. "It used to be much more common to see artists stop in Caracas," festival spokesperson Pedro Rodriguez explained. Organizers hoped to attract around 30,000 people each day to the festival, which was being staged at the Central University of Venezuela's Olympic Stadium. For her performance, Christina was wearing a skin-tight, all-black, cat suit-type ensemble that included a typical Christina touch: a zipper that opened up right up to her waist and exposed her tummy but she was wearing a gold bandeau top underneath to cover up her chest. She performed the third day of the festival, which was an excellent promotional opportunity for *Mi Reflejo* in Venezuela, where the album gained platinum certification.

In February, Irving Azoff told *Billboard* that Christina would not be touring that summer. According to Azoff, she would instead focus on recording her new album for RCA. By February, Christina's debut album had declined precipitously down the charts. As her Ricky Martin duet raced to No. 14 on the *Hot 100*, jumping from a previous low of 16, in the Latin tracks department it was at No. 3 with a bullet. For the people who had purchased a copy of *Sound Loaded* and wanted the revamped version of "Nobody Wants To Be Lonely" featuring Christina, Columbia Records was allowing people to download the song from the singer's official website in Windows Media audio format. As far as Christina's solo career, her latest Spanish single "Pero Me Acuerdo De Ti" held steady at No. 11 with a bullet. When the Grammy nominations had been announced the previous month, Christina racked up two: Best Latin Pop Album for *Mi Reflejo* and Best Female Pop Vocal Performance for "What A Girl Wants." Her nominations assured Christina an invitation to perform at the Grammys.

In fact, the first Latin choice to perform at the ceremony had actually been Grammy-award winning romantic Mexican crooner Luis Miguel. According to the show's producer, Ken Ehrlich, Luis Miguel was invited to the show but never confirmed his appearance. However, a high-placed source said that Luis Miguel did confirm at least a month prior to the show, but at the 11th hour he demanded to sing in English. Then he bowed out of the performance altogether. The demand seemed odd if for no other reason that Luis Miguel had once and again declined offers to sing in English on his records or even put out an entire English-language album. With worldwide record sales of almost 40 million, he felt he did not have to "sell out" and sing in English to achieve success. He already had it. Other Latin pop nominees were considered for the show, including Spanish singer Alejandro Sanz who ended up performing at the 2002 ceremony. In the end, Christina was selected.

Producer Ehrlich denied that Christina's performance in Spanish (she could have sung in English as she was nominated in the

Female Pop Vocal Performance category for "What A Girl Wants") had anything to do with Luis Miguel's absence. "As we move along with [the production of] the show, we don't decide what to do until the picture becomes clearer," he explained rather vaguely. NARAS president/CEO Michael Greene did point out: "We had another artist in addition to Christina set to perform in the Latin field, and at the last minute they pulled out."

On the night of Sunday, February 18, wearing jeans and a t-shirt and with her hair done up in tight braids, Christina, ever the consummate professional, was at the Staples Center rehearsing and doing sound checks for her performance. Three days later, Christina arrived at the Staples Center decked out in a skin-tight, high-slit persimmon gown with plunging front sparsely laced together at the bodice and dipping in back, revealing a large temporary tattoo. "In case that didn't attract enough attention," wrote one fashion critic, "she also wore her hair (plus extensions) in tight braids highlighted with jewels." She looked stunning. For her actual performance, Christina changed into a cream-colored gown on top of which she had placed a crocheted shawl.

She descended onto the stage sitting inside one of the O's that became her logo after the release of her first album. Her energetic performance of "Pero Me Acuerdo de Tí" and "Falsas Esperanzas" drew much applause from the audience, even if one publication noted, "She sounded remarkably mainstream, like any other pop act performing anywhere but here." Actually, Christina was her usual self; her trademark mannerisms flowing as she effortlessly glided from lower range sultriness to her goose bump-producing upper register. She also strutted around in a stunning choreography that included Christina being lifted by her dancers. She was passed up for both awards, and Shakira took home the Grammy for Best Latin Pop Album for her *MTV Unplugged*.

By February, Christina was quietly laboring on her sophomore album; working on songwriting, production and collaborating with other artists as she strove to make a record that would represent her real personality and that would signal a change in direction toward the kind of music, and image, that she had originally wanted to project. In the meantime, she wanted to keep her voice and music out there, so her fans would be pacified until the new album was actually released.

That month, Christina signed on to collaborate with rapper Lil' Kim and R&B artists Pink and Mya for a musical makeover of "Lady Marmalade," LaBelle's disco classic about a Creole courtesan, which would be featured on the soundtrack to the Nicole Kidman starring vehicle, *Moulin Rouge*. The song had already been a hit. LaBelle, the wildly costumed '70s group fronted by Patti LaBelle, originally took it to No. 1 in 1975. Regardless, Christina thrived on creativity and genuinely enjoyed collaborating with other artists. Furthermore, working with "street artists" such as Lil' Kim and the edgier Pink, would give Christina the kind of gritty credibility she so desperately seemed to crave. By doing the collaboration, perhaps inadvertently, Christina was also sending out the message that she was no longer a teen pop princess, but a serious artist who didn't mind taking creative risks that meant a significant stretch from her successful teenybopper image.

"When 'Lady Marmalade' came out, so many executives were like, 'She can't do this.' 'It's too Rockwilder and Missy.' 'It's too urban.' And I was like, 'I'm doing it,'" Christina later confessed. "Even with certain outfits that I wear, or speaking openly about my past...I'm not going to sit there and lie. Whether you like me or hate me, that's me."[2] Missy Elliott, who had previously helped Mariah Carey make the transition from virginal pop princess to credible R&B artist, would produce the tune with Rockwilder. The song would serve as the all-important first single off the soundtrack, which was due out on April 24.

Other contributors to the all-star soundtrack included Beck and Timbaland's update of David Bowie's "Diamond Dogs," Fatboy Slim's version of "The Can-Can" (titled "Because You Can-Can") and Ozzy Osbourne's reworking of Christina's earliest musical inspiration, "The Sound of Music."

FIFTEEN
Not Your Pop Tart

In a February 26 article, MTV News asked, "What do you get when you put four pop and hip-hop divas together in a recording studio? If your answer is flying fur and scratched egos, in the case of Christina Aguilera, Lil' Kim, Pink and Mya, you couldn't be more wrong." The song was actually recorded at the 6-year-old Royaltone Studios In North Hollywood, California.[1] In the article, Mya was quoted as saying: "We were all in the studio together, and we got along—no cat-fighting." She also pointed out, "It's a great thing— females getting along for a change." Mya called the song "hot."

Christina herself told MTV: "I'm a fan of all of theirs, and just to be in the same song doing something with them—collaborating, which I love to do, is a really big thing for me," she said. "And it's cool to be out there before my next album comes out there, too." (On the week of March 8, Christina's self-titled debut fell from the Top 100 of the *Billboard 200* after remaining there for 80 weeks.)

In fact, while Christina may have admired all the other women, and while Pink might have kept her emotions in check during the recording session, she later admitted that she did not like Christina. "When we first met, we definitely didn't like each other," Pink later candidly admitted.[2] "I'm not a 'yes' person... and I don't think she [Christina] liked that," Pink told Larry Rodgers. "We butted heads a little bit." Although Christina later attended Pink's 22nd birthday party that September and connected with her, in truth, initially they were anything but friends. The jealousy may have stemmed from the fact that while all of the vocalists got to perform a part of the song, it was Christina's rousing vocals that served as the climax to the tune.

Missy Elliot explained, "In listening to the record, we knew that whoever sung the lightest would sing first, and Mya has the lightest voice. So Mya would sing first, and then we would gradually build because Christina has the strongest voice, so Pink would go second, and we would put Kim in the middle, with the little rhyming part, and then we would let Christina take it out along with everybody else. So that's how we were able to fit who would go where."

When they actually recorded the song, "Pink went in and did her part, Christina went in and did her part and all of them got to sit there and listen to each person. I believe it became, not competitive, but more motivating because you had great singers and everybody wanted to make sure that their vocals were 100% so they gave 100%."

Furthermore, Christina was listed first in the credits and had the most screen time when the video for the song was shot in Los Angeles on the weekend of March 16.

Their collaboration was brought to life in a "cabaret-style video" directed by Paul Hunter, who had previously worked with Christina on her No. 1 video for "Come on Over [All I Want is You]." The clip would be choreographed by Tina Landon who had actually garnered an award for her choreography on "Come On Over."

Pink predicted the clip would be like a "circus on acid." Christina noted, "The video's going to be dope." She further explained: "We're going to be having cabaret costumes. It's something you've never seen from us before. So, it's going to be fun."

According to Hunter's office, the art direction would anachronistically merge a hip-hop sensibility with the film's French cabaret setting, thanks to some props and costumes actually used in the movie. Each of the singers would get to sing one part of the song, starting with Mya, then Pink, then a rap interlude by Lil' Kim and the song climaxed with Christina's powerful vocals. Missy Elliott also made an appearance in the video, which carried over from an interlude in the song where she announces the names of the song's vocalists. Christina's scanty attire in the video (she is literally wearing her underwear), shocking hair (a full-out blonde Afro which she later sported to the *Blockbuster* awards) and garish make-up would cause quite a sensation among her fans and her detractors. (Earlier that year, the readers of *Teen People* had named Christina "Best-Dressed Female Star.")

Christina's nose piercing caused quite a stir. In fact, according to piercer Michael Adonisio, he had also perforated Christina's chest the previous May at the Andromeda tattoo parlour on St. Marks Place in New York. "Christina had to expose her breasts to me," he explained. "But I've been doing this for 11 years," he added diplomatically, "She was just another customer."

Adonisio, who had also pierced actress Alyssa Milano's ears and Tia Carrere's navel, claimed that one of Christina's friends had called inquiring about getting her "nose or navel pierced." (Christina admitted later that she had 11 piercings, though she would not discuss where they were.)

In fact, even Christina's grandmother was shocked when she saw her granddaughter done up like a prostitute. The elderly woman asked Christina why she and the other girls were dressed up like whores. "Christina, you and the other girls look like whores in this picture! Why are you all dressed like that?" Then Christina explained the premise of the movie and how the music video was simply inspired on that movie and how they were playing a part. Grandma Fidler then responded, "Oh, okay, I get it..."

On April 14, Lady Marmalade made its "Hot Shot Debut" on the *Billboard Hot 100* at No. 70. In the grand scheme of things, many analyses of Christina's career accurately note that this is where some fans began dropping off. "Aguilera's last notable appearance was in the 'Lady Marmalade' video where her hair extensions probably weighed more than the basques she wore," noted the *Singapore Straits Times*. "It would not be difficult to imagine that she may have alienated a lot of her original fans, who still remember her as a blonde pop princess, not a neophyte Cher."

Another article pointed out, "By the time of 'Oops…I Did It Again'—the most requested video in MTV's history, thanks to a killer song, a red rubber catsuit and eyes set to Stun—Britney Spears had learned, through sheer, dweeby effort, how to hold a camera's attention...And Christina Aguilera was left to become a parody of herself playing a petulant high-class tart in the amusingly over-styled Lady Marmalade video."

But that is where they are wrong. Britney Spears is a hollow caricature of Madonna. She is Madonna without the novelty. She is Madonna without the cultural significance. While the press has consistently taken the easy route, throwing pot shots at Christina for her eccentric clothing style, the singer is actually unconcerned about breaking with tradition and deviating from the norm that all celebrities follow, whereby they only dress up in clothes that accentuate their best features, rendering them as physically perfect as possible. Christina is willing to experiment with clothes that she thinks are "fun" and daring, even if they might not make her look her best. Whether by accident or purposely, she allows outsiders to join her, and unlike Britney, she is sending the right message to teenage girls: that pretty or not, it is only her talent that has gotten her to where she is.

On April 26, Christina attended the *Billboard* Latin Music Awards. She walked away with two awards for *Mi Reflejo*, in the Female Pop Album of the Year and New Artist categories. Noted *Billboard*, "Here was an artist who had delivered devastatingly well in the mainstream pop market. She was young, talented, beautiful, had international name recognition—and a Latin surname. Could she sing in Spanish? Aguilera certainly couldn't speak her father's language, but, with Spanish teacher at hand, she was able to convincingly record in that language." Christina's friend Enrique Iglesias picked up two awards as well, and Colombian singer Shakira won for Best Latin Rock Album with her *MTV Unplugged*. Less than a week after her win, Christina traveled to Monaco to perform "Nobody Wants To Be Lonely," which had been a massive international hit, at the World Music Awards with Ricky Martin, whose album had not been propelled to the top of the charts, despite the song's success. Christina picked up yet another award recognizing her as the world's best-selling Latin female artist.

In early May, Coke once again required Christina's services. They wanted to shoot an ad featuring the singer, to support a Coke contest with a top prize that included five $1 million instant prizes as well as a backstage tour and a meeting with Christina. Coke's summer promotion would also encompass a group of radio spots with Christina and full-page ads in *People* magazine, *Entertainment Weekly* and *Rolling Stone*. By then in its fourth chart week, "Lady Marmalade" effortlessly strode into the Top 10 of the *Billboard Hot 100,* making a quicker journey to the top than its celebrated predecessor.

Starting on May 14, Christina's first American Coke commercial began airing in the United States. The Leo Burnett advertising company produced the 30-second spot. The commercial was shot on a mock video set and Christina dyed her hair red and white to include the famous signature colors of the company. Every time she approached a shy male fan visiting the set of her "latest music video," the boy fainted. At the end of the spot he remarks, "I think she might be in love with me." "The setup—she's 20 and the kid a few years younger—is sweet. That's in contrast to the sleazy Lolita effect achieved in Britney Spears' Pepsi spot," opined *Adweek*.[3]

Coke followed up the ad by ordering point-of-sale displays with larger-than-life images of Christina. Scenes from the commercial were stitched together to create an in-theater ad that showed up on 11,000 movie theater screens that summer. Christina was also the focus of the summer promotion website, cokepopthetop.com. The singer certainly needed the exposure she would be getting with the Coke deal, since the release of her new album was still more than a year away. "My fans have seen me on stage," Christina said. "This gives them a chance to see another side of me." It was another side of her that would conveniently keep her in their minds, and not tire them of her music. In keeping with her low profile, two days after the debut of the commercial spot, Christina attended the Beverly Hills premiere of *Moulin Rouge* with Jorge Santos in tow. Wearing a tiny white bandeau top with an elegant jacket on top and with her hair done up in braids, Christina made her desired impression. She complemented her look with numerous small gold necklaces and huge dangling earrings, which were almost hidden from view by a large white hat that had two khaki-colored stripes.

It remained in the air whether Christina would do another ad for Coke. Her ads certainly did not achieve the notoriety, or resonance, of Britney Spear's Pepsi ad, which made its high-profile debut on the night of the Oscar telecast and featured her singing a new version of the Pepsi jingle, "The Joy of Pepsi." The commercial gained significant exposure because of its shot of Bob Dole watching the commercial next to his dog who starts barking at Britney's image. "Down boy!" Dole chastises. Britney's follow-up ad debuted during the 2002 Superbowl broadcast.

Because Britney's Pepsi ad aired before Christina's American Coke ad came out, the tabloid press had a field day with the coincidence, and many believed that Britney had been signed to Pepsi before Christina had been with Coke. "Britney Spears and Christina Aguilera have extended their rivalry to the cola wars," reported the *Post-Gazette*. "Aguilera just signed a U.S. sponsorship deal with Coca-Cola, only a month after Spears agreed to promote Pespi." In fact, Christina's Coca-Cola sponsorship deal dated back to September of 2000. (Rather ironically, on October 3 2000, the Pittsburgh *Post-Gazette* had reported: "Christina Aguilera has a rival. No, not Britney Spears. It's that cute little girl from the Pepsi commercials. Wexford's most famous pop star has signed a deal to appear in print and TV ads for Coca-Cola." Their original statement turned out to be true.)

"You can't deny the irony that we already have a Christina-vs.-Britney situation among the pop princesses, and now the cola wars are taking the same two figureheads and putting them into battle," said senior *Billboard* writer Chuck Taylor. It was ironic, but also a carefully planned coincidence that would ignite publicity just for the spectacle of it. The news magazine *Extra* breathlessly announced: "It's the new cola war between; Britney Spears versus Christina Aguilera. These dueling divas of pop are duking it out for billions in the fizz biz!" This despite the fact that they quoted Wade Robson, the 18-year-old who had choreographed Britney's spot, as saying, "She [Britney] doesn't care. She's doing her thing. Christina's doing her thing."

The *Industry Standard.com* pointed out, "The strategy isn't necessarily a bad idea, but it might not be worth the money. The two singers' heavily choreographed dance moves are so similar to each other that the spots run into the typical Cola Wars problem: We can't remember who's promoting what."[4]

The launch of the Coke campaign coincided with Christina's filing of a federal lawsuit in U.S. District Court in Los Angeles against two record companies and producers Robert Allecca and Michael Brown, hoping to stop them from releasing, as a complete album, the demos she had recorded after leaving *The New Mickey Mouse Club*.

The suit sought an injunction to prevent the release of *Just Be Free*, a disc featuring the title track and the 12 other songs Christina had recorded with producers Robert Allecca and Michael Brown. Allecca and Brown sold the recordings to Warlock Records, which planned to release *Just Be Free* on June 19.

Warlock Records is an opportunistic music distribution label, which constantly seeks to exploit artists with whom they have little or no connection, once they achieve significant notoriety.

The Tokens were a California-based popular music and singing group, before live audiences and on commercial recordings, for more than 30 years. The brothers Mitchell and Philip Margo were two members of the original Tokens group. In 1994, they sued Warlock Records, Inc. and Ornyx Records, Inc. [the same companies behind the distribution of Christina's demo tapes] because Warlock produced and distributed a compact disc recording entitled The Tokens—Silver Anniversary Greatest Hits—*Collector's Edition*.

That distribution was preceded by a few months by the release of a compact disc produced by the brothers themselves entitled "The Tokens—Oldies Are New." What explained the sudden renaissance of "The Tokens"? One of the group's songs, "The Lion Sleeps Tonight" was revived as a featured song in the Disney film *The Lion King*. In any event, Warlock used the name "The Tokens" on the cover of their disc, and included in the liner notes caricature figures bearing the first names of the original group, "Phil" and "Mitch" being among them. Just as they had proceeded to release *Just Be Free* without Christina's authorization, Warlock did not obtain the brothers' permission before releasing their album.

Christina's fans had been inquiring about *Just Be Free* months, even a year, before word got out that these demos were being released as a full-length album. In fact, they were available as commercial singles from Amazon.com and had somehow ended up on music download sites Audiogalaxy and Napster. Fans were clamoring for an official single of the song. Christina's management noted in her website: "*Just Be Free* is not even an authorized release, and we urge you not to purchase it."

"She did them in the basement of a house, and they're just not the quality her fans expect," Christina's lawyer, Carla Christofferson, told reporters after the lawsuit was filed. "They sold the distribution rights to Warlock Records, put some new music on the tracks and sent advance pictures to Amazon [and other music sites]," she added. The lawsuit claimed there had been an "implied agreement" with producers that the tracks were for demo purposes only. "Despite the rough and unfinished nature of these recordings and the agreement that these demos were recorded for a limited purpose, defendants nevertheless seek to sell these demos for widespread commercial distribution," the suit noted. Christina was suing for breach of contract and improper use of her name, voice and likeness for the forthcoming album.

"We think the world of Christina as an artist," Adam Levy of Warlock Records explained from his New York office. "The truth is, we went to court first because we wanted to seek a declaration as to who owned the rights before releasing it, because we take that stuff very seriously." They had gone to court the previous week asking for a judgment that would clear up the question of who actually owned the recordings. Although it would appear that they were the property of producers Alleca and Brown, because Christina had originally recorded them solely for demo purposes, their actual copyright as commercial recordings was certainly an issue for dispute. Levy was upbeat about their chances of releasing the record, as he sensed a possible settlement. "We are waiting the determination of that before we go forward or do anything else. In addition, we've been talking to

Christina's management and legal counsel as to what we think the final position of this case will end up being, and I think we're pretty close to resolving the matter to everybody's satisfaction."[5]

That week, Warlock's legal team was scheduled to speak with Christina's camp. "It might be [resolved this week]," said Christofferson. "It would be nice if it is. Stranger things have happened. I would say there's a 50-50 chance it's resolved by [that] afternoon."

On June 2, "Lady Marmalade" jumped to pole position on the *Billboard Hot 100*, thus becoming the third airplay-only track in the history of the chart to make it to the top. In December 1998, *Billboard* changed the eligibility rule for charting, and all songs charting on the upper echelon of the airplay chart could appear on the *Billboard Hot 100* regardless of whether a single was available for retail sale. Since then, only Aaliyah's "Try Again" (June 2000) and "Angel" by Shaggy Featuring Rayvon (the previous March) ever made it to No. 1 without any sales points. Christina was making history. Two weeks later, Christina performed the song along with the rest of the "girls" at the Wango Tango concert in Los Angeles, a two-day extravaganza that was expected to draw over 50,000 fans to Dodger Stadium. That month, Christina sang "Run To You" in tribute to Whitney Houston, who won the Lifetime Achievement Award at the first ever Black Entertainment Television Awards.

On July 5, after a number of negotiations, Christina's lawyer announced a settlement with Warlock Records that would allow the label to release *Just Be Free* in August. Although financial details of the settlement were not disclosed, Christina would allow the album's release provided it included the following statement from her explaining the disc's origins. In her album message to fans, Christina explained:

> "*Just Be Free* was recorded when I was only 14 and 15 years old. At that young age, I made the recordings as a possible stepping stone to a career in music, which is my ultimate passion.

They were made just so that I could get my foot in the door of the music business. I did not intend that the recordings would be widely released, especially after I signed with a major record label.

I have not updated or finished the versions recorded in my childhood and they are being released 'as is,' although I tried to prevent the release for several years.

The recordings do not in any way reflect my current musical taste and where I am as an artist. The growth and vocal development I experienced as I matured into young adulthood is not reflected in the recordings."

The album of new recordings that I intend to release this fall will be the album that truly reflects my artistry, my vision and my passion. The *Just Be Free* recordings will hopefully be a footnote in a musical career that I dream will last for many years to come.

To further put the album in context, *Just Be Free* would feature cover art provided by Christina from when she was only 14 years old.

On July 17, the nominations for the second annual Latin Grammy awards were announced in Miami. Christina obtained two nominations. One was a Record of the Year nomination for "Pero Me Acuerdo De Tí", and the other was a nomination for Best Female Pop Vocal Album for *Mi Reflejo*.

With just three weeks remaining until show time, the Recording Academy had moved the Latin Grammy Awards from Miami to Los Angeles due to protests planned by Cuban exile groups against artists living under Fidel Castro's communist regime (including Isaac Delgado and Omara Portuondo). The last-minute decision came on the afternoon of August 20th, after a coalition of more than a 100 Cuban-American groups compromised with Miami city officials and promised to keep their demonstrations within a designated area near the American Airlines Arena. But the agreed-upon location was still too close for the Academy.

The Latin Grammys were scheduled to air on CBS on September 11 and would be held at the Forum in Inglewood, California, near Los Angeles. The devastating events of September 11 could not have made the awards more ill-timed. Although many believed that awards and a celebration could heal a wounded nation, the frivolity of such an affair in the midst of so much human loss would have been incredibly inappropriate.

On August 29, *Just Be Free*, debuted at No. 71 on the *Billboard 200*, and topped the *Independent Albums* chart, where it would remain for a number of weeks despite the lack of publicity and support from its main vocalist. In September, *Time* magazine caught up with Christina as she relaxed in her new Beverly Hills home with her puppy Stinky, a papillon that had been a gift from Santos. She talked to the magazine about her next album and her "new life" as an adult star. According to Christina herself, on September 11 she broke up with Jorge Santos.

Apparently, their similar backgrounds were not enough in the end to help them overcome the overwhelming gap in their current circumstances, which were wildly diverging. Christina had previously admitted of her relationship with Santos, "It was scary because we come from two different places, as far as, like, he's a dancer and I'm a star—as bluntly as I can put it. It can be hard for a guy's ego." In the end, it was too hard on Santos' own self-esteem. On Howard Stern, Pink said: "Oh I think they broke up. He needed to find himself." Inadvertently, Pink spurred rumors regarding Santos' sexual orientation. During a commercial break, she told Carson something that he would not divulge on-air. Many Christina fans believed that "something" had to do with Santos' sexuality. (Both *The Star* and *The National Enquirer* had featured lengthy pieces, with original reporting that even named names, suggesting Santos was bisexual or homosexual. Both sources, however, suffer from severe credibility problems.) "Even though we are not together anymore, we still work together," Christina said in an interview, "He's a really great person. And I love him."

In September Christina holed up in the studio in Los Angeles and started the intensive process of actually recording her album. Although Christina had been writing, brainstorming collaborations and dreaming about the album as early as late 1999, she had only recently put everything together to get back in the studio.

Christina was collaborating with producer Glen Ballard, who had worked with Alanis Morissette, No Doubt and Christina's idol Shakira as well as the massively successful Dave Matthews Band. He aided her in bringing a more edgy (in comparison to Christina's rather bland pop) and raw production to the album. Rockwilder, whom Christina had already worked with on the incredibly successful "Lady Marmalade," and who worked with rap artists of the stature of Jay-Z and Redman also lent a hand. Scott Storch, a little-known producer in Dr. Dre's camp whom Christina had kept her eye on for a while, was also helping with the album. Itaal Shur, co-writer of Santana's hit "Smooth," who won a Grammy for that collaboration with Rob Thomas, was also reportedly working on a song for Christina's album, but it is unclear whether it was actually included on the tracks for the album.

Most important however, was Christina's discovery of Linda Perry, a former vocalist for the girl group 4 Non Blondes. Perry had recently returned from "near oblivion" to assist Pink with her latest album, *Missundaztood*. The first single off that album, "Get the Party Started," jumped on the *Billboard Hot 100* and didn't stop until it cracked the Top 5 within weeks. It was Pink's highest and fastest-charting single. Through Pink, Christina connected with Perry.

"I heard some of [Pink's new songs], 'My Vietnam' and things like that, that I thought were so personal and so real on a level where my record was going," Christina later said. "[I thought] Linda would be a really cool person to collaborate with.... When I met her, she showed me how to sing from a different place. It's an incredible release to scream like that."[6]

Although Perry would ultimately help Christina with her album, she was unable to help her convince grunge-rocker-turned-Hollywood-diva Courtney Love to appear on her record. Desperate for collaborations with more alternative artists (alternative in comparison with Christina), Christina tried all the methods she could think of to get Love on board her project. Apparently, Christina was hoping that Perry could get Courtney to sing back-up or perhaps even duet with her on Christina's album. The attempt at musical harmony produced significant discord. "I almost had a fist-fight with Christina," Love recalled. Courtney and Linda were sitting together, talking and probably discussing Courtney's legal battles and new album. Christina came over and asked Linda, "What are you doing? Writing rock for your friend, Courtney?"

Love was in no mood for Christina's comments. Turning to the young pop diva, Love replied: "Christina, do you even know what rock is?'" According to Shelly Kearns, the exchange never happened. "The last time Christina ever even saw Courtney was in passing in a studio and they had a short but very pleasant conversation…so any negativity coming from Courtney would be a total surprise to Christina, seeing as they don't even know each other beyond the short, polite conversation."

Despite Shelly's denials, Courtney was adamant that Christina had tried to contact her, even through the internet. "I got an e-mail from Christina Aguilera," Love explained. "Know what she wrote? 'Na na, wass up?' You know what I wrote back? 'I'm in bed watching an Eleanor of Aquitaine documentary.'" Love's voice grew sarcastic as she recalled patronizingly asking: "'Do you know who Eleanor of Aquitaine was?' I am not gonna sit there and go, '*Wass up?*' That fucking Disney tutor should be shot! And Christina doesn't understand why I don't want to sing back-up on her record!"

Love was certainly not one of the people involved in Christina's album, despite Linda Perry's intense involvement in it.

Christina wrote four songs with Linda; "Beautiful," (the collaboration as far as this song, was limited to vocals as it was written entirely by Perry) "Cruz," "Make Over," and "I'm OK." Many of the more introspective songs were difficult for Christina. "One track in particular that I wrote with Linda, it sounds like a twisted lullaby," she said. "It's about my childhood and past. Not to get too specific, but I've spoken openly about trying to get the word out about domestic violence and child abuse, so one of the songs is really personal. I'm not afraid to do that, because I feel like so many other young people in certain situations like this [can see that] someone coming from that background could grow up and do something so great and use a bad experience and turn it into a good one. I turned to music originally because of my past and needing a release or an outlet to get out anger or frustration or hurt."

In a magazine interview, Perry herself predicted: "'Beautiful' is going to win a Grammy. I just know it in my heart. It's such a beautiful song—no pun intended."

According to Perry, Christina was taking a more organic, harder-edged approach on the new songs. "It's so different from her," she explained. "There's not a trace of Christina Aguilera on these songs. I know that she's got to do something incredible in order to survive. People have been waiting for her record, and she's got an amazing voice on her. The trick with her is to get her to use it differently."

Linda said that she was surprised when the response from RCA and Irving Azoff was positive. "I was afraid that they were going to go, 'Um, this is too left-field for her,'" Perry recalled. "They didn't, and I'm really excited about that. It shows that she's definitely taking control of this record. She definitely knows what kind of record she wants to make, and her management and her company are letting her make it." In fact, it had been clear to most inside Christina's camp that she was now entirely in control of her career as well as her artistic destiny, and this "unexpected" turn was going to happen whether people liked it or not.

Previously Ron Fair had explained: "Obviously, if she says, 'I want to do an opera-polka album,' we're going to say 'Probably not,'" but beyond that, they would be supportive of any direction Christina wanted to take.

Christina did not mind the polarizing effect she had on fans of pop music or her peers in the industry. She knew that some of her decisions would not result with her winning the popularity contest, but she had no qualms about remaining true to herself.

Christina's choice of collaborations was interesting, if for no other reason that they represented her growth as an artist since the release of her first album and had all been carefully chosen by her. On September 6, wearing jeans, a white blouse, braids and a blue beret, Christina picked up two accolades at the MTV Video Music Awards, held, as usual, at the New York Metropolitan Opera House. The four women also performed "Lady Marmalade," for what was only the second live performance of it, wearing their provocative garb. They won accolades for Best Video From a Film (for *Moulin Rouge* of course) and, rather importantly, Video of the Year. Christina's risk had paid off handsomely once again.

At Pink's birthday party on September 22, Christina and her "talked for a really long time. We've gone through a lot of the same crap," Pink recounted. According to Pink, Christina became "one of my closest friends in the business." At the party, they played Spin the Bottle and, at one point, Pink kissed Christina. "No tongue," she noted, "I put my hand over her mouth." The next day, a rumor started that the two were bisexual lovers. It was a shocking rumor, and an indication of just how much Christina's image had evolved and shifted to the fringe.

On October 26, Christina hosted the Radio Music Awards in Las Vegas, an awards show notorious for its consistently low ratings. The singer was sporting her blonde hair in curls and wearing a demure black dress, and picked up an award for Top 40 song for "Lady Marmalade." Elton John, Mariah Carey, Sugar Ray and Lifehouse were some of the performing entertainers. Upon receiving her own award, Christina told the crowd: "Thank you so much. I had so much fun making that record, and I feel kind of weird because I don't have my girls with me to accept this award. But first and foremost on behalf of—on behalf of all the girls and I, thank you to radio so much for playing that song. It was such a fun project. And thank you to all the girls, to Pink, Mya, Lil' Kim. I love you girls and I had so much fun with you guys. This is for you guys, and none of this would be possible without everyone's support. Thank you so much to the fans, too."

On October 31, Christina won a Latin Grammy at a press conference that was organized in place of the actual ceremony, which had finally been cancelled. The conference was held at the Conga Room

Nightclub and the Latin Recording Academy showed a five minute video chronicling preparations for the ceremony that never happened, including rehearsal footage of scheduled performers Destiny's Child and Marc Anthony. *Mi Reflejo* was named Best Female Pop Vocal Album. Christina was scheduled to co-host the press conference with actor Jimmy Smits, but she was kept at home by the flu. Smits accepted her trophy and read a statement she sent thanking the Latin Recording Academy for its support. "Unfortunately Christina's got the flu. She's at a hotel, like, a mile away and she's got the flu," Smits told the crowd. "But she asked us to convey this message: 'I'm sorry that I cannot be here in person. It's an honor for me to receive this award,' so says Christina, 'and I would like to thank everyone at the Latin Recording Academy for their support.' So, Christina, it's waiting here for you. Well deserved."

Noted the *San Diego Tribune*, "Aguilera...won Best Female Pop Vocal Album for *Mi Reflejo*, in spite of her marginal Spanish abilities. Her victory will probably fuel charges that the Latin Grammys, like the Grammy Awards, favor commercial success over artistic innovation." Alejandro Sanz was the big winner, taking home awards for Album of the Year and Best Pop Male Vocal Album for *El Alma Al Aire*, and Record of the Year and Song of the Year for the album's title song.

On December 18, 2001, Christina's 21st birthday party was celebrated in high-profile celebrity style. The disparate guest list included Mike from the "Real World" and "Baywatch" babe Carmen Elektra, as well as Christina's close friends and her loyal dance troop. The party was held at the new Hollywood nightclub, Deep. The place used to be a restaurant, and stainless-steel fridge rooms were turned into V.I.P. rooms, which could hold 25 people each. Ivan Kane, the owner, and Fred Sutherland, the designer, decked out one V.I.P. room with a video monitor containing four screens that offered views of the happenings in the rest of the club and, just out of sight, a strippers' pole. According to Kane, the aim of the club is "to push the envelope in terms of sexuality, decadence and voyeurism." According to *The New York Times*, "Deep is one of several clubs that have opened recently on or close to the near-mythical Hollywood Boulevard, which had fallen into deep decline but is now enjoying a revival."

The place was even decorated with a neon light sign spelling out Christina's nickname: X-TINA. Waiting expectantly outside the club, the guests were rather taken aback upon hearing the unmistakable gunning and roaring of motorcycles. All of a sudden, Christina, wearing a black leather ensemble very similar to the one she had worn for the opening ceremony of the Olympic games, came into view in one of the black Harleys. Right behind her were ten other motorcycles. She sashayed into the club and there were cameras on the Harley's grill recording her every move. The crowd of guests walked in behind her. It was open bar that night, courtesy of Christina, and Mike from the "Real World" recalled "right then and there I knew this was going to be a good night."

Toward the end of the party, Christina got up on a special stage where her big birthday cake had been placed, right in front of the X-TINA sign. She took a quick look at the cake, blew out the candles, and said her one wish was for "everyone to get fucked up."

SIXTEEN
A New Beginning

In January 2002, Christina was spotted with producer Dallas Austin, who had been one of the producers for Pink's album, at South City Kitchen in Midtown on New Year's Day. They had crab cakes and crab soup for appetizers. For dinner, Christina opted for fried chicken with mashed potatoes while Austin ate grouper with black beans and rice with hush puppies. They were reportedly working on tracks for Christina's album.[1]

Months later, a rumor regarding a Christina Aguilera "sex tape" circulating on the internet grew so intense, that Christina's website was forced to issue an official denial. "It has recently come to our attention that certain pornographic Web sites are posting sexually explicit photographs and video footage on the Internet fraudulently representing that it is Christina," the statement read. "The video clips advertised on the Web sites are of a woman with blonde hair shown only from the back—the person in the video is not Christina."

"In addition," the statement continued, "the person who claims to have taken the video is not, and has never been, associated with Christina or her management. Christina's legal representatives have contacted the Web site hosts, and Christina plans to vigorously pursue all necessary action against the individuals responsible, including, if necessary, initiating criminal proceedings. We regret that there are individuals who engage in such fraud with no regard for the injury to Christina's feelings or reputation." It certainly was not Christina. Porn sites advertise "hidden cameras" and "voyeur pictures" of celebrities all the time, sending their advertisements through junk mail to anyone with a hotmail or yahoo account.

As far as Internet intrigues went, a situation that Christina was probably unaware of was brewing behind the scenes of her own official website. Kerry Walsh, the webmaster of one of the most complete Christina Aguilera fan sites on the internet (www.christina-aguilera.to) recalled: "For many months, I [had] heard that Al Gomes, the official site webmaster [had] been rude to Christina's fans." Kerry herself had previously complained that Gomes had stolen content from her website. She constantly updated her own site with clear screen captures and fun news bits and most importantly, her updates came almost right after an event or television appearance, whereas the updates to Christina's official site were far between and usually small. "He stole much of my content for months, but as a webmaster, I was used to it," Kerry explained.

One week, Gomes posted a message on his website stating that anybody who had content on Christina's official website and wanted credit for it should e-mail him. "I thought it was worth a try," Kerry recalled. "I e-mailed him very politely asking for credit on one specific gallery of my pictures. I got a response from him soon after, and he hinted that I was lying and trying to get credit for someone else's work, who goes by VAAV." Rather upset that her work on behalf of Christina was being questioned and credited to someone else, Kerry searched for VAAV. She recalls: "So I found this VAAV person, and she said that she never claimed the pictures I made were her own. So basically, Al made up this story. I pointed that out, and he still didn't give me credit, was rude to me, and said that I could not e-mail him again."

Other people were equally upset about the stolen content as well as Gomes' rude attitude, so a petition was made against the official site. "I sent in my e-mails with Al," Kerry remembered, "along with a few other people. Al must have come across it, because he said that he would sue us, because we were lying. He obviously got Shelly's trust too, because she stated on the *Live Daily* message board that the 'e-mails weren't legit.'"

The scandal reached legitimate proportions when *Popstar Magazine* published information about the petition and discussed how some of Christina's internet fans were upset about her official site taking their content without giving due credit. Kearns had in fact sided with the official webmaster and nothing was done to correct the situation.

As the Grammys were approximating, MSN music experts gave their predictions as to who would win the Grammy in the category of Best Pop Collaboration with Vocals (in which Christina was also nominated for her Ricky Martin duet, "Nobody Wants To Be Lonely"): "My pick: the remake of 'Lady Marmalade' by Christina Aguilera, Lil' Kim, Mya and Pink."

In fact, the song's incredible success meant that the four divas were in great demand for performances of it, although they would only perform it together on three separate occasions. Every time they performed the song live, Christina's choice of raunchy clothes and make-up sparked controversy. Regardless, when they rehearsed the song for the Grammy ceremony, it appeared that everyone with Grammy-related business had made a point of being on hand to watch the proceedings, and special instructions had to be given to keep the stage and floor cleared so that the rehearsal could proceed.

On February 24, Christina unveiled a new song as part of her set during the closing ceremonies of the Winter Olympic Games. Christina came onstage wearing black pants, a black top and what seemed to be a garter belt. She also had a shiny black beret; similar to the one she had worn for the MTV Video Music Awards, which had started a trend among Hollywood celebrities. The song she chose, "Infatuation," was not the first single from the album and seemed to be an honest chronicle of her relationship with Jorge Santos. MTV later pointed out: "As those who caught her black-leather-clad act at Sunday night's closing ceremony of the Olympics may have been able to guess, Christina Aguilera is no longer the pop princess next door." The day of the performance, which excitedly culminated with confetti raining upon Christina and her back-up dancers, Jorge Santos was nowhere to be seen.

Three days later, Christina attended her third Grammy ceremony, causing a stir with the outfit she selected. According to the

Daily News, she "was obviously shooting for a Hollywood glamour look with red lipstick, penciled eyebrows and platinum blond curls. But it came off more Mae West than Marilyn Monroe." Christina admitted she had been inspired by her idol Marilyn when choosing her look for the night.

The Australian noted, "the...singer guaranteed to look a disaster, Aguilera...looked great in a '60s vintage black Madam Gres. Aguilera, who has a penchant for blue eye shadow and clothes from the wardrobe of "I Dream of Jeannie," looked like she forgot she was at the Grammys and had turned up for the Academy Awards."[2] The *Post-Gazette* opined, "When she wasn't dressed as a wannabe New Orleans hooker for the 'Lady Marmalade' performance, [Christina] did a 360-degree turn from last year's Grammy fashion fiasco. While the makeup was a tad heavy, her '40s-inspired curly 'do and vintage '60s black dress was a good choice for the red carpet. Had she left even one of her necklaces at home, she would have been perfect."[3]

A press release from the Grammys called Christina's performance of the song, along with the three other singers and a guest appearance from Patti Labelle, "a historic meeting of the divas."

The set was spectacular, bedecked with red velvet and hundreds of gold lights effectively converting the left side of the Grammy stage into a grand approximation of a house of ill repute. When the four performers began to trade vocal lines against the powerful groove of the backup band, "the musical temperature in the room rose to feverish heights." Amid this fever, Missy 'Misdemeanor' Elliott scampered out to serve as emcee during the section of the song when each singer took a brief solo turn. Then, Elliott called attention to the rear of the stage and announced the arrival of the first diva of "Lady Marmalade" fame—Patti LaBelle.

LaBelle "entered into majestic diva fashion, hitting a soaring soprano note so powerful and soulful that it had Pink dropping to her knees to genuflect." The collected ladies were all smiles as they all pitched in to bring the song to a spectacular close. Even legendary divas are fallible—after LaBelle soared even higher during a final, power-packed finish, she laughed, 'So help me Jesus, that's all I can do!'

Later in the evening, the winner for Best Pop Collaboration with Vocals was announced; it was the women of "Lady Marmalade." Christina was actually the only performer nominated twice in that category. Upon receiving the award, Christina told the audience, "Oh, man! Where's Patti? Oh, my gosh! This was so unexpected. Thank you to the academy and everybody thank you mom and dad and Michael [her little brother which her mom had with Jim Kearns in 1996] and my family. And my girls right here, thank you guys." Lil' Kim added, "I...we want to say thank you God for blessing us and whoever made the decision to give us this award, we want to thank you." Mya effusively said, "I would like to say hi to my mom and dad and thank you Jimmy Ivy for fighting for me to be on this project, and Ron Fair and Missy, everybody there incorporated in this project, thank you so much." For her part, Pink limited herself to a cheerful: "Hi, mom." Backstage, Lil' Kim noted: "Right now, I'm wearing a 2.5 Harry Winston diamond ring that they let me (borrow)."

Unlike the night three years earlier when Christina had been the glittering gem of her label's artist roster at the post-Grammy party, there was a new girl in town. It was now Alicia Keys, "reigning queen of the Grammys," who held court at BMG's posh Argyle Hotel bash that night. The champagne flowed freely as Bertelsmann Music Group Chairman Rolf Schmidt-Holtz toasted the victory of his latest star. The 21-year-old Keys, whose soulful debut had opened at the charts at pole position and whose first single off the album spent six weeks at the top of the singles chart, won five separate Grammys, including Best R&B Song, R&B Album and Female R&B Vocal. She said the experience left her "shocked, exhilarated—it was a feeling of wow!"

Not far away from her was mentor and J Records founder Clive Davis, who said, "The breadth of her awards is stunning. To have Best New Artist and Song of the Year is a special milestone." J Records was Alicia's RCA. Clive Davis was Alicia's Bob Jamieson. *Songs in A Minor* was akin to Christina's self-titled debut, give or take 3 million albums.

The rise of another young female Pop/R&B superstar seemed imminent. Christina later appeared to be unaffected. She made a big impression when she arrived at the party wearing an outrageous outfit similar to the one she had worn during her performance at the closing ceremonies for the Winter Olympics.

As fans started congregating at the Argyle to scream for their favorite stars on the red carpet, police ushered them back a few feet. There was a special section set aside for the press and fans were to stay behind it. A young lady with a headset on stood by the red carpet, ushering the celebrities inside the party. Pink suddenly arrived, followed by Chris Kirkpatrick of the Backstreet Boys. Fellow boy-band member Kevin Richardson lingered on the carpet with his wife for approximately 15 minutes. But, in a sign that Christina was still one of the hottest young music stars, a buzz came to the young lady's headset. Following instructions, she told Kevin, "I'm sorry, but we need to get you inside. Christina Aguilera's one block away." When she arrived, her fans frantically called out her name, "Christina, Christina!" Her pants rode low on her hips, and over the black and white squared fabric was a black material that appeared to symbolize a garter. She was also wearing a tiny, white bandeau top, a black leather jacket, a small white purse, a red, woven scarf tied around her neck, a cross slung over her chest, and she topped it all off with a black leather beret. Fan Robbie Nicholson recalled, "She's REALLY SMALL when you see her in person... which makes her even more phenomenal. Itty bitty girl...big voice."

Once at the party, Christina mingled cheerfully as she munched on the multitude of hors d'oeuvres.

Now fully in control of her career, and finally successful in removing her name from the list of pre-fab pop stars, Christina was comfortable with her musical direction and confident of her progress with regards to her sophomore album. Apparently, she managed to talk to Alicia Keys that night, because they would end up collaborating for a song on Christina's sophomore album.

Christina's career is only starting, and her impulsive, chameleon-like transformations seem to point toward very interesting things for the future. Her sophomore album will mark an important, and interesting, turning point in her career. Although she hinted at her change of direction through her spiced up singles, it was still her original album that sold eight million copies. After the devastating fracas that Mariah Carey suffered when she decided to shift gears from Pop ingénue to sultry R&B diva, will Christina's own decision result in a similar fiasco? Her stardom was carefully constructed, and in the end, a star was made. The question now is, will she burn as brightly on her own?

Discography

Mulan (June 1998)
Disney
Singles: "Reflection" was #15 on Adult Contemporary Chart

Christina Aguilera (August 1999)
BMG/RCA Records
1. Genie In A Bottle
2. What A Girl Wants
3. What A Girl Wants (single remix)
4. I Turn To You
5. So Emotional
6. Come On Over (All I Want Is You)
7. Come On Over Baby (single remix)
8. Reflection
9. Love For All Seasons
10. Somebody's Somebody
11. When You Put Your Hands On Me
12. Blessed
13. Love Will Find A Way
14. Obvious

Notes: The first edition of the album did not include the remixes of "What A Girl Wants" or "Come On Over (All I Want Is You)." The second pressing included the remix of "What A Girl Wants" and the third pressing came out with the "Come On Over Baby" remix. The album itself spent only one week, the week of its debut, at No. 1 on the *Billboard 200 Albums* chart, but it spent 80 weeks in the Top 100 and was certified for sales of 8 million copies. A video accompanying this album was released shortly after. Titled "Genie Gets Her Wish" it was certified platinum and reached No. 1 on the Video Sales Chart.

Singles: "Genie In A Bottle" spent five weeks at No. 1 on the *Billboard Hot 100* and was certified platinum, selling *over* one million copies. It also garnered Christina a Grammy nomination for Best Female Pop Vocal. "What A Girl Wants" was also nominated for Best Female Pop Vocal the following year, spent two weeks at No. 1 and was certified gold. "I Turn To You" spent two weeks at No. 3. "Come On Over Baby" spent four weeks at No. 1.

Pokémon [Soundtrack] (November 1999)
Atlantic Records

Single: "We're A Miracle" was the first song Christina released to the public in which she had actually participated in the writing. It was not released as a single and did not chart.

The Next Best Thing: Music From The Motion Picture (February 2000)
Warner Brothers

Single: "Don't Make Me Love You (Til I'm Ready)" was part of the soundtrack to Madonna's movie. The fact that she approached Christina instead of Britney for a contribution to her soundtrack says something about whom she really respects. It was not released as a single and did not chart.

Mi Reflejo (September 2000)
RCA/BMG International
1. Genio Atrapado
2. Esperanzas
3. El Beso Del Final
4. Pero Me Acuerdo De Tí
5. Ven Conmigo (Solamente Tú)
6. Si No Te Hubiera Conocido

7. Contigo En La Distancia
8. Cuando No Es Contigo
9. Por Siempre Tú
10. Una Mujer
11. Mi Reflejo

Notes: The album made its debut at No. 1 and spent 19 weeks there on the Latin Albums chart. It also debuted at No. 27 on the *Billboard 200 Albums* chart, a phenomenal number for a Spanish-language album. It was certified three times platinum by the Latin RIAA, which means 600,000 copies shipped in the United States. Actually, it has sold just under 500,000 copies in the United States which also meant it was certified gold. The album was nominated for Best Latin Pop Album in the Grammy awards, and won Christina two Latin Grammy Awards in the second ceremony.

Singles: "Genio Atrapado" did not chart, but it garnered Christina her first nomination for the Latin Grammy Awards for Best Female Pop Vocal. "Por Siempre Tú" and "Pero Me Acuerdo de Tí" both made the Top 10 of the *Billboard Latin Tracks* chart but only "Ven Conmigo (Solamente Tú)" reached pole position, and spent three weeks there. "Falsas Esperanzas" was made into a video using footage from Christina's tour, but as a single it failed to achieve the success of the first four.

My Kind of Christmas (October 2000)
BMG/RCA Records
1. Christmas Time
2. This Year
3. Have Yourself a Merry Little Christmas
4. Angles We Have Heard On High
5. Merry Christmas Baby (Featuring Dr. John)
6. Oh Holy Night (Featuring Billy Preston)
7. These Are The Special Times
8. This Christmas
9. The Christmas Song (Chestnuts Roasting…)
10. Xtina's Xmas
11. Christmas Song (Holiday Remix) (Thunderpuss 2000 version)

Notes: The album made its debut at No. 38 and managed to peak at No. 28 on the *Billboard 200 Album*s chart. On the *Holiday Albums* chart, however, it spent numerous weeks at No. 1 and later achieved platinum certification, for shipment of one million copies. There appeared to be two versions of the album cover; one with Christina's face turned sideways and dark coloring, the other one with Christina facing the camera and green colored.

Singles: "The Christmas Song" was released as a single, with a video, and actually made the Top 20 of the *Billboard Hot 100* before quickly tumbling down once the Holiday season was over. After the release of the album, none of the singles released charted. One interesting side note is that just as they had done with "I Turn To You" on Christina's debut, RCA recycled another Diane Warren song, "These Are The Special Times", which was actually the title song of Celine Dion's own multi-platinum Christmas album.

Sound Loaded (November 2000)
Sony/Columbia Records

Single: "Nobody Wants To Be Lonely" was part of Ricky Martin's double-platinum follow-up to his breakthrough self-titled debut. The original version of the song was a ballad, and he teamed up with Christina for a video and a remixed dance version of the song. The single reached No. 13 on the *Hot 100 Billboard* chart. His Spanish version of the song, without Christina, reached the pinnacle of the *Latin Tracks* chart. A single of the song was appended to the *Sound Loaded* albums that had already been pressed, and the second edition included the Christina version.

Moulin Rouge [Soundtrack] (May 2001)
Interscope Records

Single: "Lady Marmalade" smashed onto the *Hot 100* as the Hotshot Debut and raced to the No. 1 position, where it perched itself for five weeks. The actual soundtrack was certified double-platinum.

Just Be Free (August 2001)
Warlock Records
1. Just Be Free
2. By Your Side
3. Move It [Dance Mix]
4. Our Day Will Come
5. Believe Me
6. Make Me Happy
7. Dream A Dream
8. Move It
9. Way You Talk To Me
10. Running Out Of Time
11. Believe Me [Dance Remix]
12. Just Be Free [Dance Remix]

Notes: The controversy surrounding the album's release probably helped the sales that Christina tried to curtail by refusing to authorize it. Still, the album debuted at No. 71 on the *Billboard 200 Albums* chart, more than respectable for an album entirely lacking in promotion. It went on to sell more than 100,000 copies. There was also an unauthorized single of "Just Be Free," but it is impossible to know how many copies of it were sold.

What's Going On (October 2001)
Sony

Single: "What's Going On" Christina contributed vocals to this single, which actually managed to climb into the Top 20 of the *Billboard Hot 100* chart. Christina also lent her vocals to a Spanish version of the song, "El Ultimo Adíos" which opened at No. 3 on the *Billboard Top Latin Album* chart.

Stripped (October 2002)
BMG/RCA Records
1. Walk Away
2. Fighter

3. Infatuation (Interlude)
4. Infatuation
5. Loving Me For Me (interlude)
6. Loving Me For Me
7. Impossible
8. Underappreciated
9. Beautiful
10. Make Over
11. Cruz
12. Soar
13. Get Mine, Get Yours
14. Dirrty
15. Stripped pt. 2
16. A Voice Within
17. I'm OK
18. Singing My Song

End Notes

Introduction
1. The Arts/Show Business: Christina Aguilera BUILDING A 21ST CENTURY STAR Date: 03-06-2000; *Time*; Author: Christopher John Farley With David E. Thigpen/Los Angeles

Chapter 1
1. *The Price of Experience: Money, Power, Image and Murder in Los Angeles*. Randall Sullivan. Atlantic Monthly Press, 1996.
2. http://www.ci.nyc.ny.us/ New York City Department of Planning
3. Christina Aguilera website
4. Internet chat
5. Blessed by a Genie, August 13, 1999, Ed Masley; Pittsburgh *Post-Gazette*
6. MTV July, 1999: Christina Aguilera: I Dream of Genie
7. MTV's New Sensation. When Christina mentioned to the interviewer that she loved the "Sound of Music," the reporter pointed out that the Sound of Music used to give her nightmares when she was a little girl.
8. *Daily News*, June 23, 2000 Christina Aguilera
9. Blessed by a Genie, August 13, 1999, Ed Masley; Pittsburgh *Post-Gazette*
10. Christina Aguilera interview, MTV's New Sensation
11. AOL Live chat
12. Internet Chatroom
13. *Daily News*, June 23, 2000: Gossip
14. *The Plain Dealer*; August 18, 2000, Battle for Fandom; John Soeder
15. Spanish Eyes on a Dream, Lily Chin, *The Sunday Telegraph*; October 22, 2000
16. *The Washington Post*, February 13, 2000 Christina Aguilera's Fast Track; Ex-Mouseketeer Has the Voice to Pull Away From Teen pop Pack, Richard Harrington

17. *AllPop*, February 8, 2002, Stephanie McGrath
18. http://www.christina-a.com/
19. *Star-Ledger*, June 2000
20. Rather awkwardly because she did so in an interview, in Spanish with *People* en espa-nol.
21. MTV News, TLC & Christina Aguilera: Together on Tour
22. *Daily News*, June 23, 2000; Christina Aguilera

Chapter 2

1. Pittsburgh *Post-Gazette*, July 30, 1998: THE RIGHT NOTE; Wexford Teen Lands RCA Records Contract and a deal to sing hit song for 'Mulan'
2. Blessed by a Genie, Ed Masley, Pittsburgh *Post-Gazette*, August 13, 1999
3. *Bliss* Magazine, October 2001, Genie in a Bottle
4. MTV Christina Aguilera: I Dream of Genie; July 1999
5. Interview with Shelly Kearns, MTV's New Sensation
6. Blessed by a Genie, Ed Masley, Pittsburgh *Post-Gazette*, August 13, 1999
7. *AllPop*, February 8, 2002
8. *Entertainment Weekly*
9. E-mail from Shelly Kearns to the author
10. Miss Click interview
11. Internet Chat
12. E-mail from Shelly Kearns to author
13. Interview with Miss Click
14. Christina Aguilera interview, New Sensation

Chapter 3

1. "When they arrived in Orlando…" Pittsburgh *Post-Gazette*, "They have kept the dog…", http://www.christina-a.com
2. *The Washington Post*, February 13, 2000
   Christina Aguilera's Fast Track; Ex-Mouseketeer Has the Voice to Pull Away From Teenpop Pack, Richard Harrington
3. MTV Icon, Janet Jackson
4. July 8, 2000
5. E-mail from Lindsey Alley to author, Re: Christina Aguilera

6. *Singapore Strait-Times*
7. *The New York Beacon*
8. Interview with Shelly Kearns, MTV's New Sensation
9. Pittsburgh *Post-Gazette*
10. Ruth Inniss Lawsuit
11. *Teen People* Magazine

Chapter 4

1. E-mail to the author from Shelly Kearns
2. *Bangkok Post*, August 18, 1999, Stop Taking the Mickey!
3. *The Washington Post*, February 13, 2000
   Christina Aguilera's Fast Track; Ex-Mouseketeer Has the Voice to Pull Away From Teenpop Pack, Richard Harrington
4. Warlock Records Lawsuit
5. Lawsuit, Christina Aguilera vs. Warlock Records
6. Christina Aguilera biography from Marquee Entertainment
7. *Bangkok Post*, August 18, 1999: Stop taking the Mickey!
8. Blessed by a Genie; Ed Masley, Pittsburgh *Post-Gazette*, August 13, 1999

Chapter 5

1. *Los Angeles Times,* July 26, 1999, GENIE BEHIND 'BOTTLE'; SEEMING TO POP UP OUT OF NOWHERE, EX- MOUSEKETEER CHRISTINA AGUILERA SCURRIES TO THE TOP OF THE POP CHARTS. ALISA VALDES-RODRIGUEZ, TIMES STAFF WRITER
2. Jackie Robb, *Christina Aguilera: An Unauthorized Biography*, HarperCollins Publishers, Incorporated: October1999
3. http://www.christina-a.com/skshelly12102.html
4. MTV News, Christina Aguilera: I Dream of Genie; July 1999
5. Ruth Inniss vs. Marquee Entertainment, Steve Kurtz
6. Interview with Miss Click
7. According to the woman who fielded my call from Marquee, Kurtz refused to answer because he did not want to give Christina's team an excuse to reply.
8. Lawsuit, Christina Aguilera vs. Steve Kurtz, Marquee Entertainment

9. *The Washington Post*, February 13, 2000; Christina Aguilera's Fast Track; Ex-Mouseketeer Has the Voice to Pull Away From Teenpop Pack, Richard Harrington
10. Ibid.
11. Ron Fair interview, MTV's New Sensation
12. *The Washington Post*, February 13, 2000
   Christina Aguilera's Fast Track; Ex-Mouseketeer Has the Voice to Pull Away From Teenpop Pack, Richard Harrington
13. Ibid.
14. Ron Fair interview, MTV's New Sensation program
15. Ibid.
16. *Newsweek* Magazine
17. *Bangkok Post*, August 18, 1999: Stop taking the Mickey!
18. Pittsburgh *Post-Gazette*

Chapter 6

1. *The Washington Post*, February 13, 2000
   Christina Aguilera's Fast Track; Ex-Mouseketeer Has the Voice to Pull Away From Teenpop Pack, Richard Harrington
2. MSN Chat
3. *The Washington Post*, February 13, 2000
   Christina Aguilera's Fast Track; Ex-Mouseketeer Has the Voice to Pull Away From Teenpop Pack, Richard Harrington
4. Ibid.
5. *South China Morning Post*; July 30, 1999: Mickey's pal with the big, bold voice
6. *The Washington Post*, February 13, 2000
   Christina Aguilera's Fast Track; Ex-Mouseketeer Has the Voice to Pull Away From Teenpop Pack, Richard Harrington
7. *Bangkok Post*, August 18, 1999: Stop taking the Mickey!
8. Elaine Rivera, *Time* Magazine, September 25, 2001
9. *The Washington Post*, February 13, 2000
   Christina Aguilera's Fast Track; Ex-Mouseketeer Has the Voice to Pull Away From Teenpop Pack, Richard Harrington
10. Ibid.

End Notes

11. *The San Diego Union Tribune*, January 19, 2000: From the Top of Pop, Christina Aguilera seeks new heights

Chapter 7
1. *Teen People* Magazine
2. July 26, 1999, *Los Angeles Times*; Genie Behind the Bottle
3. *South China Morning Post*; July 30, 1999: Mickey's pal with the big, bold voice
4. *Entertainment Weekly*
5. AOL chat
6. *People* Magazine
7. E-mail to the author from Shelly Kearns
8. *Teen People* Magazine, Special Year-End issue for 2000 with Christina on the cover
9. The Arts/Show Business: Christina Aguilera BUILDING A 21ST CENTURY STAR, 03-06-2000; *Time*; Author: Christopher John Farley With David E. Thigpen/Los Angeles
10. "Christina Aguilera", CD Liner notes
11. *South China Morning Post*; July 30, 1999: Mickey's pal with the big, bold voice
12. *Bliss*, October 2001; Genie in a Bottle
13. Kristen Baldwin, The Best Next Thing A popster with (gasp!) talent, CHRISTINA AGUILERA is go-going her way to the top—and is part of a dizzying music-biz shake-up., *Entertainment Weekly*, 03-31-2000, pp 20+.
14. MSN Chat

Chapter 8
1. *Billboard* Magazine
2. Blessed by a Genie, Ed Masley, Pittsburgh *Post-Gazette*, August 13, 1999
3. Blessed by a Genie, Ed Masley, Pittsburgh *Post-Gazette*, August 13, 1999
4. *San Diego Union Tribune*
5. *South China Morning Post*, July 30, 1999; Mickey's pal with the big, bold voice
6. Carson Daly Interview, New Sensation
7. *People* Magazine, Genie out of her Bottle

Chapter 9

1. This included *Time* magazine, which called Christina "one of the most strikingly gifted singers to come along since Mariah Carey"
2. *Mariah Carey: The Unauthorized Biography*, March Shapiro, ECW Press, 2001
3. *Teen People* Magazine
4. *The Washington Post*, February 13, 2000
Christina Aguilera's Fast Track; Ex-Mouseketeer Has the Voice to Pull Away From Teenpop Pack, Richard Harrington
5. *Boston Herald*
6. It is impossible to know exactly what Christina meant when she said they were in Europe together. If she meant her European promotional appearances (including one in "Top of the Pops") before her self-title debut was released there, then this is more evidence that points to the fact that their relationship had already started at this point. If she meant her European promotional tour for "I Turn To You," then she could not have been entirely truthful because that was only a month before her interview with Heidi Sherman, which means that Christina had fallen "head over heels in love" with Santos in less than one month, and had felt it was important enough to discuss in an interview, which appears highly unlikely.
7. MTV News, TLC & Christina Aguilera: Together on Tour

Chapter 10

1. *Rolling Stone*, July 6, 2000; Christina Aguilera
2. Ibid.
3. Pittsburgh *Post-Gazette*, Genie at the Superbowl, January 11, 2000
4. MTV News, TLC & Christina Aguilera: Together on Tour
5. *Boston Globe*, What Christina Aguilera Wanst, January 14, 2000
6. MTV News, TLC & Christina Aguilera: Together on Tour
7. Ibid.
8. October 4, 2000; LiveDaily post
9. MTV News, TLC & Christina Aguilera: Together on Tour
10. December 30, 2000, 887 words, Rudy Prez Tops Hot Latin Tracks Producers List For 2000, Miami
11. *Billboard*, Leila Cobo

End Notes

12. *People* en espa-nol, Maria Morales; Diciembre 2000; Un Nuevo Reflejo; Con su primer disco en espanol, Mi reflejo, Christina Aguilera pone broche de oro a un ano deslumbrante y sale en busca de sus raices
13. *Billboard*, Leila Cobo
14. *The San Diego Union-Tribune*; October 5, 2000, Thursday; Mikel Toombs; The genie grants her wish
15. MTV News, Christina Aguilera: Platinum Blonde
16. Thursday, March 2, 2000 Christina on the Grammys and her future; *AllPop*
17. Kristen Baldwin, EW Online, Christina's Whirl
18. Shelly Kearns, writing in her daughter's website
19. Shelly Kearns, writing in her daughter's website
20. The Arts/Show Business: Christina Aguilera BUILDING A 21ST CENTURY STAR, 03-06-2000; *Time*; Author: Christopher John Farley With David E. Thigpen/Los Angeles
21. April 14, 2000 *The New York Post*
22. Wednesday, May 17, 2000 The Christina Aguilera interview By Stephanie McGrath—All Pop
23. E-mail to author from Ed Masley; RE: Christina, Mon, 11 Mar 2002
24. Kristen Baldwin, The Best Next Thing A popster with (gasp!) talent, CHRISTINA AGUILERA is go-going her way to the top—and is part of a dizzying music-biz shake-up., *Entertainment Weekly*, 03-31-2000, pp 20+.
25. *Angry Blond*, by Eminem. © November 21, 2000, Regan Books
26. *Rolling Stone*, July 6, 2000: Christina Aguilera
27. Ibid.
28. *The Toronto Sun*, October 26, 2000, Thursday, Final EDITION DURST TAKES THE BIZKIT JANE STEVENSON, TORONTO SUN
29. *The New York Times*; At 18, Singer Seeks to Prove She's Not a One-Hit Wonder; LUISITA LOPEZ TORREGROSA;09/06/99
30. Christina's world: a hit debut album, a tour and a feud with Eminem; 09/05/00 By Jay Lustig *Star-Ledger*

Chapter 11

1. Isaac Guzman; *The Daily News*, September 21, 2000
2. *The Hartford Courant* August 31, 2000 Thursday, STATEWIDE PG. 10 GOT ADS? MUSICIANS FOR HIRE ROGER CATLIN; Courant Rock Critic
3. *The New York Post*. Despite the fact this was reported in the *New York Post*, its veracity cannot be questioned because Christina had previously told MTV: "I always wanted to work the window at a drive-thru fast food restaurant. I always thought it was a cool thing to do." It is incidents like these that made me question Shelly Kearns' constant rebuttal of what was in the tabloids, when in fact they were right so many times.
4. Digital Dish Diva, 'I Turn To You' / 'Por Siempre Tu' / Tour 2000, June 8, 2000
5. Tuesday, June 6, 2000 Christina in L.A.
6. Wednesday, May 17, 2000 The Christina Aguilera interview by Stephanie McGrath—*All Pop*
7. Wednesday, May 17, 2000 The Christina Aguilera interview by Stephanie McGrath—*All Pop*
8. MSN Live Presents Christina Aguilera'I Turn To You' / 'Por Siempre Tu' / Tour 2000 June 8, 2000
9. Invitation from the Prince of Wales Trust, posted: http://www.christina-a.com/
10. Fans Keep Watch for Weary star, June 11, 2000, AllPop
11. Friday, July 14, 2000 Christina plies pipes in 'Peg studio by John Kendle, *Winnipeg Sun*
12. March 2001, Pg. 46; ISSN: 0149-5380, 02796823, 1295 words, Pop Fetish

Chapter 12

1. Christina Aguilera: Not Your Puppet; MTV News Online, February 27, 2002
2. *People* en espa-nol, Maria Morales; Diciembre 2000; Un Nuevo Reflejo; Con su primer disco en espanol, Mi reflejo, Christina Aguilera pone broche de oro a un ano deslumbrante y sale en busca de sus raices
3. James Herbert; Public Eye; *The San Diego Union-Tribune* September 15, 2000, Friday
4. *Time* Magazine, 2001

End Notes

5. E-mail to author from Leila Cobo; Re: Christina Aguilera, Mon, 9 March 2002
6. E-mail to author from Leila Cobo; Mon, 11 March 2002
7. Christina Aguilera Prepares Spanish Debut by Leila Cobo; *Billboard* September, 2000
8. Alisa Valdez-Rodriguez; September 16, 2000; *Pop Beat*
9. *The San Diego Union-Tribune*; October 5, 2000, Thursday; Mikel Toombs; The genie grants her wish
10. *Teen People*, December 2000 special year-end issue
11. *Teen People*, December 2000 special year-end issue

Chapter 13

1. February 16, 2001, 331 words, otr Westlife delighted to play Glasgow, JOHN DINGWALL EXCLUSIVE
2. *Teen People*, December 2000 special year-end issue
3. *Teen People,* December 2000 special year-end issue
4. *Teen People*, December 2000 special year-end issue

Chapter 14

1. January 20, 2001, 353 words, SINGLE SPOTLIGHT REVIEW: RICKY MARTIN WITH CHRISTINA AGUILERA
2. Christina Aguilera; Not Your Puppet; MTV News;

Chapter 15

1. December 1, 2001, *Spotlight*; Articles; 3285 words, THE BILLBOARD SPOTLIGHT ON RECORDING STUDIOS - ROOMS AT THE TOP: The year's top-rated recording, mixing and mastering studios, CHRISTOPHER WALSH
2. *Teen People* Magazine, April 2002
3. May 21, 2001, National Edition, 668 words, Barbara Lippert's critique Girl Power Christina hypes Coke, wows fan
4. June 13, 2001, Wednesday, 770 words, Cultural Piggybacking, Steven M. Zeitchik
5. Tuesday, May 22, 2001 Fate of Christina album unsure by Stephanie McGrath—*AllPop*
6. MTV News; Christina Aguilera: Not Your Puppet

Chapter 16

1. *The Atlanta Journal and Constitution* January 3, 2002 Thursday, Home Edition Section: Features; Pg. 2B; Peach Buzz 'Nursery' revisits Hardwick case Byline: Richard L. Eldredge
2. (*The Australian* March 8, 2002, Friday Features Section; Pg. 19, Barbies, rocks and clean hair on the rise)
3. February 28, 2002 Thursday Sooner Edition Section: Arts & Entertainment, Pg.D-1; 420 Words; In Fashion: O J-Lo, Where Art Thou?; Monica L. Haynes, *Post-Gazette* Staff Writer

www.ingramcontent.com/pod-product-compliance
Lightning Source LLC
Chambersburg PA
CBHW061636040426
42446CB00010B/1437